Explaining Railway Reform in China

Having been state-owned for decades, the railway reform in China confused many people, particularly in terms of its ownership and property rights arrangements. Western literature always prescribes that the best model for railway reform is privatization. China's leadership has also declared the state's determination to re-arrange property rights and rejuvenate corporate governance. But is China's railway reform really a story of convergence and will the Chinese government follow the Western model of railway reform?

Addressing these questions, this book provides a positive explanation of the reform in China's railway sector between 1978 and the dissolution of the Ministry of Railways. It bridges the socialist reform and transport policy literature, and studies the empirical changes of the property rights arrangements in China's railway system. Refuting the convergence theory, it concludes that the cyclical reform policies of decentralization and re-centralization were actually an exploratory and interactive mechanism of "assets discovery" and "assets recovery." This in-depth study is based on 21 face-to-face interviews with railway cadres, as well as field trips to collect first-hand information in Guangzhou, Beijing, Shanghai, Tianjin, and Wuhan.

As one of the only empirical studies on the reform of the railway sector in China, this book will be of interest to students and scholars of China studies, transport studies, and political economy.

Linda Tjia Yin-nor teaches at the Department of Geography of the University of Hong Kong. She is affiliated with the Center for Third Sector Studies of the Hong Kong Polytechnic University.

Routledge contemporary China series

1 **Nationalism, Democracy and National Integration in China**
Leong Liew and
Wang Shaoguang

2 **Hong Kong's Tortuous Democratization**
A comparative analysis
Ming Sing

3 **China's Business Reforms**
Institutional challenges in a globalised economy
Edited by Russell Smyth and
Cherrie Zhu

4 **Challenges for China's Development**
An enterprise perspective
Edited by David H. Brown and
Alasdair MacBean

5 **New Crime in China**
Public order and human rights
Ron Keith and Zhiqiu Lin

6 **Non-Governmental Organizations in Contemporary China**
Paving the way to civil society?
Qiusha Ma

7 **Globalization and the Chinese City**
Fulong Wu

8 **The Politics of China's Accession to the World Trade Organization**
The dragon goes global
Hui Feng

9 **Narrating China**
Jia Pingwa and his fictional world
Yiyan Wang

10 **Sex, Science and Morality in China**
Joanne McMillan

11 **Politics in China Since 1949**
Legitimizing authoritarian rule
Robert Weatherley

12 **International Human Resource Management in Chinese Multinationals**
Jie Shen and Vincent Edwards

13 **Unemployment in China**
Economy, human resources and labour markets
Edited by Grace Lee and
Malcolm Warner

14 **China and Africa**
Engagement and compromise
Ian Taylor

15 **Gender and Education in China**
Gender discourses and women's schooling in the early twentieth century
Paul J. Bailey

16 **SARS**
Reception and interpretation in three Chinese cities
Edited by Deborah Davis and Helen Siu

17 **Human Security and the Chinese State**
Historical transformations and the modern quest for sovereignty
Robert E. Bedeski

18 **Gender and Work in Urban China**
Women workers of the unlucky generation
Liu Jieyu

19 **China's State Enterprise Reform**
From Marx to the market
John Hassard, Jackie Sheehan, Meixiang Zhou, Jane Terpstra-Tong, and Jonathan Morris

20 **Cultural Heritage Management in China**
Preserving the cities of the Pear River Delta
Edited by Hilary du Cros and Yok-shiu F. Lee

21 **Paying for Progress**
Public finance, human welfare and inequality in China
Edited by Vivienne Shue and Christine Wong

22 **China's Foreign Trade Policy**
The new constituencies
Edited by Ka Zeng

23 **Hong Kong, China**
Learning to belong to a nation
Gordon Mathews, Tai-lok Lui, and Eric Kit-wai Ma

24 **China Turns to Multilateralism**
Foreign policy and regional security
Edited by Guoguang Wu and Helen Lansdowne

25 **Tourism and Tibetan Culture in Transition**
A place called Shangrila
Åshild Kolås

26 **China's Emerging Cities**
The making of new urbanism
Edited by Fulong Wu

27 **China–US Relations Transformed**
Perceptions and strategic interactions
Edited by Suisheng Zhao

28 **The Chinese Party-State in the 21st Century**
Adaptation and the reinvention of legitimacy
Edited by André Laliberté and Marc Lanteigne

29 **Political Change in Macao**
Sonny Shiu-Hing Lo

30 **China's Energy Geopolitics**
The Shanghai cooperation
organization and Central
Asia
Thrassy N. Marketos

31 **Regime Legitimacy in
Contemporary China**
Institutional change and
stability
*Edited by Thomas Heberer
and Gunter Schubert*

32 **U.S.–China Relations**
China policy on Capitol Hill
Tao Xie

33 **Chinese Kinship**
Contemporary anthropological
perspectives
*Edited by Susanne Brandtstädter
and Gonçalo D. Santos*

34 **Politics and Government in
Hong Kong**
Crisis under Chinese
sovereignty
Edited by Ming Sing

35 **Rethinking Chinese Popular
Culture**
Cannibalizations of the canon
*Edited by Carlos Rojas and
Eileen Cheng-yin Chow*

36 **Institutional Balancing in the
Asia Pacific**
Economic interdependence and
China's rise
Kai He

37 **Rent Seeking in China**
*Edited by Tak-Wing Ngo and
Yongping Wu*

38 **China, Xinjiang and Central
Asia**
History, transition and
crossborder interaction into the
21st century
*Edited by Colin Mackerras and
Michael Clarke*

39 **Intellectual Property Rights in
China**
Politics of piracy, trade and
protection
Gordon Cheung

40 **Developing China**
Land, politics and social
conditions
George C.S. Lin

41 **State and Society Responses
to Social Welfare Needs in
China**
Serving the people
*Edited by Jonathan Schwartz
and Shawn Shieh*

42 **Gay and Lesbian Subculture
in Urban China**
Loretta Wing Wah Ho

43 **The Politics of Heritage
Tourism in China**
A view from Lijiang
Xiaobo Su and Peggy Teo

44 **Suicide and Justice**
A Chinese perspective
Wu Fei

45 **Management Training and
Development in China**
Educating managers in a
globalized economy
*Edited by Malcolm Warner and
Keith Goodall*

46 **Patron–Client Politics and Elections in Hong Kong**
Bruce Kam-kwan Kwong

47 **Chinese Family Business and the Equal Inheritance System**
Unravelling the myth
Victor Zheng

48 **Reconciling State, Market and Civil Society in China**
The long march towards prosperity
Paolo Urio

49 **Innovation in China**
The Chinese software industry
Shang-Ling Jui

50 **Mobility, Migration and the Chinese Scientific Research System**
Koen Jonkers

51 **Chinese Film Stars**
Edited by Mary Farquhar and Yingjin Zhang

52 **Chinese Male Homosexualities**
Memba, Tongzhi and Golden Boy
Travis S.K. Kong

53 **Industrialisation and Rural Livelihoods in China**
Agricultural processing in Sichuan
Susanne Lingohr-Wolf

54 **Law, Policy and Practice on China's Periphery**
Selective adaptation and institutional capacity
Pitman B. Potter

55 **China–Africa Development Relations**
Edited by Christopher M. Dent

56 **Neoliberalism and Culture in China and Hong Kong**
The countdown of time
Hai Ren

57 **China's Higher Education Reform and Internationalisation**
Edited by Janette Ryan

58 **Law, Wealth and Power in China**
Commercial law reforms in context
Edited by John Garrick

59 **Religion in Contemporary China**
Revitalization and innovation
Edited by Adam Yuet Chau

60 **Consumer-Citizens of China**
The role of foreign brands in the imagined future china
Kelly Tian and Lily Dong

61 **The Chinese Communist Party and China's Capitalist Revolution**
The political impact of the market
Lance L.P. Gore

62 **China's Homeless Generation**
Voices from the veterans of the Chinese civil war, 1940s–1990s
Joshua Fan

63 **In Search of China's Development Model**
Beyond the Beijing consensus
Edited by S. Philip Hsu, Suisheng Zhao and Yu-Shan Wu

64 **Xinjiang and China's Rise in Central Asia, 1949–2009**
A history
Michael E. Clarke

65 **Trade Unions in China**
The challenge of labour unrest
Tim Pringle

66 **China's Changing Workplace**
Dynamism, diversity and disparity
Edited by Peter Sheldon, Sunghoon Kim, Yiqiong Li, and Malcolm Warner

67 **Leisure and Power in Urban China**
Everyday life in a medium-sized Chinese city
Unn Målfrid H. Rolandsen

68 **China, Oil and Global Politics**
Philip Andrews-Speed and Roland Dannreuther

69 **Education Reform in China**
Edited by Janette Ryan

70 **Social Policy and Migration in China**
Lida Fan

71 **China's One Child Policy and Multiple Caregiving**
Raising little Suns in Xiamen
Esther C.L. Goh

72 **Politics and Markets in Rural China**
Edited by Björn Alpermann

73 **China's New Underclass**
Paid domestic labour
Xinying Hu

74 **Poverty and Development in China**
Alternative approaches to poverty assessment
Lu Caizhen

75 **International Governance and Regimes**
A Chinese perspective
Peter Kien-Hong YU

76 **HIV/AIDS in China**
The economic and social determinants
Dylan Sutherland and Jennifer Y.J. Hsu

77 **Looking for Work in Post-Socialist China**
Governance, active job seekers and the new Chinese labour market
Feng Xu

78 **Sino-Latin American Relations**
Edited by K.C. Fung and Alicia Garcia-Herrero

79 **Mao's China and the Sino-Soviet Split**
Ideological dilemma
Mingjiang Li

80 **Law and Policy for China's Market Socialism**
Edited by John Garrick

81 **China–Taiwan Relations in a Global Context**
Taiwan's foreign policy and relations
Edited by C.X. George Wei

82 **The Chinese Transformation of Corporate Culture**
Colin S.C. Hawes

83 **Mapping Media in China**
Region, province, locality
*Edited by Wanning Sun and
Jenny Chio*

84 **China, the West and the Myth
of New Public Management**
Neoliberalism and its discontents
Paolo Urio

85 **The Lahu Minority in
Southwest China**
A response to ethnic
marginalization on the frontier
Jianxiong Ma

86 **Social Capital and Institutional
Constraints**
A comparative analysis of China,
Taiwan and the US
Joonmo Son

87 **Southern China**
Industry, development and
industrial policy
*Marco R. Di Tommaso,
Lauretta Rubini, and
Elisa Barbieri*

88 **State–Market Interactions in
China's Reform Era**
Local state competition and
global market building in the
tobacco industry
Junmin Wang

89 **The Reception and Rendition
of Freud in China**
China's Freudian slip
*Edited by Tao Jiang and
Philip J. Ivanhoe*

90 **Sinologism**
An alternative to Orientalism and
Postcolonialism
Ming Dong Gu

91 **The Middle Class in Neoliberal
China**
Governing risk, life-building, and
themed spaces
Hai Ren

92 **The Chinese Corporatist State**
Adaption, survival and resistance
*Edited by Jennifer Y.J. Hsu and
Reza Hasmath*

93 **Law and Fair Work in China**
*Sean Cooney, Sarah Biddulph,
and Ying Zhu*

94 **Guangdong and Chinese
Diaspora**
The changing landscape of
qiaoxiang
Yow Cheun Hoe

95 **The Shanghai Alleyway House**
A vanishing urban vernacular
Gregory Bracken

96 **Chinese Globalization**
A profile of people-based global
connections in China
Jiaming Sun and Scott Lancaster

97 **Disruptive Innovation in
Chinese and Indian Businesses**
The strategic implications for
local entrepreneurs and global
incumbents
Peter Ping Li

98 **Corporate Governance and
Banking in China**
Michael Tan

99 **Gender, Modernity and Male
Migrant Workers in China**
Becoming a 'modern' man
Xiaodong Lin

100 **Emissions, Pollutants and Environmental Policy in China**
Designing a national emissions trading system
Bo Miao

101 **Sustainable Development in China**
Edited by Curtis Andressen, Mubarak A.R., and Xiaoyi Wang

102 **Islam and China's Hong Kong**
Ethnic identity, Muslim networks and the new Silk Road
Wai-Yip Ho

103 **International Regimes in China**
Domestic implementation of the international fisheries agreements
Gianluca Ferraro

104 **Rural Migrants in Urban China**
Enclaves and transient urbanism
Fulong Wu, Fangzhu Zhang, and Chris Webster

105 **State-Led Privatization in China**
The politics of economic reform
Jin Zeng

106 **China's Supreme Court**
Ronald C. Keith, Zhiqiu Lin, and Shumei Hou

107 **Queer Sinophone Cultures**
Howard Chiang and Ari Larissa Heinrich

108 **New Confucianism in Twenty-First Century China**
The construction of a discourse
Jesús Solé-Farràs

109 **Christian Values in Communist China**
Gerda Wielander

110 **China and Global Trade Governance**
China's first decade in the World Trade Organization
Edited by Ka Zeng and Wei Liang

111 **The China Model and Global Political Economy**
Comparison, impact, and interaction
Ming Wan

112 **Chinese Middle Classes**
China, Taiwan, Macao and Hong Kong
Edited by Hsin-Huang Michael Hsiao

113 **Economy Hotels in China**
A glocalized innovative hospitality sector
Songshan Sam Huang and Xuhua Michael Sun

114 **The Uyghur Lobby**
Global networks, coalitions and strategies of the World Uyghur Congress
Yu-Wen Chen

115 **Housing Inequality in Chinese Cities**
Edited by Youqin Huang and Si-ming Li

116 **Transforming Chinese Cities**
Edited by Mark Y. Wang, Pookong Kee and Jia Gao

117 **Popular Media, Social Emotion and Public Discourse in Contemporary China**
Shuyu Kong

118 **Globalization and Public Sector Reform in China**
Kjeld Erik Brødsgaard

119 **Religion and Ecological Sustainability in China**
Edited by James Miller, Dan Smyer Yu and Peter van der Veer

120 **Comparatizing Taiwan**
Edited by Shu-mei Shih and Ping-hui Liao

121 **Entertaining the Nation**
Chinese television in the twenty-first century
Edited by Ruoyun Bai and Geng Song

122 **Local Governance Innovation in China**
Experimentation, diffusion, and defiance
Edited by Jessica C. Teets and William Hurst

123 **Footbinding and Women's Labor in Sichuan**
Hill Gates

124 **Incentives for Innovation in China**
Building an innovative economy
Xuedong Ding and Jun Li

125 **Conflict and Cooperation in Sino-US Relations**
Change and continuity, causes and cures
Edited by Jean-Marc F. Blanchard and Simon Shen

126 **Chinese Environmental Aesthetics**
Wangheng Chen, translated by Feng Su, edited by Gerald Cipriani

127 **China's Military Procurement in the Reform Era**
The setting of new directions
Yoram Evron

128 **Forecasting China's Future**
Dominance or collapse?
Roger Irvine

129 **Chinese Migration and Economic Relations with Europe**
Edited by Marco Sanfilippo and Agnieszka Weinar

130 **Party Hegemony and Entrepreneurial Power in China**
Institutional change in the film and music industries
Elena Meyer-Clement

131 **Explaining Railway Reform in China**
A train of property rights re-arrangements
Linda Tjia Yin-nor

132 **Irony, Cynicism and the Chinese State**
Edited by Hans Steinmüller and Susanne Brandtstädter

133 **Animation in China**
History, aesthetics, media
Sean Macdonald

Explaining Railway Reform in China

A train of property rights re-arrangements

Linda Tjia Yin-nor

Routledge
Taylor & Francis Group

LONDON AND NEW YORK

First published 2016 by Routledge

2 Park Square, Milton Park, Abingdon, Oxfordshire OX14 4RN

52 Vanderbilt Avenue, New York, NY 10017

Routledge is an imprint of the Taylor & Francis Group, an informa business

First issued in paperback 2020

British Library Cataloguing in Publication Data
A catalogue record for this book is available from the British Library

Library of Congress Cataloging-in-Publication Data
Tjia, Linda Yin-Nor.
Explaining railway reform in China : a train of property rights re-arrangements / Linda Yin-Nor Tjia. – 1 Edition.
    pages cm. – (Routledge contemporary China series ; 131)
    Includes bibliographical references and index.
    1. Railroads–China. 2. Railroads and state–China.
    3. Transportation–China. 4. Infrastructure (Economics)–China.
    5. China–Economic policy–21st century. I. Title.
    HE3287.T53 2015
    385.0951–dc23   2015017540

ISBN: 978-0-415-63305-5 (hbk)
ISBN: 978-0-367-59794-8 (pbk)

Typeset in Times New Roman
by Wearset Ltd, Boldon, Tyne and Wear

Contents

List of figures	xvi
List of tables	xviii
Acknowledgments	xx

	Introduction	1
1	**Property rights, ownership changes, and the puzzles**	3
	Overview 3	
	Conceptualizing "property rights" 5	
	Explaining ownership changes 11	
	The puzzle 17	
	Research methodology 19	
2	**The best railway reform model**	28
	Overview 28	
	The economic model of railway reform 28	
3	**China's railway reform in context**	41
	A chronicle of China's railway reform 41	
	Research hypotheses 55	
4	**(De)centralization policies**	61
	Overview 61	
	China's railway: a three-dimensional integrated structure 62	
	Economic explanation of railway reform 65	
	Economic imperatives, decentralization, and property rights arrangements 66	
	Railway reform: the search beyond efficiency 79	

5   Great-Leap-Forward approach of railway reform   85
Overview 85
Before the Great-Leap-Forward approach 86
The Great-Leap approach 107
A peep into the railway sub-sectors 112

**6   The railway's transport sub-sector: top down
re-centralization and local cadres' survival strategies**   118
Overview 118
*Reviewing the concept of extra-budgetary production
     resources 120*
Local railway cadres' survival strategies 121
Picking the right assets 142

**7   The railway's construction sub-sector: emergence of a
multi-layered, state-owned enterprise group**   147
Overview 147
*Discovery of excessive construction assets before spinning off from
     the MOR 149*
Re-centralization of selected state-owned property rights 154
*Further discovery and recovery of construction assets under the
     SASAC 158*
*The emergence of a construction business group: a property rights
     hybrid 163*
Iron grip control 168

8   The railway's telecommunications sub-sector   174
Overview 174
Telecommunications availability and economic development 175
State-led telecommunications reform in China 176
*Property rights re-arrangements for rail-borne
     telecommunications assets 182*
Mixed policies of decentralization and re-centralization 201

9   Conclusion   206
Confusing property rights re-arrangement policies 206
Property rights re-arrangements as a discovery process 207
*Recovery of state assets: consolidation and specialization of
     business groups 208*
"Statization" versus "privatization" 210
*Emergence of a multi-tiered hybrid: dilution of state
     ownership 210*

Appendix: list of interviewees 213

Bibliography 214
Index 232

Figures

2.1	The best railway reform model	31
2.2	Fully integrated model	32
2.3	Vertically separated and horizontally integrated model	32
2.4	Vertically and horizontally separated model	33
2.5	Dominant integrated and horizontally separated model	33
2.6	Vertically integrated and geographically separated model	33
2.7	Vertically disintegrated and geographically separated model	34
4.1	Functional and social integration of the MOR	63
4.2	Annual handling volume and net profit/loss, railway sector, 1987–2005	68
4.3	Passenger transport market share, 1949–2005	69
4.4	Freight transport market share, 1949–2005	70
4.5	Labour productivity, transport sector, 1990–2005	72
5.1	State allocation of fixed assets investment in the transport sector, 1985–2005	94
5.2	Length of China's railways vs. highways, 1978–2005	95
5.3	Number of China's railway freight cars vs. motor trucks, 1978–2005	96
6.1	Operating cost and net profit/loss, Chinese railway, 1984–2005	123
6.2	Number of staff members, revenue, and profit in diversified businesses of the MOR's transport sub-sector vs the MOR, 1991–2005	127
6.3	Total workforces in the MOR, 1978–2005	132
6.4a	MOR's organizational chart, 1999	133
6.4b	MOR's organizational chart, 2003	134
7.1	Re-organization of CRCC	162
7.2	Number of and total profit generated by SOEs, 1997–2004	164
7.3	The CRCC organizational chart II	166
8.1	Personnel reshuffle in China's telecommunications sector in 2004	183
8.2	Ownership arrangements for China Telecommunications Corporation	184

8.3	Ownership arrangements for China United Telecommunications Corporation	185
8.4	Ownership arrangements for China Mobile Corporation	186
8.5	Ownership arrangements for China Network Communications Group Corporation	187
8.6	Ownership arrangement for China Satellite Communications Corporation	188
8.7	Ownership arrangement of China TieTong Corporation	190
8.8	Restructuring of the telecommunications assets in the MOR, 1995, 2000, 2004	198
8.9	China Railcom's property rights hybrid	200

Tables

1.1 Ownership changing models 18
2.1 A list of railways undertaking various structural separations 38
3.1 Time frame for vertical separation of the MOR 43
4.1 For-profit enterprises and offices in the sideline sector of the MOR 1999 65
5.1 China's Medium to Long-term Railway Construction Plan, 2004–2020 89
5.2 China's railway Eleventh Five-Year Plan, 2006–2010 90
5.3 Railway statistics, China, India, Britain, the United States and Japan, 1994 and 1995 97
5.4 Comparative cost of logistics as a percentage of GDP, wholesale price, total revenue, and total cost, 1987–2005 100
5.5 Highway vs. railway: length and freight transport product, 1952–2005 102–103
5.6 Turnaround time, handling time and speed of railway freight cars, 1991–2005 104
5.7 Distribution of goods lifted by China's railway, 1990–2005 105
5.8 Distribution of goods lifted by railways in China, India, United Kingdom, Sweden, Spain, and France, 1994 and 1995 106
5.9 Railway administrations and sub-administrations in the transport services sub-sector, the MOR, 1999 and 2005 109
6.1 No. of enterprises, no. of staff members, revenue and profit: diversified business of the MOR's transport sub-sector vs. the MOR, 1990–2005 124
6.2 A sample form of a regional unit's budgetary plan, 2003 127
6.3 China's exports and imports volume, 1978–2005 138
6.4 Share of world trade volume, 2003 139
6.5 WTO timetable for foreign participation in China's logistics sector 140
7.1 Total value of construction projects undertaken by the CRCC, 1992–2002 (RMB 100 million) 153
7.2 The SASAC's missions 156

7.3   China's 11th Five-Year Plan for transport infrastructure   159
7.4   Selected CRCC joint ventures   169
8.1   Maximum share of foreign investment in telecommunications
      joint venture after WTO accession   180

Acknowledgments

The journey of my PhD research and this book manuscript was full of tears and laughter.

Two weeks before my qualifying examination, my father passed away. This was the second time I lost someone important in my life—my loving mother had passed away before I started my undergraduate study. I regret so much that my parents could not see their daughter complete her doctoral degree. From the bottom of my heart, I thank them for their courage to travel from their birth place in Indonesia to China, and from China to Hong Kong, looking for ways to improve the quality of life of their two daughters, Tiffany and myself. They are always my great models, giving me the wisdom and persistence to overcome the challenges in life and study. Tiffany is the best-ever sister in the world. Her love continues to remind me of my happiest memories with my family.

The search for knowledge was a joyful experience. I would like to thank many people who assisted me directly throughout the production of this dissertation. In the first place I show my heartfelt gratitude to Professor David Zweig, my thesis supervisor, for his encouragement from the outset. He was always confident that I would do fine, and this helped me more than he knew.

Special thanks go to Professor Barry Naughton, Professor James Kung, Professor Lin Yi-min, and Professor Larry Farh for serving as external and internal examiners on my thesis committee and providing constructive comments during the oral defense. I had met Professor Naughton only once at a workshop in Hong Kong, and yet he was interested in my research and agreed to fly all the way to attend my oral examination in person. His substantial comments on both my theoretical framework and case studies were very useful at the final stage of my thesis revision. Professor Kung spent an enormous amount of time reading the final draft of my lengthy thesis during the festive season and amid his busy schedule as the Acting Head of the Division of Social Science. Professor Lin has been very supportive of my study since I enrolled in the Master in China Studies program ten years ago. Professor Farh teaches at the Department of Management of Organization; his knowledge in business and management in the Chinese community added value to the conceptual framework of the thesis.

For some technical reasons, Professor Ma Ngok was unable to examine my thesis, but his prior teaching on the economic reform of the Eastern European countries opened up unknown areas to me. His critical comments at the early stage of my research were vital for me to develop my theoretical framework.

I am also grateful to Professor Rong Chaohe, Professor Ou Guoli, and Dr. Li Hongchang at the Transport Management Department of the Beijing Jiaotong University. They were all enthusiastic in sharing with me their professional knowledge and personal views as regards various reform policies in the Chinese railway sector.

During my research trips in China, my two personal friends went out of their way to introduce me to a network of railway cadres. For research ethics reasons, I have to thank them anonymously. But I want them to know that I would not be able to see the patterns of property rights changes in the field and come up with these interesting research findings without their kind assistance.

In the winter of 2003, Auntie Sun and Jiwen allowed me to stay at their homes in Beijing and Shanghai, respectively, so that I did not need to burn money on hotel expenses while I was trying to arrange interviews with and wait for responses from those busy railway officials. I thank both of them and their families for their great hospitality.

For financial support, I thank the Sir Edward Youde Memorial Fund Council for awarding the Sir Edward Youde Memorial Fellowship in 2002, in recognition of the importance of my research. I also thank the School of Humanities and Social Science of the Hong Kong University of Science and Technology (HKUST) for providing two consecutive research travel grants for me to travel to Beijing, Shanghai, Tianjin, Wuhan, and Guangzhou to conduct in-depth interviews. In addition, the Center on China's Transnational Relations and the University Grants Committee of HKUST supported my travel to present different parts of my thesis at the Business History Conference in Le Creusot, France in 2004, the Association of Pacific Rim Universities Doctoral Students Conference in Tokyo, Japan in 2007, and the All China Economics International Conference, Hong Kong in 2007.

I convey my acknowledgment to my colleagues and friends at HKUST— Karen, Wai-yip, Joshua, Sam, Jason, Emily, Andrew, Valerie, Phoebe, Marina, Alvin, Channey, Pearl, Mandy, Connie, Iris, and Connie—for their advice, support, and assistance in innumerable ways over the years.

Finally, my deepest debt goes to Kong, my husband. My life would not have been the same without his support. I am grateful for his patience in listening to me when I was stuck in the middle of making sense of my research data; his understanding when I needed to travel away from home for data collection, interviews, and conference presentations; and his willingness to share the household work at home. Thank you for brightening my days with your love.

Introduction

Western literature always prescribes that the best model for railway reform is privatization. China's leadership also declared the state's determination to re-arrange property rights and rejuvenate corporate governance. But is China's railway reform really a story of convergence? Will the property rights of railway assets be clearly demarcated, if not privatized, eventually? To answer these questions, this book bridges the socialist reform and transport policy literature, and studies the empirical changes of the property rights arrangements in China's railway system. Refuting the convergence theory, this book concludes that the cyclical reform policies of decentralization and re-centralization were actually an exploratory and interactive mechanism of "assets discovery" and "assets recovery."

The surface appearances of decentralization and profit sharing reforms served two purposes. First, the profit sharing approach was a mere mimic of the Western model. By complying with the Western style, the Chinese government could be legitimized in terms of obtaining financial and technological assistance from various international funding sources. But the so-called decentralization reform policies did not lead to partial or full-scale privatization.

Second, decentralization did not clarify property rights arrangements, which could have helped the state leadership to gradually identify the right person to inherit the state assets. Rather, during the initial phase of reform, the state administered the dual-track system, resulting in an unexpected situation of asset ambiguity, and encouraging local cadres to discover and rejuvenate the extra-budgetary productive resources.

After the discovery of the idle productive assets, the central government began to recover these newly discovered resources. For those productive assets of the industries which required significant upfront investment, produced public goods, or were vulnerable to market competition, the Chinese government re-centralized or consolidated the respective property rights; otherwise the government decentralized and, perhaps, privatized them.

This book is largely based on the research for my doctoral thesis and provides a positive explanation of the reform in China's railway sector between 1978 and the dissolution of the Ministry of Railways (MOR). Chapter 1 conceptualizes the idea of property rights by referring to orthodox property rights theory. The proposed "assets discovery mechanism" will be hinted at here by putting forward an alternative view that focuses on the capture of the residual property rights of the state assets.

Chapter 2 discusses the economic logic of railway reform in orthodox transport studies. Although the book focuses more on the positive theory of reform, it is necessary to set the scene by first introducing the normative origin of the reform theory and describing where reality falls short of the conditions to realize the normative implication. Combining the relevant theoretical puzzles, this chapter paves the way for the next chapter, which will bring in the railway reform theories and set four working hypotheses.

Chapter 3 describes the evolutionary development of the railway reform in China between 1978 and 2013, which resulted in various conflicting and confusing reform outcomes, and cast doubt on the explanatory power of the efficiency model. Bridging the general socialist reform theories, and the specific railway reform policies, the conclusion translates the theoretical puzzles into a set of specific research questions and puts forward four research hypotheses:

H1   Economic imperatives do not necessarily lead to decentralization.
H2   Decentralization does not necessarily lead to privatization.
H3   Decentralization identifies idle assets—i.e., "picks the right assets"—but not "picks the winners."
H4   The more strategically important the newly identified assets, the more they will be centralized by the state.

Chapter 4 examines the overall railway reform policy, and validates the hypothesis (H1) that there is indeed no direct relationship between the economic imperatives and the degree of decentralization.

By comparing the transport sub-sector of the railway system with other modes of transport, and reviewing the overall top-down reform policies, Chapter 5 describes the great leap in rail development, and argues for the hypothesis (H2) that various decentralization policies do not necessarily lead to privatization arrangements. Rather, it was part of the state's strategic move to, on the one hand, mimic the Western capitalist model selectively, and, on the other hand, discover the idle production assets.

Chapter 6 continues to focus on the MOR's transport sub-sector and zoom in on local cadres' survival strategies to examine the hypothesis (H3) that the assets discovery mechanism—the MOR's leakage of authority and the dual track policy—unexpectedly enabled local cadres to discover idle productive resources, i.e., to "pick the right assets," not to "pick the right owners."

Chapters 7 and 8 study the construction and signaling sub-sectors of the MOR. In addition to providing evidence to support the asset discovery mechanism, they also demonstrate cases of asset recovery, supporting the last hypothesis that the more strategically important the newly identified assets, the more they will be centralized by the state.

Chapter 9 provides concluding remarks on the asset discovery and recovery experiences of the railway sector in China.

1 Property rights, ownership changes, and the puzzles

Overview

Despite the importance of the railway sector in China, both in terms of its strategic role and economic values, there is little in the way of a thorough empirical study of its reform. Having been state-owned and centrally regulated for decades, the railway reform in China confused many people, particularly in terms of its ownership and property rights arrangements. Western literature on railway reform focused on how to induce competition and enhance profitability. As a result, any discrepancy in the course of reform would be considered as a deviation from the best reform model. In view of the influence of the property rights theory and the global trend on privatization, it was not surprising to see China's leadership enunciate the state's determination to restructure the property rights arrangements and rejuvenate corporate governance.

In fact, during the mid-1990s, rural enterprises in China had already undergone massive privatization. But such privatization was different from the type proposed by the Western model, in which the property rights of the state assets are expected to be transferred to outsiders. What happened in China was that most of the rural enterprises were sold to insiders, and yet they were able to improve the performance.[1] So the question becomes whether the Chinese government will follow the Western model of railway reform, or copy the successful experience from its other enterprises, or develop a different strategy to reform the country's last batch of centralized sectors?

To answer these questions, this book bridges the gap between socialist reform literature and transport policy, and studies the empirical changes of property rights arrangements in China's railway system. The research questions that guide this research to understand China's railway reform can broadly be divided into two areas.

The first set of questions target the normative approach of socialist reform theory and ask: Was China's railway reform a story of convergence to the Western model? Were the property rights of the railway assets clearly demarcated, if not privatized eventually? Was China's leadership willing to give up its control over railway assets? Did the Chinese government pay lip service to the idea of decentralization, and if so, why? Did China's railway reform deviate from the efficiency model of reform, and if so, how?

The second set of questions was a response to the positive research on various reform experiences, and asks: What were the differences between the property rights changes of the railway sector and those of the rural enterprises? What were the endowments or institutional factors that contribute to the differences? Could the experience of the reform of rural enterprises aid in understanding China's railway reform?

In brief, this book concludes that the convergence theory of privatization cannot explain China's railway reform. Although the positive characteristics of property rights theory are appealing for their logical and forceful policy implications, it remains a theoretical reference and fails to explain the actual property rights re-arrangements in the real world.

What we have seen in the past two decades in China was that the central government undertook a problem-solving approach to decentralize and re-centralize the property rights arrangements of many large-scale state sectors, including the railway system. In responding to such cyclical reform policies and the resulting fuzzy fiscal arrangements, local cadres rushed to discover the idle or hidden productive resources. This "assets discovery process" has not been described in detail in the reform literature, mostly because the reform of the strategically important, longstanding, and highly centralized state sectors was more complicated than that of the rural enterprises, and thus the central government had to grope for the most feasible way to restructure the last batch of state sectors.

In view of the limited information on these huge state sectors and the finite computational resources, the central government could hardly have a very long-term view down the road of reform. However, it was indeed these short-sighted but pragmatic measures that together shaped the reform in a way that encouraged local cadres to uncover the idle productive assets. Without committing to a process of outright privatization, the central government was able to recover the recently discovered assets. For productive assets relating to those industries in which market competition alone could not improve the efficiency, the Chinese government would maintain the state's ownership in order to re-regulate and re-arrange the respective property rights; otherwise the government would decentralize and, perhaps, privatize them. By studying the railway reform in China, this book is thus aimed at uncovering the "assets discovery mechanism" and the "assets recovery mechanism."

This chapter first conceptualizes the idea of property rights by referring to the orthodox property rights theory. Although the book focuses more on the positive theory of reform, it is necessary to set the scene by first introducing the normative origin of the reform theory and describing where reality falls short of the conditions to realize the normative implication. In fact, the newly developed "assets discovery mechanism" will be hinted at from here by putting forward an alternative view that focuses on the capture of the residual property rights of the state assets.

The second section shifts to review various positive theories of ownership change. While most of the positive literature focuses on local cadres and how they shape the transformation process, the "assets discovery mechanism" brings in the role of the central government and explains the exploratory process through which idle state assets are gradually discovered. This discovery mechanism is followed by a closely related "assets recovery mechanism" through which the central government gradually realizes the existence of idle assets and selectively re-organizes these newly discovered assets to form a state-owned property rights hybrid. This chapter will conclude by combining the relevant theoretical puzzles and paving the way for the next chapter, which will bring in the railway reform theories and set four working hypotheses.

Conceptualizing "property rights"

There are many views as to the definition of property rights and how they can be used to explain economic behavior. The orthodox property rights theory comprises the control, income, and transfer of rights, and argues that the best way to coordinate resources is to concentrate the ownership of the three bundles of rights by privatization and de-politicization.

Economic theory of property rights bundles

Economic analysis of property rights assumes that, under two sets of conditions, individuals will always maximize self-profits, optimize resources distribution, and benefit the society as a whole. First, property rights have to be legally enforced and explicitly protected so that the related parties can negotiate for the best possible allocation of the rights of the resources exclusively.[2] Second, property rights can be clearly dissociated into three bundles: the right to use an asset; the right to retain the returns from an asset; and the right to transfer an asset to others.[3]

Accordingly, under the pure private ownership arrangement, all three bundles of rights are concentrated in the same owner, who is bound to put the assets in the best use in order to maximize the reward. The owner will take into consideration not only the instant result, but also any future possible impact.[4] Pushing the claim to the extreme case, the owner "will attempt to take into account the supply and demand conditions that he thinks will exist after his death."[5] Since people have different talents with different assets, the comparative advantage can only be materialized if ownership rights are transferable.[6] Hence the right to transfer assets is no less important than the use and income rights. Otherwise people are prevented from acquiring property with which they could produce more effective outcomes than others.

To recap, property rights theory logically deduces that the best way to restructure ownership is to delineate clearly the trio of rights and legally enforce the transferability of property rights. Market transactions will mold the ownership structure into the most effective arrangements, under which the three bundles of rights are concentrated in the same owner, who can make the best use of the assets for his own benefit and for the sake of the society.

Communal and state ownership

Theoretically, communal ownership refers to a collective property rights arrangement in which all members of the community have equal right of access to the trio of rights. In practice, communist and post-communist countries lack well-developed systems of property protection and contract enforcement. The idea of collectivity thus results in not only ineffective ownership arrangements, but also unfair allocation of resources to the people who are in power as gate-keepers to the common resources. Since everyone in the community is said to possess the right to claim the award from the resources and bear the cost of the use of the resources, the gatekeeper would exhaust the available resources, maximize their personal gains, and ignore the detrimental effects of the excessive use of the common resources. After all, such costs will be diluted and shared among all the members of the community.[7]

State ownership is even more problematic than communal ownership, as the party/state confiscates private property and puts it under state control in the people's name.[8] Generally speaking, the central leadership controls the right to transfer the property, the state treasury controls the right to receive and allocate the reward, and the local cadres control the right to use the productive assets. Very often the central leadership also exerts its influence in the income and control rights as well.[9]

Since the central leadership does not have direct cash flow rights, they are not necessarily motivated by efficiency concerns. In addition, different pressure groups may lobby the politicians for various political and social interests other than efficiency. On the other hand, loss-making cadres always expect external financial assistance from the state in terms of subsidies, tax exemptions, generous credits, state loans, or other preferential policies. They are, strictly speaking, spared from any disciplinary consequences of inefficient operation. As such, price responsiveness declines, entrepreneurial innovations dissipate and excessive demand for inputs leads to what Kornai refers to as the "soft budget constraint" and "shortage economy."[10]

Moreover, benevolent politicians are rare. Many of them favor private gains over efficiency. Knowing that any improvement in the business performance would only invite the supervising treasury to set more demanding targets in the next year's budget, cadres tend to under-perform, which leads to inefficient performance. In addition, assuming partial or *de jure* property rights of the state assets, local cadres are opportunistic and tend to carry out unproductive rent-seeking behavior.[11] Boykco *et al.* concludes that state ownership implies "political control of poorly defined property rights," which further endangers the problematic communal ownership. [12]

De-collectivization and de-politicization of state ownership

State and communal ownership is characterized by political control of economic activities and lack of well-developed systems for property protection and contract enforcement. To solve the problem of poor property rights arrangements, state- or collective-owned assets should de-collectivized and de-politicized by re-allocating the trio of rights from politicians and state treasury to private owners.

In addition, the neoliberal theory, encompassing the classical liberal theory, public choice theory, and free market theory, suggests that government should promote freedom through minimizing coercion and transferring state power back to the "liberated," "risk-taking," and "competitive" individuals.[13] Agency theory also believes that highly vertical and bureaucratic integration will induce interlocking constraints and inflict ineffective monitoring of multi-level principal–agent relationships. Accordingly, property rights reform should include de-collectivization and de-politicization.[14]

However, the planned system was embedded with interlocking links which cannot be simply cut across and taken away. These networks are ready to undergo re-composition and adaptation in the process of disintegration, and are likely to integrate again in another form. In fact, in spite of the collapse of the communist regime in many Eastern European countries and the subsequent political compromise, it has already been proved extremely difficult to de-collectivize and de-politicize the ineffective system.[15] Without doubt, it is complicated to regularize the planned system so as to deregulate it. The Eastern European countries had tried various forms of privatization, such as spontaneous privatization, direct sale, management buy-out, and voucher privatization, but many resulted in unsatisfactory outcomes, including disastrous assets stripping and insider control.[16]

Beyond the trio of rights

In reality, the trio of rights is hardly exhaustive and *de jure* clarification of each and every right is costly. Even the Western capitalist system relies on the broader social and legal systems to set the generic framework for the proper use of various rights. It is only with such mutually accepted legal and social norms that the rest of the unspecified rights were well recognized and constrained, and the clarification of the trio of rights becomes meaningful.[17]

In socialist systems, where the broader social and legal systems are not well in place, clarification of the trio of rights becomes insufficient. Without external constraints, there are many unspecified ways to deploy the resources, and one needs to identify various resources and assets before one can demarcate the ownership of the property rights.

Williamson's new institutional economic theory argues that the institutional environment includes a number of legal, social, and cultural rules which will alter the governance of a firm by changing its comparative cost of contractual relations.[18] During the reform era, the external environment is changing dynamically, and the unpredictability inevitably increases the costs of contractual relations and productive activities. Firms are always in need of production resources which are risky and uncertain to secure.[19] They will, therefore, make use of the existing (or pre-reform) inter-firm linkages to guarantee adequate supply of existing resources and to identify unused and idle resources. It was through such local survival strategies that the cadres indeed helped with the process of "asset picking." The newly picked assets would later be assessed by the government to decide whether they should be eventually decentralized or re-centralized.

Hidden productive resources

The orthodox property rights theory takes into consideration only production assets which are in operation, such as factory buildings, production lines, and machinery. This book, however, shows that as property rights take various forms, in particular during the reform era when productive resources are being identified and put into operation, some of these hidden resources are idle machinery, while others are intangible resources which have never been listed as fixed assets of the company. During the reform era, the changing top-down reform initiatives brought out the latent potential of these hidden resources, which then manifested themselves in a series of production activities. These hidden assets are embedded in the state firms and do not come to the attention of the supervising body, mostly because of their fluid nature. For the same reason, the property rights of these hidden assets cannot be demarcated, at least during the stage when these hidden assets are being recovered. In fact, the fuzzier the property rights arrangements, the more the room for manipulation and further discovery.

The following section describes the characteristics of hidden resources which are discovered and made visible by localities during the reform era. In order to uncover the "assets discovery mechanism," it is important to distinguish these intangible productive resources from other physical productive assets.

Intangible resources: technocratic, managerial, and political capital

In the Walrasian model of a neoclassical firm, the size and scope of a firm are determined by the list of assets it possesses to convert inputs into outputs. Such an economic approach assumes that the legal and social systems are in place to settle the property relations of different parties involved in the business operations, and therefore focuses only on restructuring the tangible productive assets. Such a perspective, however, ignores intangible productive resources, which are often rented or owned by different parties,[20] and whose property relations are not well specified during the reform era.[21]

For example, one such intangible resource is human capital. In China, during the planned regime, the supervisory units fixed production targets for their subordinates and provided them with the necessary, and often abundant, personnel establishments. However, for various reasons, such as the problems of principal–agent relations and asymmetric information, state personnel were underutilized. During the transition era, when the labor market could not serve as a "credentialing mechanism" to signify managerial abilities,[22] there was no way to ensure that cadres would stretch their abilities to the utmost. Moreover, financial and product markets were not in place to link cadres' rewards with the company's performance. As a result, human capital as important productive resources was embedded as an individual's latent abilities, which was intangible and invisible until the cadres decided that they should work to the best of their abilities because of various incentives.

Other intangible assets included different "extra-budgetary production capacities," which were either not well developed or simply "non-existent" during the planned regime. Very often, these extra production capacities were closely associated with cadres who possessed special bureaucratic status and worked at particular positions to assume the power and retain and re-allocate the assets. In theory, the earlier-mentioned human capital refers to the technocratic and managerial ability, and the discussion on the use of idle assets here requires another kind of intangible resources—"political capital." While human capital involves technocratic and managerial knowledge, political capital involves longstanding working relations, which the cadres accumulated during the planned regime. In practice, cadres combine their human capital and political capital to survive, or even thrive during the reform era.

Individually based resources

The efficiency model emphasizes the importance of clearly defining the ownership of the three bundles of property rights. However, it is not necessary to decide on the most capable owner because, under perfect market competition, property rights will eventually be transferred to the person who is most capable of making a profit. Such a concept assumes that the trio of rights is attached to the physical assets and can be transferred from one owner to another.

However, such a conceptual framework fails to capture the intangible characteristics of the assets, which are largely based on individual economic actors, and cannot be channeled away by transferring the physical assets. Rather, they are largely based on individual cadres, who can rejuvenate and channel the resources in a productive way by their technocratic, managerial, and political capital. Hu asserts that: "in this initial stage of property transformation, some seminal political factors and crucial institutional changes opened up new avenues for whoever was in the right place at the right time."[23]

"Floating" resources

An economic analysis of property rights also assumes that the three bundles of property rights are permanently associated with the physical production assets.[24] The transfer of the physical assets implies the transfer of the property rights as well. However, during the transitional economy in China, various extra-budgetary production capacities were in fact "floating" resources embedded within the state sector which required special coordination to get hold of and to put into production. Barzel contends that:

the most valued uses of an asset usually require the cooperation of other asset owners.... [E]fficient firm must locate a piece of equipment needed to produce its output next to where it operates, but it needs not own it. Ownership per se does not matter.[25]

In China, the local cadres who stake claims to use the idle assets were usually not the owners of the assets, but had influence on the deployment of the assets. This was known as the right of allocation (*fenpei quan*). Local cadres "redefined and recombined" resources, which were not rigidly attached to the physical assets of a company, but were "floating" within the organization.[26] King refers to such rights as "social property rights."[27]

Informally recognized resources

The fact that the economic theory of property rights emphasizes the clear demarcation of the trio of rights implies that the rights have to be formally recognized by "the institutions of corporate, contract, bankruptcy, tort and property law."[28] On the other hand, Weimer and Hu argue separately that there are also "informal rights" which are not legally, explicitly, or formally recognized, and yet all related parties endorse the rightful claim.[29] This was especially true during the transitional period when reform policies changed from time to time. In order to adapt better to the different and sometimes conflicting policies, informal arrangements of property rights emerged.

The gray area encouraged local cadres to identify and make use of available but unclaimed productive resources within the state sector. These informal resources, usually intangible, individually based, and floating in nature, may eventually be formalized and converge to the Western property rights system—at that time, the economic theory of property rights may become more useful in explaining various economic behavior; or it may develop into a different kind of property rights arrangement, with Chinese characteristics.

Normative model and positive constraints of reform

The normative conceptualization of property rights is the foundation of the efficiency model of reform, under which policy makers are advised to prescribe various ways to distribute the inefficient property rights. The communal and state ownership, however, carry certain positive constraints so that efficiency theory alone is insufficient in explaining the reality of the reform. As a result, while the normative model is useful in setting the idealistic scene, a positive approach is important in understanding the process pragmatically.

One widely concerning phenomenon is principle–agent problems. On the one hand, having limited information and finite computational resources, the reformers are working with their bounded rationality in the process of policy planning. On the other hand, local cadres would respond in different ways to the reform policies, and the result of the transformation largely depends on whether local agents shape the process in an entrepreneurial or parasitic way. In view of such a theoretical dilemma, most empirical research focuses on picking the right person to receive the state assets.

For example, La Porta and Lopez-de-Silanes' research on 97 percent of the non-financial firms privatized in Mexico during 1983–1991 suggests that outsider privatization improves productivity more than insider privatization, and the stronger the government's determination to deregulate the market, by removing price and quantity control as well as trade barriers, the faster the convergence to the benchmark performance.[30] The problem of insider privatization was largely due to what Milgrom and Roberts refer to as moral hazard, which is commonly found when local agents, who have critical information about the to-be-privatized firms and different interests from those of the central leadership, pursue private interests at others' expense.[31]

However, what happened in China's rural reform was that decentralized insider privatization was not only a predominant way of privatization, but also a successful way of doing so. Li and Rozelle's research in China suggests that local governments employed a screening contract to differentiate good managers from bad managers during insider privatization of rural enterprises: while good managers would pay a higher price for the firm and keep all the firm's future profits, bad managers would pay a lower price but agree to share future profits with the government.[32]

Such a "value discovery mechanism" helped local governments elicit information about a firm's true value. The positive constraint of privatization of rural enterprises in China was that, during the transition era, incumbent managers developed firm-specific skills which made the firms more valuable to them than outsiders. The research thus illustrates that local governments, in coping with the positive constraints of insider privatization, managed to arrive at the second best strategy to differentiate between good and bad owners among insiders.

However, when the Chinese government started to reform the last batch of its state enterprises, namely the centralized, large-scale, and strategic state-owned enterprises, it did not follow the same pattern of insider privatization and property rights changes as that of the rural enterprises. This time, the reform focused more on the top-level decision makers. Since they had not yet decided whether they would privatize the entire centralized sector, the screening mechanism was not applicable. Rather, a different kind of asset discovery mechanism was developed to discover the idle assets and help the leaders understand what they really possessed. The following literature review of various theories in explaining ownership changes thus fits the asset discovery mechanism into the broader reform literature.

Explaining ownership changes

With the conceptual building block of "property rights" in place, this section consolidates and reviews three major theoretical frameworks developed for studying the reform of the socialist planned economy. Each theory has its own vantage point, but all intend to explain the re-arrangements of property rights and transformation of ownership types. The efficiency model focuses on the normative prescription of ownership structure. The evolutionary and ownership conversion models adopt the positive approach to describe what has really happened; the former model traces the ownership heritage and the latter concerns the transformational mechanism.

The efficiency model

The efficiency model focuses on deductive reasoning of the optimal way and destiny of reform. This school of thought is associated with the economic concept of property rights. The discussion centers on the debate between big bang and gradual reform strategies.

Ownership concentration theory

The big bang advocates assert that rapid convergence to a Western style of market economy is the only way out for socialist reform.[33] Embracing Adam Smith's free market model and "invisible hand" principal,[34] the Coase Theorem of exclusive property rights,[35] and Demsetz's truncation of property rights into three bundles of rights,[36] neoclassical economists derive a set of comprehensive shock therapy for socialist reform,[37] which I call the "Ownership Concentration Theory." In short, big bang advocates believe that, under public ownership, people exhaust the available resources, maximize personal gains, and disregard the detrimental effects of the use of collective resources. Hence they argue that the essence of socialist reform is to streamline the ownership structure, which means to concentrate the control, income, and transfer rights of all productive assets into the hand of private owners.[38] The neoliberal further argues that the state should retreat from the market as soon and as far as possible. They believe that minimal state intervention is the essence of reform because concentrated ownership structure will allocate resources in the most effective way by itself.

Ownership delineation theory

The logic of the ownership concentration theory is straightforward, but its underlying assumptions of zero transaction costs, clear-cut boundaries of production assets, and universal social development fail to stand the test of reality, particularly in socialist economies.[39] Seeing that parts of Eastern Europe have endured prolonged economic stagnation after undertaking shock therapy, and that China has been one of the fastest-growing economies despite its reservation about massive privatization, the ownership concentration theory is fiercely attacked by a variant of the efficiency model, which I call the "Ownership Delineation Theory."

This school of thought largely agrees in principle that clearly defined and legally enforceable property rights are important to induce incentives and enhance efficiency. However, they cast doubts on the feasibility and necessity to undertake full-fledged outright privatization all at once.[40] These gradualists argue that, in the absence of advanced accounting, legal, and social institutions, bureaucratic coordination could be more efficient than, and far preferable to, market coordination during the transition era. Accordingly, one-stroke reform is subject to a high risk of disruptive consequences which are disastrous and irreversible.[41] Hence this school advocates a gradual and incremental engineering of the three bundles of property rights.[42] The gradualists also attribute China's stunning economic growth to piecemeal delineation of property rights, which gradually pushes back the frontiers of the socialist regime and facilitates the conversion to a market economy.[43]

The evolutionary model

Both the "ownership concentration" and "ownership delineation" theories focus on the property rights of production assets and explain ownership changes by state-led and efficiency-driven reasons. Such an efficiency model explains quite well why the responsibility contract system succeeded in the agricultural reform of China. However, when it comes to explaining the proliferation of rural industry in China, the efficiency model fails to explain the conflicting relationship between privatization and performance—many village and township enterprises did not respond to property rights incentives in a predictable way.[44] Studies of large-scale, state-owned enterprises also demonstrate that, in addition to internal work incentives, external market conditions also matter.[45]

In brief, privatization theories and effective ownership structure alone cannot explain the great variety of ownership arrangements in China.[46] Hence, the evolutionary model shifts to focus on the peculiarities of each reform experience empirically. Instead of prescribing what should be done and achieved, the evolutionary researchers study what has actually happened. This model also comprises two main theoretical variants: path dependency theory and institutional theory.

Path dependency theory

Path dependency theory focuses on the cumulative effects of pre-reform endowments on the processes of property rights re-arrangements.[47] Specifically, regional variations on the evolution of different property rights arrangements are found to be linked with endowment factors, such as the existing economic situation and marketization development, the power base of the commune and brigade enterprises,[48] the indigenous bureaucratic, market, and familial coordination,[49] the availability of kinship ties and access to overseas remittances,[50] the central state capacity,[51] and the provincial leadership quality.[52]

Institutional theory

The institutional theory, on the other hand, focuses on the effects of organizational constraints on the evolution of property rights arrangements, such as firm size and business diversity,[53] financial debts, and employment burdens,[54] multiple levels of administrative jurisdiction (the problem of too many "mothers-in-law"),[55] and the hierarchical level at which the firms are situated.[56]

The evolutionary model provides insightful accounts of the unfolding of various property rights arrangements in China. Piecing together the findings of both the path dependent and institutional studies, we are well informed on the peculiarities of different reform experiences. Instead of prescribing a theoretically optimal ownership structure, the evolutionary model demonstrates empirically the existence of a hybrid mix of ownership arrangements and fuzzy boundaries between firms and markets. The evolutionary pattern of ownership changes provides a very solid knowledge base for further research, but both the path dependent and institutional theories fail to spell out the causal mechanism.

The ownership conversion model

Building on the knowledge of the efficiency and evolutionary studies, the ownership conversion model looks into the reform patterns and generalizes about the transformation mechanism of property rights arrangements. In brief, the existing ownership conversion theories focus on how the local cadres responded to the top-down reform policy and resulted in various unexpected property rights arrangements—some local cadres dragged the entire reform process out and maintained the state ownership, some facilitated but shaped the transformation to serve their own interest, and a combination of these led to conflicting and confusing property rights outcomes. Thus, many state enterprises did not respond to the carefully designed incentives in the way many neoclassical economists had expected. While the first two ownership conversion theories address the problem of finding the right owners to receive the state assets, I put forward a newly formulated theory which addresses the problem of identifying the right assets to be restructured.

Political capitalism

Communist cadres are powerful and influential during the transition era because they are in a position to execute the state's policy of bureaucratic coordination just before the start of the reform. It is not at all surprising that they do not want to be marginalized during the reform process. One way of remaining powerful is to manage the reform so that as the system becomes less centralized, they have more room to retain personal gain. These cadres want to make sure that the system would not be further liberalized so that they can continue to be the gatekeepers and keep various rent-seeking activities going.

Staniszkis refers to this conversion of political power into economic power as "political capitalism."[57] Such local reform resistance is prominent during fiscal decentralization, when the state allows local cadres to retain more profits than in the pre-reform era, and results in asset stripping and unsatisfactory performance.[58]

Walder contends that cadres' abilities to resist the reform as such are largely determined by the extent of regime change. If the regime change is limited and cadres are able to retain their posts, it is highly likely that the incumbents will make use of their officialdom to extract income both legally and illegally.[59]

The result for local cadres employing political capitalism is the stalling of further reform and the emergence of a property rights hybrid in which state ownership co-exists with the dummy companies which have acquired assets from the state firms.

Technocratic managerialism

In opposite to the above-mentioned parasitic mechanism, capable cadres can also make use of their human capital in a positive way to survive and remain powerful during the market transition era. In this case, socialist cadres realize that they will be better off not by appropriating short-term benefits, but by aligning their long-term interests with their company's business performance.

Such a mechanism involves a certain level of revitalization of the hidden production resources—the human capital which had not been used before the reform era.[60] Szalai refers to such a conversion of technocratic power into economic power as "technocratic continuity."[61] This mechanism is particularly prominent in a mixed economy, where market competition begins to play a greater role than bureaucratic coordination. Szelenyi and Kostello's study of post-communist transformation in Eastern Europe after 1989 also contends that the technocratic faction was the main beneficiary and would easily enter the propertied class as a "corporate bourgeoisie."[62] Eyal *et al.* later researched class formation in post-communist Central Europe and put forward a similar theory of managerialism. They proclaim that the communist technocrats retained power by assuming the role of a "cultural bourgeoisie" who were not property owners in any sense, but were influential in managing the emerging "capitalist economy."[63]

The theory of technocratic managerialism is useful in explaining the property rights arrangements in sectors where the top leadership adopts the policy of decentralization during the reform era. The vast literature on local state corporatism also demonstrates the prevalence of entrepreneurialism in the decentralized village economy in China.[64] The resulting property rights arrangements were the emergence of fief-like enterprises regulated by local officialdom, followed by insider privatization. What remains unsure is whether the same arrangement is replicable in centralized state firms and strategic industries.

Assets discovery mechanism

Both the theories of political capitalism and technocratic managerialism focus on individual cadres as the subject of analysis. Accordingly, the results of the reform policies depend partly on whether local cadres stall or facilitate the effective use of state assets. The policy implication is therefore to "pick the winners," or, to put it under the schema of ownership and property rights discussion, to "pick the owners." In other words, before giving away the property rights, even partially, the reformers are bound to take a step backwards to identify the suitable incumbent stakeholders.[65] In the case of any constraints which complicate the selection of outside owners, the local government would at least try to differentiate the good insider from the bad insider. By allowing "bad" owners to pay less in obtaining the state assets, local governments retain the right to receive profits made from these partially privatized firms in the future.[66]

While the theories of "picking the owners" are useful in understanding local cadres' behavior during the reform and post-reform era, they fail to explain the intricacies of the early stage of reform of centralized enterprises in strategic industrial sectors. The third type of ownership conversion mechanism that I put forward adopts a more encompassing subject of analysis. Instead of focusing on individual cadres, this mechanism focuses on the hidden productive resources and explains the relation between such resources and the dynamics of the ownership arrangements during the transition period.

Many productive resources became idle during the planned regime, and such hidden resources are usually intangible, individually based, floating, and informal in nature. This includes not only the unused physical machinery, but also the potential production capacities which are non-existent before the reform, and the latent local cadres' capabilities which they refuse to devote to the firm during the planned regime.

Logically, the first step in state sector reform is for the reformer to "pick the right assets," not to "pick the right owners." By energizing these hidden productive assets, the reformer expects them to come into operation eventually. Such an "assets discovery mechanism" explains why, sometimes, decentralization does not lead to privatization, but rather encourages local cadres to search for hidden productive assets and does not promise to grant ownership to the cadres. Whether the newly discovered assets would be privatized or "statized" would be a matter to be dealt with in the second phase of reform.

The assets discovery mechanism does not require the acquisition of the productive assets. It is therefore less obvious than, and easily confused with, the other two ownership conversion mechanisms. Political capitalism and technocratic managerialism explain how local cadres use their bureaucratic relations and technocratic capital to survive and advance during the transition era. The assets discovery mechanism takes a different vantage point and refers to the latent productive capacity. As such, it focuses more on how central leaders identify hidden productive assets, including local cadres' human capital, as well as other idle productive assets, by re-arranging the respective property relations among the state firms.[67] After discovering what the state really possesses and how to make the most valuable use of it, the top-level actors recover and re-centralize some of the assets.

Recap: the three reform models and China's railway reform

The efficiency model, the evolutionary model, and the ownership conversion model all provide insightful perspectives in analyzing socialist reform (Table 1.1). The efficiency model alone fails to explain the complicated railway reform, but it provides a normative framework for policy planners to formulate a well-packed and big bang reform, or to benchmark the real-life reform agenda.

The evolutionary model, which originated from the studies of rural economy and township and village enterprises (TVE) development, calls for a more empirical and inductive reasoning of the property rights re-arrangements within the railway regime. Not surprisingly, such a path-dependent approach helps identify the particularities of China's railway reform and triggers the need to understand various ownership conversion mechanisms.

The ownership conversion model focuses on the transformation mechanism. While political capitalism and technocratic managerialism study how local railway cadres made use of their positions, network, jobs skills, and various abilities to survive during the conflicting railway reform policies, the assets recovery mechanism brings in a new vantage to study how central leadership identify the embedded productive resources.

The puzzle

Oi and Walder outline five major types of ownership arrangements in China during the reform era, including traditional state or collective enterprises, management responsibility contracts, government–management partnerships, government–leaseholder relationships, and private enterprises.[68] Such variation implies the diversity of property rights arrangements other than pure state-owned and pure privatized enterprises. If we assume that the hybrid is representing a kind of unidirectional property rights re-arrangement by privatization and decentralization, we would conclude that China's railway sector was moving from being a traditional state-owned sector to a decentralized public sector managed by responsibility contracts. However, in reality, the transformation process was complicated by a series of multi-directional decentralization and re-centralization shifts in different sub-sectors. The book therefore explains the intricacies of such conflicting reform policies, and the resulting property rights arrangements.

In fact, research on the post-socialist economy and the organizational structure of various reformed enterprises in Eastern Europe sheds light on the fact that re-arranging property rights does not necessarily clarify property rights. Stark argues that the post-socialist actors rebuilt the organizations "with the ruins of communism" as they adapt to the uncertainties and redeploy available resources.[69] In order to streamline the property relations, local cadres coordinate the productive resources and result in various unexpected and unintended organizational forms, such as cross-ownership. Stark refers to the resulting property rights arrangements as recombinant property:

Table 1.1 Ownership changing models

	The efficiency model		The evolutionary model		The ownership conversion model		
Areas of concern	Ways and destiny of ownership changes		Peculiarities of ownership changes		Mechanism of ownership changes		
Theoretical variants	Big bang theory	Gradualism theory	Path dependency theory	Institutional theory	Technocratic managerialism	Political capitalism	Assets recovery mechanism
Theoretical approach	Ownership concentration approach	Ownership delineation approach	Historical developmental approach	Organizational structural approach	Human capital approach	Power conversion approach	Embedded theory
Explanations for ownership changes	A state-led search for reform to achieve optimal efficiency	A local unfolding of reform to improve efficiency	Regional endowments predispose historical evolution to particular ownership changes	Organizational complexities predispose structural evolution to particular ownership changes	Cadres' survival strategies result in positive ownership changes	Cadres' survival strategies result in negative ownership changes	State-led decentralization and re-centralization policies result in a mix of ownership changes
Policy implications	One-stroke concentration of control, income and transfer rights	Piece-meal engineering of property rights demarcation	Ownership reform may lead to problems of regional disparities	Ownership reform may be impeded by problems of "too many mother-in-laws"	The successful conversion of cadres' technocratic and managerial ability suggests the need to pick the right owners	The successful conversion of cadres' positional power to economic power suggests the need to combat corruptive activities	The successful discovery and recovery of extra-budgetary productive resources suggests the need to pick the right assets

Recombinant property is a form of organizational hedging, or portfolio management, in which actors respond to uncertainty in the organizational environment by diversifying their assets, redefining and recombining resources. It is an attempt to hold resources that can be justified or assessed by more than one standard of measure.[70]

The experience of such Eastern European reform highlights the possibility of recombinant property, organizational hedging, and portfolio management, and reflects the potential value of idle productive assets embedded within the planned regime under the socialist economy. The focus on the assets discovery mechanism further formulates the causal relationship between the state-led reform policy and the resulting recombination productive relations and poses the following research questions.

1   If socialist reform does not necessarily follow the economic theory of property rights which lead to outright privatization and concentrated ownership arrangements, what kind of property rights changes should we expect to see?
2   What are the key factors which determine the assets discovery and assets recovery processes?
3   Did the variance in the top-down reform policies matter? Did the variance in local survival strategies matter?

Research methodology

The railway sector in China was characterized as being *"Gao-da-ban,"* i.e., highly centralized and unified, huge and comprehensive, and semi-militaristically administered (*gaodu jizhong tongyi, da'er quan, ban junshihua guanli*). The bureaucratic and enclosure system rendered the empirical research extraordinarily problematic. Yet the very fact that the system could hardly be opened up induced a burning research curiosity to understand the transformation process of the regime.

Guided by the three ownership explanatory models, this book resolves the research puzzle from two vantage points: documentary review and face-to-face in-depth interviews.

Making sense of the state-led reform policy

To explain how and why the empirical reform experience was different from what the efficiency model predicted, I first searched for the archival documents and compiled a comprehensive and thorough account of the state policies on railway reform since 1978. The railway sector has its own publisher, the China Railway Publisher (*Zhongguo tielu chuban she*) in Beijing, which has been publishing volumes of railway rules, regulations, reform directives, newspapers, magazines, journals, and annual reports. In addition, the library of the Beijing

Jiaotong University, the Universities Service Center at the Chinese University of Hong Kong, and the Intercity Services Department of the Kowloon-Canton Railway Corporation also contains secondary resources, such as dissertations, statistical yearbooks, annual reports, magazines, etc.

I also interviewed railway cadres who vividly supplemented the archival information with personal views and insider stories. Following the efficiency logic, I asked a set of open-ended questions relating to reform polices:

- What railway reform policies were advocated in the past two decades?
- Did the railway reform policies gradually mold the railway sector into a market-oriented entity of which the modus operandi would be based on market coordination rather than bureaucratic coordination?
- How would you evaluate the reform policies and outcomes?
- What were the resulting property rights arrangements in the work units?

Chinese policy papers and state documents are characterized by stretching to great lengths and sloganeering empty rhetoric. It was only through repeated and persistent discussion with railway cadres that the papers and documents eventually make coherent sense.

Three case studies: digging up local survival strategies

After compiling the reform profile and detailing the unexpected reform results for the railway sector, I narrowed down to studying three sub-sectors—one was the core business sub-sector, i.e., the transport sub-sector, and the other two were the infrastructure-support sub-sectors, i.e., the construction and the signaling sub-sectors.

I chose these three sub-sectors as case studies for three major reasons. First, these three sub-sectors demonstrated two different restructuring varieties: the transport sub-sector remained with the railway sector while the construction and signaling sub-sectors were detached and subsumed under another state agency. Second, the three sub-sectors were at quite different stages of reform and thus could be taken as a set of complementary case studies to illustrate the transformation pattern. Third, my personal connections linked me to interview cadres mainly working in these three sub-sectors and they provided me with enormous insights into the process of ownership conversion and assets discovery.

The second part of the book deals with the questions of how local cadres reacted to the changing reform policies and how unexpected property rights arrangements emerged. Focusing on the railway cadres' power relations and railway firms' resource relations, I asked another set of questions:

- Did local cadres manage to retain their power?
- How could cadres survive in the midst of the transition regime?
- What resources, positional or technocratic, did they identify and deploy?

- How did they retain, re-arrange, and recompose the existing or newly defined productive resources?
- Did they eventually receive the productive resources from the MOR and own the spin-off?

Groping in the field

Between September 2003 and January 2004, I made three research trips to five cities in China, including Guangzhou, Beijing, Shanghai, Tianjin, and Wuhan. In November 2006 I made another follow-up trip to Beijing. The fieldwork was not as smooth as expected. The major reason was that in 2003, Liu Zhijun, the then Vice Railway Minister, had just been promoted to Railway Minister right before I started conducting interviews in Beijing. Once Liu assumed the authority as the new Minister, he quickly called off the previous reform policy of vertical separation and put forward the Great-Leap style of railway development. The reform policy of vertical separation was advocated by the railway expert at the World Bank, and was thought to be an important milestone toward at least partial privatization of the railway assets. Amid such a rosy picture of reform, the sudden policy twist was quite a shock to railway cadres. Since they were not sure which was the right bandwagon on which to jump, many of them were very reluctant to comment on either the previous policy or the current one.

Fortunately, by means of the personal contacts I had developed during my previous work, I was introduced to 21 cadres working in different railway subsectors to carry out in-depth interviews. Although these interviews were not formally arranged by the Ministry, many of the cadres I talked to were actively involved in identifying hidden productive resources during the reform era. Some of them were initially hesitant to talk about their sideline businesses but gradually became enthusiastic because they considered me as a Hong Kong scholar who may eventually be able to advise them on how to diversify their businesses (see the Appendix for a list of interviewees).

Also, the policy twist, which had once been seen as a major obstacle to arranging in-depth interviews, turned out to be an important event throughout my research. The conflicting reform policy cast doubt on the efficiency model as it represented a state-led effort to re-centralize the strategic assets after recovering the newly discovered idle assets from the local railway cadres. It was actually through the controversial discussion of such conflicting policies with local cadres that I gradually formulated the asset discovery and recovery mechanisms.

Another major administrative reform took place in 2013 when I was in the middle of revising my research output into this book manuscript—the entire MOR was dissolved and a new agency, China Railway Corporation (CRC), was established and subsumed under the Ministry of Transport and Communication. The collapse of the MOR demonstrates a full-scale re-centralization of the railway assets in China.

Notes

1 Li and Rozelle completed 670 enterprise surveys in China's Yangtze Delta region and found out that more than half of the rural enterprises had been privatized by 2000. They believe that, in general, more than a million firms in rural China were privatized. They also concluded that the premium-paying privatized firms successfully caught up with private firms in terms of accounts receivable management, profit rate, and value added per worker. Li Hongbin and Scott Rozelle, "Privatizing Rural China: Insider Privatization, Innovative Contracts and the Performance of Township Enterprises," *The China Quarterly*, vol. 176 (2003): 981–1005.
2 Ronald H. Coase, "The Federal Communications Commission," *Journal of Law and Economics* vol. 2 (1959): 1–40.
3 Harold Demsetz, *Ownership, Control, and the Firm: The Organization of Economic Activity*, (Oxford: Blackwell, 1988), pp. 104–116.
4 Demsetz, *Ownership Control and the Firm*, p. 18.
5 Harold Demsetz, "Towards a Theory of Property Rights," *American Economic Review*, vol. 57, no. 2 (1967): 355.
6 Armen Alchian, "Some Economics of Property Rights," *Economic Forces at Work*, vol. 30 (1977): 142.
7 Demsetz, "Towards a Theory of Property Rights."
8 Demsetz, *Ownership Control and the Firm*, p. 18.
9 M. Boycko, A. Shleifer, and R. Vishny, *Privatizing Russia* (Cambridge, MA: MIT, 1996).
10 Janos Kornai, *Vision and Reality, Market and State: Contradictions and Dilemmas Revisited* (New York: Routledge, 1990).
11 Mark Allen Groombridge, "The Politics of Industrial Bargaining: The Restructuring of State-owned Enterprises in the People's Republic of China, 1978–1995" (PhD dissertation, Columbia University, 1998).
12 Boycko *et al.*, *Privatizing Russia*.
13 Jon Shaw, *Competition, Regulation and the Privatization of British Rail* (Aldershot: Ashgate, 2000), pp. 9–15.
14 John McMillan, "Market in Transition" (Symposium address at the Seventh World Congress of the Econometric Society, Tokyo, August 1995); John Vickers and George Yarrow, *Privatization: An Economic Analysis* (Cambridge, MA: MIT Press, 1988); Belen Villalonga, "Privatization and Efficiency: Differentiating Ownership Effects from Political, Organizational, and Dynamic Effects," *Journal of Economic Behavior & Organization*, vol. 42 (2000): 43–47; and Meryem Duygun Fethi, "Measuring the Efficiency of European Airlines: An Application of DEA and Tobit Analysis," Discussion paper in Management and Organization Studies, University of Leicester School of Management, No. 01/20.
15 Moris Bornstein, "Non-standard Methods in the Privatization Strategies of the Czech Republic, Hungary and Poland," *Economics of Transition*, vol. 5, no. 2 (1997): 323–338; Boycko *et al.*, *Privatizing Russia*; John S. Earle and Almos Telegdy, "The Results of 'Mass Privatization' in Romania: A First Empirical Study," *Economics of Transition*, vol. 6, no. 2 (1998): 313–332; Roman Frydman and Andrzej Rapaczynski, *Privatization in Eastern Europe: Is the State Withering Away* (Budapest: CEU, 1994).
16 Eva Voszka, "Centralization, Re-Nationalization, and Redistribution: Government's Role in Changing Hungary's Ownership Structure," in Jerzy Hausner, Bob Jessop, and Klaus Nielsen, eds., *Strategic Choice and Path-Dependency in Post-Socialism: Institutional Dynamics in the Transformation Process* (Aldershot: Edward Elgar, 1995); Boycko *et al.*, *Privatizing Russia*, p. 72; and Wojciech Bienkowski, "The Bermuda Triangle: Why Self-governed Firms Work for their Own Destruction," *Journal of Comparative Economics*, vol. 16, no. 4 (1992): 750–762.

17 Weimer's example on home ownership illustrates that even the property rights of a residential place involves different sets of legal and social constraints without which the trio rights cannot be properly demarcated. We may not be aware of such constraints because they are so well established and Western society simply takes it for granted:

> Consider, for instance, a house on a city lot. The owner of this asset has a right to live in it, but zoning laws may deny her the right to use it to house a business. She may have the right to sell it, but civil rights laws may deny her the right to close the sale to protected classes of people. She may have the right to the income stream generated from renting the house, but she may not have the right to rent it to three or more unrelated adults.

See David L. Weimer, "The Political Economy of Property Rights," in David L. Weimer, ed., *The Political Economy of Property Rights* (Cambridge: Cambridge University Press, 1997), p. 3.

18 Oliver E. Williamson, "Transaction Cost Economics and Organization Theory," in Neil J. Smelser and Richard Swedberg, eds., *The Handbook of Economic Sociology* (Princeton, NJ: Princeton University Press, 1994), pp. 77–107.

19 Jeffrey Pfeffer and Gerald R. Salancik, *The External Control of Organizations: A Resource Dependence Perspective* (New York: Harper & Row, 1978).

20 Yoram Barzel, "Property Rights in the Firm," in Terry Anderson and Fred McChesney, eds., *Property Rights: Cooperation Conflict and Law* (Princeton, NJ: Princeton University Press, 2003), p. 45.

21 Lee's study in Chinese firms during transition also contends that "property rights are not simply owner's rights over things, but are more importantly 'relations among people.' Accordingly, forms of property are determined by relations among people, as well as rights contained in the 'bundle.' " See Kuen Lee, *Chinese Firms and the State in Transition: Property Rights and Agency Problems in the Reform Era* (London: M.E. Sharpe, 1991), p. 20.

22 McMillan, "Markets in Transition."

23 See Hu Xiaobo, "Choices and Path-Dependency of China's Property Rights Transformation: The Institutional Origins" (working paper presented at the Social Science Seminar, the Hong Kong University of Science and Technology, 8 December 2003), p. 10.

24 Ivan Szelenyi, "The rise of Managerialism: The 'New Class' after the Fall of Communism" (Discussion paper 16, Collegiums Budapest, Public Lecture Series, October 1995, p. 5). In the study of the post-communist societies, Szelenyi also contends that "managers ... are exercising power which is far greater than the property they own").

25 Barzel, "Property Rights in the Firm," pp. 43–45.

26 David Stark, "Networks of Assets, Chains of Debt: Recombinant Property in Hungary," in Roman Frydman, Cheryl Gray, and Andrzej Rapaczynski, eds., *Corporate Governance in Central Europe & Russia*, vol. 2 (Budapest: Central European University Press, 1996), p. 112.

27 Lawrence P. King, *The Basic Features of Postcommunist Capitalism in Eastern Europe* (Westport, CT: Praeger, 2000), p. 76.

28 Weimer, "The Political Economy of Property Rights," p. 3.

29 Weimer, "The Political Economy of Property Rights," pp. 1–19; and Xiaobo, "Choices and Path-Dependency of China's Property Rights Transformation."

30 Rafael La Porta and Florencio López-de-Silanes, "The Benefits of Privatization: Evidence from Mexico," *The Quarterly Journal of Economics*, vol. 114, no. 4 (1999): 1193–1242.

31 Paul Milgrom and John Roberts, "Moral Hazard and Performance Incentives" in Paul Milgrom and John Roberts, *Economics, Organization and Management* (Englewood Cliffs, NJ: Prentice-Hall, 1992), ch. 6.

32 Li and Rozelle, "Privatizing Rural China: Insider Privatization, Innovative Contracts and the Performance of Township Enterprises," and Li Hongbin and Scott Rozelle, "Insider Privatization with a Tail: the Screening Contract and Performance of Privatized Firms in Rural China," *Journal of Development Economics*, 75 (2004): 1–26.
33 Wing Thye Woo, "The Real Reasons for China's Growth," *The China Journal*, vol. 41 (1999): 115–137.
34 Adam Smith's model of free market and "invisible hand" assumes that individuals tend to maximize self-profit. Such dynamics bring forth an optimum distribution of resources and an overall beneficiary of the society. See Adam Smith, *An Inquiry into the Nature and Causes of the Wealth of Nation* (London: Printed for A. Strahan, T. Cadell and W. Davies, 1796).
35 Coase contends that clearly specified and exclusive property rights are conducive to self-maximized negotiations between related parties, mutually agreed terms of contract, and optimal allocation of resources. See Coase, "The Federal Communications Commission."
36 Demsetz, "Towards a Theory of Property Rights."
37 Prybala advocates a comprehensive shock therapy which includes "privatization, deregulation, decentralization, price reform and legal system reform, and shall be undertaken once and for all. See Jan Prybyla, "The Road from Socialism: Why, Where, What and How," *Problems of Communism*, 40 (1991): 1–17.
38 See Demsetz, "Towards a Theory of Property Rights," and Boycko *et al.*, *Privatizing Russia.*
39 Williamson sets out a schema for economic theories of firm and market organization and suggests that the neoclassical approach is to view the firm in technological terms in which "(1) the boundary of the firm was taken as given…, (2) property rights were assumed to be well-defined, and (3) disputes, if any, were assume to be costlessly and efficaciously decided by the courts." See Oliver E. Williamson, "A Comparison of Alternative Approaches to Economic Organization," *Journal of Institutional and Theoretical Economics*, vol. 146 (1990): 61–71.
40 Walder and Oi contend that it is not the underlying principle of privatization that is disputable, but the specific arrangements such as the exact clarity and predictability of property rights demarcation that is required, and the practical way of achieving such clarity and predictability. See Oi and Walder, "Property Rights in the Chinese Economy: Contours of the Process of Change," in Jean C. Oi and Andrew G. Walder, eds., *Property Rights and Economic Reform in China* (Stanford, CA: Stanford University Press, 1999), pp. 1–24.
41 See Peter Murrell, "Conservative Political Philosophy and Strategy of Economic Transition," *East European Politics and Societies*, vol. 6, no. 1 (1992): 3–16; and Andreas Pickel, "Jump-Starting a Market Economy: A Critique of the Radical Strategy for Economic Reform in Light of the East German Experience," *Studies in Comparative Communism*, vol. 25, no. 2 (1992): 177–191.
42 Vedat Milor, "Changing Political Economies: An Introduction," in Vedat Milor, ed., *Changing Political Economies: Privatization in Post-Communist and Reforming Communist States* (Boulder, CO and London: Lynne Rienner Publishers, 1994), pp. 1–23.
43 Barry Naughton, *Growing Out of the Plan: Chinese Economic Reform, 1978–1993* (Cambridge: Cambridge University Press, 1995).
44 Lina Song and Du He, "The Role of Township Governments in Rural Industrialization," in William A. Byrd and Lin Qingsong, eds., *China's Rural Industry: Structure, Development, and Reform* (New York: Oxford University Press, 1990), pp. 342–357.
45 Byrd concludes that the first round of China's state-owned enterprise reform has made considerable progress in reinstitution of financial incentives. The in-depth case studies of seven industrial firms, however, demonstrate that "the effectiveness of reform in promoting improved efficiency has been severely hampered by chronic sellers'

markets for industrial products." See William A Byrd, *Chinese Industrial Firms under Reform* (Oxford: Oxford University Press, 1992), pp. 2–48; Steinfeld's study of the steel sector in China also suggests that "it is not the corporatized, partially 'privatized' SOE that responds in what would be considered a market-oriented fashion but instead the firm that has, in a sense, been drawn closer to the state rather than pushed father away." See Edward Steinfeld, *Forging Reform in China: The Fate of State-owned Industry* (Cambridge: Cambridge University Press, 1998); see also Vladimir Popov, "Shock Therapy Versus Gradualism: The End of the Debate (Explaining the Magnitude of Transformational Recession)," *Comparative Economic Studies*, vol. 42, no. 1 (2000): 1–57.

46 Lin suggests that there are more than seven or eight models identified for rural economies in China, such as the Wenzhou model, the Sunan model, the Fuyan model, the Gengche model, and the Jinhua model. He argues that each model has its own local roots and economic paradigm. See Nan Lin, "Local Market Socialism: Local Corporatism in Action in Rural China," *Theory and Society*, vol. 24 (1995): 301–354; Lin Yi-min's recent study also provides a comprehensive description on the sectoral and regional variations in ownership arrangements. Lin Yi-min, "Economic Institutional Change in Post-Mao China: Reflections on the Triggering, Orienting, and Sustaining Mechanisms," *Asian Perspective*, vol. 25, no. 4 (2001): 33–66; and in Alvin Y. So, ed., *China's Development Miracle: Origins, Transformation, and Challenges* (Armonk, NY: M.E. Sharpe, 2003), pp. 29–57.

47 Path dependency theory is also prominent in studies of Eastern European countries. See David Stark, "Path Dependence and Privatization Strategies in Eastern Europe," *East European Politics and Societies*, vol. 6, no. 1 (1992): 17–54.

48 James Kai-sing Kung, "The Evolution of Property Rights in Village Enterprises: The Case of Wuxi County," in Jean C. Oi and Andrew G. Walder, eds., *Property Rights and Economic Reform in China* (Stanford, CA: Stanford University Press, 1999), pp. 95–122; Susan H. Whiting, "The Regional Evolution of Ownership Forms: Shareholding Cooperatives and Rural Industry in Shanghai and Wenzhou," in Jean C. Oi and Andrew G. Walder, eds., *Property Rights and Economic Reform in China* (Stanford, CA: Stanford University Press, 1999), pp. 171–202; Gregory A. Ruf, "Collective Enterprise and Property Rights in a Sichuan Village: The Rise and Decline of Managerial Corporatism," in Jean C. Oi and Andrew G. Walder, eds., *Property Rights and Economic Reform in China* (Stanford, CA: Stanford University Press, 1999), pp. 27–48; Gary H. Jefferson and Thomas G. Rawski, "Enterprise Reform in Chinese Industry," *Journal of Economic Perspectives*, vol. 8, no. 2 (1994): 47–70; James Kai-sing Kung and Lin Yi-min, "Markets, the Local State, and Ownership Transformation: The Rise and Decline of Local Public Enterprises in China's Economic Transition," forthcoming.

49 Lin explains the reform of the Daqiuzhuang by the concept of local market socialism, which captures the pivotal role of political, economic, and socio-cultural roots in the village. See Nan Lin, "Local market socialism: local corporatism in action in rural China," *Theory and Society*, vol. 24 (1995): 301–354.

50 Chih-Jou Jay Chen, "Local Institutions and the Transformation of Property Rights in Southern Fujian," in Jean C. Oi and Andrew G. Walder, eds., *Property Rights and Economic Reform in China* (Stanford, CA: Stanford University Press, 1999), pp. 49–70.

51 Wang Shaoguang, "The Rise of the Regions: Fiscal Reform and the Decline of Central State Capacity in China," in Andrew Walder, ed., *The Waning of the Communist State* (Berkeley, CA: University of California Press, 1995), pp. 87–113.

52 Peter Cheung, J.H. Chung, and Z. Lin, *Provincial Strategies of Economic Reform in Post-Mao China: Leadership, Politics, and Implementation* (Armonk, NY: M.E. Sharpe, 1998); Dorothy Solinger, "Despite Decentralization," *China Quarterly*, vol. 145 (1996): 1–34; and Liu Yia-Ling, "Reform from Below: The Private Economy and

Local Politics in the Rural Industrialization of Wenzhou," *The China Quarterly*, 130 (1992): 293–316.

53 Andrew Walder, "Local Governments as Industrial Firms: An Organizational Analysis of China's Transitional Economy," *American Journal of Sociology*, vol. 101, no. 2 (1995): 263–301. See also Douglas Guthrie, "Between Markets and Politics: Organizational Responses to Reform in China," *American Journal of Sociology*, vol. 102 (1997): 1258–1304.

54 Lin Yi-min and Zhu Tian, "Ownership Restructuring in Chinese State Industry: An Analysis of Evidence on Initial Organizational Changes," *The China Quarterly*, vol. 166 (2001): 305–341.

55 David Granick, *Chinese State Enterprises: A Regional Property Rights Analysis* (Chicago, IL: University of Chicago Press, 1990).

56 Doug Guthrie, *Dragon in a Three-Piece Suit: The Emergence of Capitalism in China* (Princeton, NJ: Princeton University Press, 1999). Guthrie also studies the economic health, the joint venture effect, and organizational governance; see also Walder, "Local Governments as Industrial Firms."

57 Jadwiga Staniszkis, " 'Political Capitalism' in Poland," *East European Politics and Societies*, vol. 5, no. 1 (1991): 127–141.

58 Wojciech Bienkowski, "The Bermuda Triangle: Why Self-governed Firms Work for their Own Destruction," *Journal of Economic Literature*, vol. 16, no. 4 (1992): 750–762; Staniszkis, " 'Political Capitalism' in Poland"; He Qinglian, *Xiandaihua de xianjing: dangdai zhongguo de jingji shehui wenti* (*The Trap of Modernization: the Economic and Social Problems of Contemporary China*) (Beijing: Jingre zhongguo Publisher, 1998); Ding Xueliang, "The Illicit Asset Stripping of Chinese State Firms," *The China Journal*, vol. 43 (2000): 1–28; Christine Wong, "Overview of Issues in Local Public Finance in the PRC," in Christine Wong, ed., *Financing Local Government in the People's Republic of China* (Hong Kong: Oxford University Press, 1997), pp. 1–60; Christine Wong, "Central–Local Relations Revisited: The 1994 Tax-haring Reform and Public Expenditure Management in China," *China Perspectives*, vol. 31 (2000): 52–63.

59 Andrew Walder, "Politics and Property in Transitional Economies: A Theory of Elite Opportunity," Working Paper, The Asia/Pacific Research Center (2003).

60 Zhou Qiren, *"Renli zhiben dechangquan,"* ("Property Rights of Human Capital") in Zhou Qiren, *Zhengshi shijie de jingjixue* (*The Economics of the Real World*) (Beijing: Zhongguo fazhan chubanshe, 2002), pp. 11–47.

61 Erzsebet Szalai, "Political and Social Conflicts Arising from the Transformation of Property Relations in Hungary," *Journal of Communist Studies*, vol. 10, no. 3 (1994): 56–77.

62 Ivan Szelenyi and Eric Kostello, "The Market Transition Debate: Toward a Synthesis?" *American Journal of Sociology*, vol. 101, no. 4 (1996): 1082–1096.

63 Gil Eyal, Ivan Szelenyi, and Eleanor Townsley, *Making Capitalism without Capitalists: Class Formation and Elite Struggles in Post-Communist Central Europe* (London: Verso, 1998).

64 Jean Oi, "Fiscal Reform and the Economic Foundations of Local State Corporatism in China," *World Politics*, vol. 45, no. 1 (1992): 99–126; Nan Lin, "Local Market Socialism: Local Corporatism in Action in Rural China," *Theory and Society*, vol. 24, no. 3 (1995): 301–354; Jean C. Oi and Andrew G. Walder, eds., *Property Rights and Economic Reform in China* (Stanford, CA: Stanford University Press, 1999); and Jane Duckett, *The Entrepreneurial State in China: Real Estate and Commerce Departments in Reform Era Tianjin* (London: Routledge, 1998).

65 Ma Ngok, "The Political Economy of Privatization in Eastern Europe: Transformative Politics and Competing Imperatives of Privatization in Hungary, Poland and the Czech Republic," (PhD Dissertation, Political Science, University of California, Los Angeles, 1998).

66 Li and Rozelle, "Privatizing Rural China."
67 In a socialist economy, property rights are more than the control, income, and transfer rights, because various other rights have not been agreed on the external social and legal system. The whole bundle of property rights are therefore referred to as property relations. Brenner argues that the control, income, and transfer rights are a subset of what he calls "social property relations"—"the relationship among the direct producers, which specify and determine the regular and systematic access of individual economic actors (or families) to the means of production and the economic product." See Robert Brenner, "The Social Basis of Economic Development," in John Roemer, ed., *Analytical Marxis* (New York: Cambridge University Press, 1986), pp. 23–53. Pryor also refers to such property relations as "a set of relations between people with regard to some good, service, or 'thing.'" See Frederic Pryor, *Property and Industrial Organization in Communist and Capitalist Nations* (Indiana, IN: Indiana University Press, 1973), p. 2.
68 Andrew Walder and Jean Oi, "Property Rights in the Chinese Economy: Contours of the Process of Change," in Jean C. Oi and Andrew G. Walder, eds., *Property Rights and Economic Reform in China* (Stanford, CA: Stanford University Press, 1999), pp. 1–24.
69 David Stark, "Recombinant Property in East European Capitalism," in Gernot Grabher and David Stark, eds., *Restructuring Networks in Post-Socialism: Legacies, Linkages, and Localities* (Oxford: Oxford University Press, 1997), p. 36.
70 David Stark, "Recombinant Property in East European Capitalism," p. 38.

2 The best railway reform model

Overview

Research on railway reform is abundant, in particular in the field of transport policy studies, which are largely based on the economic theory of property rights. These studies are aimed at looking for the optimal model of railway operation, and the best way to mold the old system into the best possible one by introducing markets and competition. While the comprehensive reform schema was reported as drawing the policy makers' attention in the process of reforming China's railway,[1] the efficiency model did not really capture and explain the empirical discrepancies of the more complicated and puzzling reform experience in China.

This chapter first discusses the economic logic of railway reform in orthodox transport studies. Second, it describes the evolutionary development of railway reform in China between 1978 and 2013, which resulted in various conflicting and confusing reform outcomes and therefore casts doubt on the explanatory power of the efficiency model. Bridging the general socialist reform theories, and the specific railway reform policies, the conclusion translates the theoretical puzzles into a set of specific research questions and puts forward various research hypotheses.

The economic model of railway reform

Orthodox transport studies assume that the railway industry is a natural monopoly, and large economies of scale should be realized through vertical integration of rail operations.[2] At the same time, railways have to be state owned or regulated, with a view to curbing the monopolistic pricing of rail services. However, recent worldwide railway developments witness that large-scale railways are losing their competitive edge.[3] Seeing that the railway sector fails to compete with other modes of transport in the market, railway analysts try to get around the problem of natural monopoly by adopting the efficiency-driven reform theory.

Monopolistic myth

A number of network characteristics have given rise to the lumpiness and monopolistic myth of railway operations. First, the railway industry involves substantial fixed costs in infrastructure construction and thus leads to the quest for economies of scale which can only be realized through consolidation of rail operations, under either private or public control.[4] At the same time, with a view to controlling the natural monopolists, railways should be largely state-owned or state regulated to prevent the monopolists from pricing rail services above the market price.

Second, the railway transport facilities are said to be "lumpy" in the sense that the capital units, such as train cars and stations, can only be expanded discretely, while the transport demands vary continuously. The indivisibility of assets responds slowly to market information, defers R&D investment, and impedes timely improvement on service and infrastructure provision. As a result, government intervention and coordination are required to supply the necessary market information.[5]

Third, rail operators provide heterogeneous services which can be classified in terms of spatial movement (route specific), service standard (speed, frequency, comfort, and price), and carrying objects (bulk freight transport, parcel and postal goods, and intercity and domestic passenger). Since some or all of the products/services share the same sunk cost and a combination of the operating costs, the businesses require simultaneous management of different operations which favor structural integration.[6]

Fourth, operational failures and delays could lead to chain reactions and affect other scheduled rail services. So structural integration is important because it not only facilitates simultaneous timetable coordination for the provision of heterogeneous service, but also minimizes transport accidents and eliminates the transaction costs incurred in designing and implementing the compensation accounting system.[7]

Fifth, rail transportation has long been conceived of being a kind of public service for various reasons—railways are comparatively cheap as a form of mass transportation; the nationwide network is strategically important for military reasons; and the integrative system is vital for economic development of remote regions. Such public-good attributes imply that certain cost recovery is impossible and commercial operators with economic interests, per se, will not invest at a socially optimal level. Again, government regulation is essential for redistributive reasons.[8]

Lastly, the existence of negative externalities, such as congestion, noise pollution, and other environment disruptions in the railway system implies that government intervention is necessary in order to regulate railway operations and allocate the respective administration fee to the public in the form of congestion and/or pollution rates.[9]

Despite the above-mentioned arguments on state-regulated monopolization of the railway industry, recent developments witness the fact that large-scale railways are losing their competitive edge. The railway giants are criticized for being bureaucratic and unresponsive to change, and fail to compete with other non-railway sectors in the market. Since government intervention and centralized planning are thought to be the reasons for inefficient allocation of resources, most of the reform is based on the idea of breaking the myth of natural monopoly and introducing market competition in the railway sector to enhance its efficiency.

The best reform model

With a view to turning the railway businesses around, transport studies are endeavoring to look for the best reform model. In general, railway experts embrace the economic theory of property rights and believe that, under public ownership, people exhaust the available resources, maximize personal gains and disregard the detrimental effects of using collective resources. Hence, the goal of the reform of a state-owned railway sector is to streamline its ownership structure, and to concentrate the control, income, and transfer rights of all productive assets into the hand of private owners.[10] The neoliberal further argues that the state should retreat from the market as soon and as far as possible. They believe that minimal state intervention is the essence of reform, since concentrated ownership structure will itself allocate resources in the most effective way.

Following such a comprehensive reform model, railway analysts focus mainly on the issues of privatization and competition. Kopicki and Thompson, the railway experts of the World Bank, advocate disintegration and de-politicization.[11] Disintegration separates the railway's network service providers from passenger and freight transport operators, breaks the myth of natural monopolist and economy of scale, and introduces contestable markets for potential competition. The railway's network services include the provision of infrastructure, such as rail roads, bridges, signaling facilities, electrification networks, marshalling yards, and railway stations. De-politicization shields railway operations from state intervention, enhances entrepreneurial autonomy, facilitates ownership concentration, encourages various incentive designs, and finally paves the way for partial or outright privatization.

The Organization for Economic Co-operation and Development (OECD) also suggests that privatization of railways will facilitate the governance of incentives administration and that such institutional reform should be accompanied by the introduction of market competition within the industry.[12]

The logic of privatization and competition theories is clear-cut, but in practice different countries choose to reform their railway systems in different ways. Thompson and Budia map the directions of railway change in different countries in terms of private involvement and structural change (Figure 2.1).[13] Private involvement refers to the process of de-politicization under which ownership changes from public partnership to private ownership. Structural change refers to the process of disintegration under which degree of government intervention range from structurally integrated to partially separated and separated structure. China's pre-reform railway is classified as state-owned and structurally integrated. Obviously the best way to reform, according to the economic and

Figure 2.1 The best railway reform model.

efficiency model, is to move along the dotted line from the public ownership and integral structure to private ownership and separated structure.

Theoretically the best railway model is privately owned and structurally disintegrated so as to allow the maximum degree of market competition. However, we see different variations of vertical separation and ownership arrangements in the worldwide railways which clearly demonstrate an empirical deviation from the best model.[14]

Many transport economic studies explain such empirical deviations from the best railway reform in different countries based on the structural constraints of the existing market demand and movement patterns of passenger and freight services. Such structural explanation facilitates the comprehension of how different railways in the world choose to disintegrate their rail sectors along the best possible lines so as to maximize market competition.

For example, Li suggests that the underlying principle of structural separation is to facilitate competition among train service operators over the same infrastructure. As a result, there are three basic models of structural separation, as follows.[15]

Vertical separation   Vertical separation refers to the disintegration of the upper part of the railway system from the lower part. The upper parts are the operating components, such as passenger and freight transport services, locomotives, and rolling stock. The lower part refers to the infrastructure, comprising railway tracks, bridges, tunnels, stations, depots, signaling systems, train routes, and schedule planning services.

Horizontal separation   Horizontal separation refers to the disintegration between the passenger and freight transport service, within the upper part of the railway system.

Geographical separation   Geographical separation splits the national system into regional railways based on geographical boundaries. Within each regional railway, the system can be vertically and/or horizontally integrated or separated.

Li further explains that based on various combinations of the above three basic models, there are six derivatives.

1   Vertically and horizontally integrated model: This is usually the pre-reformed and unified model. The upper part and the lower part are fully integrated (Figure 2.2).

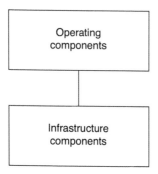

Figure 2.2 Fully integrated model.

2   Vertically separated and horizontally integrated model: This is a simple dichotomized separation between the upper part and the lower part. Both the freight and passenger transport services are integrated within the operating company in the upper part (Figure 2.3).

3   Vertically and horizontally separated model: This reform model first separates the upper and the lower parts and then further splits the upper layer into freight and passenger transport companies (Figure 2.4).

4   Dominant integrated and horizontally separated model: This model merges the lower part with some of the operating components, which is usually the dominant transport service, and forms the vertically integrated company. The rest of the operating components is separated from the integrated company and allowed to use the track in competition with the integrated operating company (Figure 2.5).

5   Vertically integrated and geographically separated model: This model divides the lower part into regional infrastructure companies, but the upper and lower parts of each regional company remains integrated (Figure 2.6).

6   Vertically disintegrated and geographically separated model: This is a model of complete separation which divides the lower part into regional companies and, at the same time, separates the upper part from the lower part.

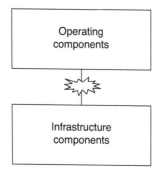

Figure 2.3 Vertically separated and horizontally integrated model.

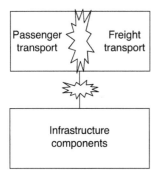

Figure 2.4 Vertically and horizontally separated model.

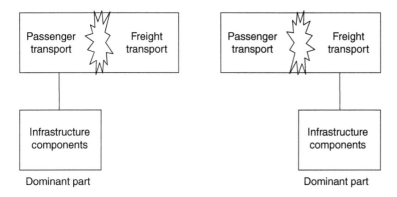

Figure 2.5 Dominant integrated and horizontally separated model.

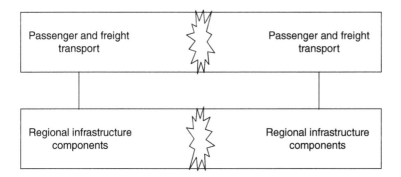

Figure 2.6 Vertically integrated and geographically separated model.

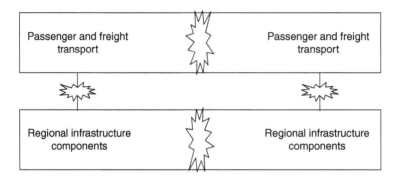

Figure 2.7 Vertically disintegrated and geographically separated model.

Structural explanation of vertical separation

With the above-mentioned different railway reform models, the focus of the reform experience was put on the structure disintegration. As a result, country variation in terms of the form and degree of separation was explained by structure difference in passenger and freight transport market. The basic idea is to explain how different railway monopolists were broken up along their weakest links with a view to placing the spin-off entities in the market for competition.

The Swedish railway reform was the first among all the member countries of the Europe Union to separate the accounting and charging arrangement for the transport services and network provision, with a view to opening the railway market to potential transport services operators through competitive tendering arrangements. The Swedes demonstrated a typical model of vertically separated and horizontally integrated railway structure; the experience was copied in the British railway system.[16]

The US and Japanese railways chose to adopt the dominant integrated and horizontally separated model. The US focuses on the freight market and therefore kept the freight transport services and the network integrated, and separated most of the regional passenger services. On the other hand, the Japanese railway focuses more on the passenger market and therefore chose to integrate the passenger transport service with the network and separated the freight transport operators. The railway passenger sector in Japan was further separated by well-defined geographical regions to induce indirect competition among the six rail passenger companies.

The New Zealand railway was characterized by its relatively low-density transport market; the government decided to pursue a unified structure in which both the principal freight transport service, the complementary passenger services, and the network are integrated. The entirety was corporatized and competition relied largely on intermodal competition before the sector was eventually sold to a private strategic consortium.

The Swedish railway

Similar to most other European railway, the Swedish railways had once been state-owned and vertically integrated. The state monopolist was not responding to market competition as quickly and accurately as other transport sectors. Harsh intermodal competition called for a review of railway reform.

In 1988, the Swedish government chose to break the myth of natural monopoly along the structural cleavage between transport services and railway infrastructure. The former was operated by the Swedish state railway, namely Järnvägar (SJ), and the latter by the national rail administration, namely Banverket (BV). The separation between the transport services and the rail network facilitated the separation of the accounting system of the two sectors. At the beginning of the restructure, SJ had to pay BV for the use of track, but the track usage fee did not reflect the real maintenance and investment cost, and the network operator was not able to recover its sunk cost by such a charging mechanism. As a result, the state had to heavily subsidize the railway industry.

Such vertical separation, however, created possible market competition among transport service operators and allowed regional authorities to procure train services by means of competitive tendering. At the same time, the railway network remained intact and under state control as a whole for the sake of economies of scale and public goods provision. Such a vertical separation arrangement served as a test for the European Community and paved the way for the Community's directive in 1991 which required all railways of its member countries to set up separate accounting and charging mechanisms for rail operations and infrastructure, and facilitate interconnecting train services throughout the rail network in Europe.[17]

In 1994 the Swedish Parliament passed a bill on deregulating transport operation so that newcomers are allowed to compete with the incumbent rail operator. In 1996 BV was allowed to make available its track capacity and other facilities to train operators other than SJ. In 2001, with a view to better competing with newcomers, SJ was further separated and corporatized into a passenger services company, a freight services company, a railway station, and real estate company, and other sideline companies. In 2010, BV merged with the road administration, Vägverket, to form the newly established traffic administration, Trafikverket, which was charged with the responsibility for planning and procuring the construction and maintenance services for all state-owned track infrastructure. The Swedish railway market was fully opened for competitive tendering in 2012.[18]

The US railway

Despite being privately owned and operated for a long time, railroad companies in the United States were regulated and controlled by the federal government. The financial deficit and the severe intermodal competition led to a more market-oriented restructuring and separation between the passenger and freight transport. Since the key railway business in the United States was freight transport, the United States opted for the structure of dominant integration and horizontal separation, and allowed private freight service operators and their respective railways to remain intact.

The regional passenger commuter service operators, on the other hand, were left to compete with each other and also had to pay for the right to use the unified freight system. Having said that, the sole intercity passenger railroad and transport service was nationalized and operated as a public enterprise. In 1970, Congress passed the Rail Passenger Service Act; National Railroad Passenger Corporation (Amtrak) was incorporated in March 1971, and took over the passenger transport services from 20 private operators.[19]

In 1980, with further liberation from federal control and regulation, the private rail freight operators initiated a series of structural consolidation operations so as to compete with other modes of transport. Such industrial segmentation has resulted in two major private carriers in the United States, a few large inter-regional carriers over high-density branches; and numerous local carriers over low-density branches.[20]

The small rail operators in the United States emerged after structural segmentation because they are capable of offering tailor-made customer services for small shippers to meet special logistical requirements. Such low-density branches would be uneconomical if they were incorporated into the larger system, especially with the severe intermodal competition from the more flexible services offered by highway- and water-based transport. As a result, railway companies operating similar train services across major cities were considered as providing parallel competition for potential customers at mutually agreed tariffs. Shippers may choose to send their goods from one railroad to another, as well as by road and water transport, and the use of rail tracks over each other's railroad is also based on voluntary and mutual negotiation.[21]

The Japanese railway

The railway sector in Japan was under the jurisdiction of the Ministry of Railways until 1949, when the Japan National Railway (JNR) was established as a public enterprise. The sheer size of JNR, covering the four islands of Japan, was found to be too large to manage in an effective fashion. The problem was further exaggerated by the bureaucratic and inefficient management. As a result, JNR lost its market share gradually to other small private railways, as well as to road and water transport, throughout 1960s and 1970s, and recorded its first operating loss in 1964.[22]

JNR had accumulated a financial deficit of more than US$300 billion by 1987,[23] right before it was dissolved into seven railway companies (JRs)—six for regional passenger transport services and one for freight transport: JR East; JR Central; JR West; the three islands JRs in Hokkaido, Shikoku, and Kyushu; and the nationwide JR Freight. At the same time, the JNR Settlement Corporation was established to hold the stock shares of the seven JRs before they were offered for sale to the potential investors, and the Shinkansen Holding

Corporation was established to lease the profitable Shinkansen (high-speed train) network to the passenger JRs.[24]

As passenger transport is the major business for Japanese railways, each passenger JR operates exclusive passenger services on their own rail track so as to facilitate unified management and enhance the benefit of economies of scale. JR Freight, on the other hand, owns no railway and has to pay for the right to use the track for freight services. Such horizontal separation of the original JNR introduces geographical competition among regional passenger companies. Although such competition is indirect and less thorough than parallel competition, the line of horizontal separation corresponds to the scope of the market demand, and is proved to be good enough to turn the passenger business around.

In 1993 and 1996, JR East and JR West were eventually listed on the stock market, respectively, and JR Central was partially listed in 1997. The three island JRs were expected not to be financially viable because of the low-density populations and will be subsidized by the interest revenues of a management stability fund on a fixed lump-sum basis.

The New Zealand railway

New Zealand has long been operating as a state-owned monopoly under the Railway Department, which owned a nationwide network linking the two major islands. The Department operated both freight and intercity passenger transport services. The freight was the key business and benefited from numerous biased policies from the government, used to protect it from the competition put forward by highway and waterway sectors. The passenger transport service was operated by using the spare capacity from the freight transport service (i.e., passenger services were scheduled to run when the freight services were not using the rail tracks).

The New Zealand railway sector was characterized by its low-density service, and the Railway Department has been used by the government as a means to serve various social, economic, and even political objectives, such as provision of employment opportunities and training for school leavers. As a result, the state had to subsidize the sector and the soft budget constraint has rendered the railway system ineffective and unprofitable. The traveling patterns in terms or the origin and destination of railway trips did not allow it to introduce geographical separation as had happened in Japan. In 1971, the Minister of Railways commissioned a US consultancy firm, Wilbur Smith and Associates, to study the state policy on the transport sector.[25] Incorporating the consultant's recommendations to enhance user choice and market forces, the New Zealand government proposed to establish a Railways Corporation.

In 1981, the New Zealand Railways Corporation Act converted the Railways Department into a Crown-owned Railways Corporation. The New Zealand government also decided to introduce market competition by reducing state regulation and intervention in the transport sector, as well as enhancing market competition and user choice. As a result, New Zealand Rail was established in

Table 2.1 A list of railways undertaking various structural separations

Country(ies)	Separation model	Definition	
Sweden	Vertically and horizontally separated model	Infrastructure Freight Passenger	} Separated
United States	Dominant integrated and horizontally separated model with access for passenger services	Infrastructure Freight Passenger	} Integrated Separated
Japan	Dominant integrated and horizontally separated model with access for freight services	Infrastructure Passenger Freight	} Integrated Separated
New Zealand	Vertically and horizontally integrated model	Infrastructure Passenger Freight	} Integrated

Source: Adapted from "Progress in Rail Reform," Australian Productivity Council, Inquiry Report no. 6, 5 August 1999.

1982 to operate on a more commercial basis. The deregulation of the transport industry in New Zealand facilitated the entry of truck operators into the market and posed intermodal competition to the railway sector.

The New Zealand Railways Corporation responded to the market environment well and managed to reduce staffing requirements and operating costs. The Railways Corporation was further restructured into New Zealand Rail Limited in 1990, the labor productivity of which has been drastically increased by over 200% since incorporation in 1982.[26] New Zealand Rail Limited was eventually sold to Tranz Rail Ltd, a consortium made up of a US railroad company, a US investment firm, and a New Zealand merchant bank in 1993. The whole process of privatization was meant to convert bureaucratic state ownership to private ownership, in which the threat of bankruptcy would enhance the service performance.[27]

Notes

1 The Economic Research Institute of the Ministry of Railway (MOR) was quoted in the newspapers advocating following the worldwide railway reform trend. See "*Wangyun fenli tielaoda zaici tixu*" ("Separating Between Rail Road and Transport Services, the MOR Will Catch Up on the Speed Again") *China Enterprise News*, 16 April 2001, Wise News, http://libwisesearch.wisers.net/wisesearch/index.do (accessed 11 April 2015).
2 Javier Campos and Pedro Cantos, "Rail Transport Regulation," World Bank Group Working Paper (1999), p. 5, http://info.worldbank.org/etools/docs/library/64576/2064rail.pdf (accessed 11 April 2015); C.A. Nash and J. Preston, "United Kingdom: Privatization of Railways," Report of the Ninetieth Round Table on Transport Economics, European Conference of Ministers of Transport (1993), pp. 91–95.
3 Kenneth Button, "Regulatory Reform," in Kenneth Button and David Pitfield, eds., *Transport Deregulation: An International Movement* (New York: St. Martin's Press,

1991), pp. 14–15; David Banister and Kenneth Button, eds., *Transport in a Free Market Economy* (Houndmills: Macmillan, 1991), pp. 7–8; and Jon Shaw, *Competition, Regulation and the Privatization of British Rail* (Aldershot: Ashgate, 2000), pp. 28–31.

4 Campos and Cantos, "Rail Transport Regulation"; Nash and Preston, "United Kingdom"

5 Mike Adamson, Wynne Jones, and Robin Pratt, "Competition Issues in Privatization: Lessons for the Railways," in David Banister and Kenneth Butlon, eds., *Transport in a Free Market Economy* (Houndmills: Macmillan, 1991), pp. 49–81; Button and Pitfield, *Transport Deregulation*; Campos and Cantos, "Rail Transport Regulation"; John Kay and David Thompson, "Regulatory Reform in Transport in the United Kingdom: Principles and Application," David Banister and Kenneth Button, eds., *Transport in a Free Market Economy* (Houndmills: Macmillan, 1991), p. 36.

6 Campos and Cantos "Rail Transport Regulation," p. 7.

7 Adamson *et al.*, "Competition Issues in Privatization," p. 7; Shaw, *Competition, Regulation and the Privatization of British Rail*, p. 61; and Campos and Cantos "Rail Transport Regulation," p. 7.

8 Button and Pitfield, *Transport Deregulation*; Campos and Cantos, "Rail Transport Regulation."

9 Button and Pitfield, *Transport Deregulation*.

10 See Harold Demsetz, "Towards a Theory of Property Rights," *American Economic Review*, vol. 57, no. 2 (1967); and M. Boycko, A. Shleifer, and R. Vishny, *Privatizing Russia* (Cambridge, MA: MIT, 1996).

11 Ron Kopicki and Louis S. Thompson, "Best Methods of Railway Restructuring and Privatization," World Bank CFS Discussion paper Series (November 1995).

12 Organization for Economic Co-operation and Development, "Railway Reform in China Promoting Competition," Proceedings of an OECD/DRC Seminar on Rail Reform in Beijing, 28–29 January 2002.

13 Louis S. Thompson and Karim-Jacques Budin, "Directions of Railway Reform" (paper presented at the International Railway Congress Association meeting in Vienna, Austria, 25–28 September 2001).

14 Thompson and Budia, "Directions of Railway Reform"; Kopicki and Thompson, "Best Methods of Railway Restructuring"; Russell Pittman, "Chinese Railway Reform and Competition: Lessons from the Experience in Other Countries," *Journal of Transport Economics and Policy*, vol. 38, no. 2 (2004): 309–332.

15 Li Wai-ching, "The Reform Programme of the Ministry of Railways and Its Impact on Rail Development in China" (MA Dissertation, the University of Hong Kong, 2001, pp. 13–32).

16 Li Wai-ching, "The Reform Programme of the Ministry of Railways," pp. 33–54.

17 Kopicki and Thompson, "Best Methods of Railway Restructuring and Privatization," pp. 169–208.

18 G. Alexandersson and K. Rigas, "Rail Liberalisation in Sweden: Policy Development in a European Context," *Research in Transportation Business & Management*, vol. 6 (2013): 88–98.

19 Amtrak website, www.amtrak.com/home (accessed 12 April 2015).

20 Kopicki and Thompson, "Best Methods of Railway Restructuring and Privatization," pp. 249–277.

21 Russell Pittman, "Railroads and Competition: The Santa Fe/Southern Pacific Merger Proposal," *Journal of Industrial Economics*, vol. 34 (1990), pp. 25–46.

22 Fumitoshi Mizutani, "An Assessment of the Japan Railway Companies Since Privatization: Performance, Local Rail Service and Debts," *Transport Review*, vol. 19, no. 2 (1999): 117–139.

23 Kopicki and Thompson, "Best Methods of Railway Restructuring and Privatization," pp. 73–97.

24 Mizutani, "An Assessment of the Japan Railway Companies."
25 Wilbur Smith and Associates, *New Zealand Transport Policy Study* (New Zealand: Ministry of Transport, Government of New Zealand, 1973).
26 R.Y. Cavana, "Restructuring the New Zealand Railway System: 1982–1993," *Transport Reviews*, vol. 15, no. 2 (1995): 119–139.
27 Kopicki and Thompson, "Best Methods of Railway Restructuring and Privatization," pp. 102–128.

3   China's railway reform in context

The previously discussed efficiency model and structural analysis of railway reform is important for its clarity and elegant reasoning. The economic logic helps to lay the foundation for policy planning. But it does not provide insights on the intricacies of the empirical implementation and unfolding of the reform. The efficiency-driven approach adopts the state-centered point of view and assumes that there exists a benevolent state leadership which is autonomous and capable of judging and implementing the best reform policies for the country.[1] This approach, however, fails to take into consideration that policies are not made in a vacuum. A thorough and profound study of railway reform should include the historical and social contexts. Previous studies of China's policies on investment,[2] rural development,[3] water,[4] energy,[5] forestry,[6] education,[7] population,[8] and science and technology[9] all demonstrate the importance of studying both the policy content and context.

A chronicle of China's railway reform

After decades of reform, China has been on the threshold of reforming its highly regularized public utilities sectors.[10] Changes are urgently needed for the country to keep pace with fast-changing economic development and to cope with the accession to the World Trade Organization. In this last set of restructuring, railway reform was one of the most challenging tasks owing to its longstanding and deep-seated structural problems, some of which were attributable to the planning heritage of the socialist system, while others were characteristics of the railway industry in particular.

The official portrayal of railway reform in China has been an efficiency-driven story. The Ministry of Railways (MOR) has been claiming for decades that the country was on the threshold of revolutionizing its rail sector in a bid to keep pace with economic growth and modernization plans, and to eradicate the longstanding structural inefficiency of the railway system.

The latest twist

In January 2002, the Development Research Centre (DRC) of the State Council and the Organization for Economic Co-operation and Development (OECD) co-hosted a seminar on China's railway reform in Beijing. Chen Qingtai, Vice Director-General of the DRC agreed that China's accession to the WTO would speed up the reform of those natural monopolistic or public utility industries. Such reform would introduce competition, corporatize state-owned enterprises, reduce government intervention, and enhance efficient practices.[11] Against this background, the OECD shared its experiences and recommendations on rail reform with China. Earlier, in March 2000, Louis S. Thompson, the Railway Advisor of the World Bank, also briefed Fu Zhihuan, then Minister of Railways on "Railway Restructuring in China: The Great Railway Challenge."[12]

Well informed by the MOR about various economic statistics, such as freight and passenger traffic density, transport volume growth, transport composition, and labor productivity, these two seminars provided well-grounded and author-itative recommendations on how to reform China's railway. In brief, both suggested that the Chinese railway reform should focus on de-politicization and disintegration.

De-politicization separates the government and ministerial interventions from the enterprise operation. By minimizing political intervention, introducing hard budget constraints, and enhancing autonomy in the pricing and scheduling of railway services, such separation improves the efficiency and governance of the state-owned sector.

Disintegration breaks the myth of natural monopoly and economies of scale, and promotes maximum competition within the sector. Based on various railway reforms undertaken in other parts of the world, the MOR compared and analyzed alternative options and decided to change from "the vertically and horizontally integrated model" to "the vertically and horizontally separated model."

In April 2000, the State Council approved the MOR's reform.[13] In 2001, the MOR had formally put forward a time frame for vertical separation (Table 3.1),[14] and in April 2001 some newspapers even reported that the MOR planned to shorten the ten-year time frame to seven years.[15] While international railway experts were keeping an eye on this breakthrough in China's railway sector, Liu Zhijun, the successor of Fu Zhihuan, played down the reform after he had been promoted from Vice Minister to Minister in 2003, and finally called the whole thing off by the end of 2003.[16]

Liu was soon given the name "Great Leap Liu" because of his ambitious approach to developing the railway network, as well as to introducing the super high-speed train in the country.[17] In view of such a Great Leap Forward approach to railway development, China has put in place the second-largest rail network, supporting the third busiest railway system, in the world in terms of combined passenger and freight traffic density in 2011.[18] There were about 17,000 kilo-meters of high-speed rail supporting high-speed trains running at an average speed of 200 km/h or higher by 2012.[19]

Table 3.1 Time frame for vertical separation of the MOR

Year	Specific plan for vertical separation
1999	Establish passenger service companies under four direct management railway administrations as pilot sites at Kunming, Hohhot, Liuzhou, and Nanchang.
2000	Establish passenger service company under the Guangzhou Railway (Group) Corporation in December.
2000–2003	Establish passenger service companies in all 14 railway administrations (corporations) with separate accounts.
2004–2006	Restructure and regroup passenger service companies into a few large-scale companies according to the modern enterprise system so that they are truly market-oriented. At the same time, proceed to set up freight companies.
2006–2010	Restructure and regroup freight companies into a few large-scale companies.
By 2010	Passenger and freight companies as well as a railway network company will have been established, thus completing the entire process of "vertical separation."

Such a huge achievement, however, has been plagued by the tragic accidents in Shandong which killed 70 people,[20] and in Hunan which killed three people in 2009.[21] Another accident in relation to the high-speed train took place in Wenzhou in 2011, killing 40 people.[22] In 2011, in the middle of these railway accidents, the then Minister Liu was dismissed and imprisoned for taking bribes and gifts of 64.6 million yuan between 1986 and 2011. In July 2013 he was sentenced to death with a two-year reprieve. Liu was also deprived of political rights for life. In the same year, the Ministry of Railways was dissolved and the China Railway Corporation (CRC) was established to operate the national railway. The administrative functions of the railway sector were transferred to the Ministry of Transport.[23]

The dramatic cancellation of the vertical separation policy during Liu's regime raised doubts about the economic explanation of railway reform. The reversal of the reform policy suggested that there were other intervening factors behind the economic imperative. The chronicle of China's railway reform suggests that many reform policies were implemented half-heartedly or terminated midway through, despite their lofty ambitions.

The separation of the administrative and commercial functions suggested that the Chinese government was neither de-politicizing nor disintegrating the railway sector as explained in the efficiency model. A thorough study of the sector reveals that the state has never let go its iron grip on a few strategically important sectors. The following section puts the evolution of the property rights arrangements and re-arrangements in China's railway sector into context, and paves the way for developing a new vantage point to study and explain the railway reform in China.

Evolution of property rights arrangements and re-arrangements

Chandler's book on the managerial revolution in American business sheds light on the development of property rights arrangements of the railway industry in capitalist economies, which is found to be very different from that in China. The first railroad in both countries was privately constructed and owned, but then the property rights arrangements of the railroad industry diverged significantly. In America, dispersed private ownership during the railway boom in the late 1840s and 1850s gave rise to the failure of nationwide coordination. A serious head-on collision of passenger trains in 1841 called for a thorough administrative reform to enhance coordination and facilitate safe operation. Chandler contends that the first administrative hierarchies in American business emerged in the form of joint stock ownership, separating ownership and management, departmentalizing organizational functions, and adopting advance accounting techniques. Soon after the railway ownership and management were separated, fund-raising firms were put in place in 1851 and 1852 to handle railroad securities, which were largely purchased by foreign capitalists in Germany, France, and Britain. Modern business managers were hired to take over the railway managerial and administrative tasks. Chandler refers to such property rights arrangement as "managerial capitalism."[24]

The property rights arrangements of China's railway evolved in a different way. The following discussion divides China's railway history into three major periods: the pre-centralization period, the centralization period, and the reform period.[25] Although this book focuses mainly on the reform period of China's railway, a brief overview of the first two phases sets the scene for discussion of the institutional change and property rights re-arrangements in China's rail sector in the twentieth century.

The pre-centralization period: 1876–1949

During the pre-centralization period, foreign construction and control of railroads in China was common and resulted in disjointed property rights arrangements. The problem of fragmentation eventually triggered a series of patriotic movements and legitimized the centralization in the next period.

In 1876, Jardine, Matheson & Company built the first railroad in China, between Shanghai and Wusong. The British company first constructed the railroad without the Qing government's consent and then requested the Qing government pay 285,000 tael of silver as compensation for not running the railroad. After paying the money in three installments, the Qing government dismantled the railroad and claimed that railways were bad based on superstitious (*fengshui*) reasons. China's resistance to foreign ownership of railroads was seen as conscious negation of foreign penetration.[26]

Five years later, in 1881, China constructed its own railway between Tangshan and Xugezhuang. The 10 km railroad was used for transporting coal from the Kaiping coal mine. The first Chinese railway company, Kaiping Railway

Company, was later established to extend the Tang-Xue line to Lutai and Tianjin. By that time, the total length of railroad in China was 130 km.

Until 1894, Chinese railroads were mostly built for coal and iron transport. Then Beiyangguan Railway Bureau was established to construct the railroad at Shanhaiguan for defense purposes. But China's international status further deteriorated after being defeated in the 1894–1895 Sino-Japanese War. Between 1896 and 1903, a number of unfair treaties were signed to grant the imperialist countries—such as France, Germany, Britain, Belgium, Russia, and America—railway concessions in regions of economic interest. As a result, 41 percent of China's railroads were controlled by imperialist countries, and another 39 percent were under foreign control in the form of loan agreements.[27] Such foreign railway loans were seen as a form of foreign aggression, as the terms of the loans were often unfair to China:

> Again the terms of the loans are often objectionable. In addition to the high rate of interest and extravagant guarantee, certain powers invariably exact as many special privileges as seem permissible in the face of international jealousy. They insist in nearly every railway loan that the engineers, accountants, and comptrollers must be their subjects, that the power to judge and receive material must rest in their hands, and that material itself must also be bought from their merchants. In short, these powers in trying to lend money to China, want to get everything which they can possibly lay claim to through the loan.[28]

Later, when the Qing government collapsed and Yuan Shikai ruled between 1912 and 1916, he put up for auction the right of way of China's railroad, which became the collateral for foreign loans. In addition, Japan also controlled the right of way, construction, and loan management of most railroads in Manchuria.

Foreign ownership of railroads was seen as a kind of invasive imperialism and instigated waves of patriotic movements. Between 1904 and 1907, 19 railway rights-recovery groups were established to raise capital and buy out foreign railroad rights. Such localized patriotic movements eventually led to the well-known Sichuan Railroad Recovery Movement and the establishment of a so-called "shadow provincial government."[29] The Nanjing government later determined to nationalize and expand China's rail network, but was jeopardized by the Sino-Japanese war and the civil war. The foreign, unstable, scattered, sometimes illegal, and very often unregulated property rights arrangements of the railway sector in China were a result of the bargaining between foreign and indigenous powers. The former wanted to transport their economic goods and expand their mercantile interests in China and thus used diplomatic pressure to control railway ownership. The latter wanted to maintain nationalistic pride and refute imperialistic invasion by nationalizing the railway ownership.[30]

The result of such a disjointed property rights arrangements are as follows: First, before 1949, around 20,000 km of railroad was built, mostly in the northeast region along the coastline; only around 6 percent of the railroad was in the northwest and southwest regions. Second, the British, German, Belgian, Russian, Japanese, and American authorities had built their railroads with different standards and specifications, technically and administratively. In 1907, the Republican government began to design a national railway network, and between 1912 and 1915 it nationalized those important railroads. But the regional railways were still operated with different fund-raising and book-keeping systems.[31] These railroads were not easy to integrate, and problems of fragmentation legitimized the one-off centralization during the New China era.

The centralization period: 1949–1978

During the Sino-Japanese War between 1894 and 1895, and the civil war between 1927 and 1949, most battles took place along the railway lines, and the railroad became militarily important.[32] The Chinese Communist Party (CCP) had a specific team of railway soldiers which built and repaired rail lines in the liberated areas. In January 1949, the Chinese People's Revolutionary Army Railway Bureau (*Zhongguo renmin geming junshi weiyuanhui tiedaobu*) was established, and in May of the same year, the Chinese People's Liberation Army Corps of Railway Soldiers was formed (*Zhongguo renmin jiefangjun tielubing*) to repair railroad damaged during war time.[33] After the establishment of the People's Republic of China in 1949, the government inherited a fragmented railway system of which only half was operative.[34] The Chinese People's Revolutionary Army Railway Bureau was renamed as the Ministry of Railways of the Central People's Government (*Zhongyang renmin zhengfu tiedaobu*, the MOR).

At that time, the CCP had advocated "abolishing of private property" and asserted that private property was "based on the exploitation of the many by the few."[35] As the vanguard of the world revolution of proletariats, the CCP aimed at confiscating all private property, putting it under communal ownership, and coordinating all economic activities in the name of the people. To revitalize the country after years of wars, China adopted the strategy of the planned economy and combined government and enterprise functions (*zhengqi heyi*).

Teng Daiyuan, the first railway minister, was charged with integrating the nationwide railway network. By June 1950, the entire rail system was reported to follow the uniform set of "Railway Technical Administration Rules and Regulations";[36] the nation-wide "transportation schedules" were launched the same year.[37] By that time there were 15 regional railway administrations.[38]

After the so-called "Period of Economic Recovery" (1950–1952), China entered its first Five-Year Plan (1953–1957). Following the general economic directive, the railway undertook the Soviet model of centralized planning. Regional railway cadres did not own any state assets and their overall production and financial targets were centrally planned. They were also required to generate and turn in revenues to the MOR annually and to submit their expenditure budgets to the finance department of the MOR for approval. The state would then allocate the necessary fixed assets, working capital, and other production materials. Such practice was commonly known as maintaining two separate lines of income and expenditure (*shouzhi liangtiaoxian*), or unification of income and expenditure (*tongshou tongzhi*). By 1956, various bonus systems were designed to allow regional railway administrations and other units to retain a fixed percentage of the extra revenue made against the planned targets.[39] But the policy of bonus systems was soon abolished.

Between 1958 and 1960, during the "Great Leap Forward," Mao wanted to hasten the pace of economic development in China and to surpass the United Kingdom in 15 years and the United States in 50–70 years. He thus urged for a boost to steel and iron production. In March 1958, the Chinese government urged localities to develop regional self-sufficiency. To stay in line with the central directives, the MOR set up 29 regional railway administrations, one in each province. Since administrative, functional, or professional specialization was criticized as "departmentalism" (*danwei zhuyi*),[40] the rail sector adopted the policy of "Large-scale Railway Construction by All the People" (*Quanmin daban tielu*). Urged on by the unreasonable production targets and the quest for full-scale self-sufficiency (*daerquan xiaoerquan*), local railway administrations rushed to complete the constructions targets. The result was irrational and uncoordinated investments in "under-quality railways" (*tu tielu*), crowded and unsafe scheduling among different railway administrations, and false regional reports of production outputs. The Great Leap Forward lasted three years and its failure called for another wave of re-centralization to curb the chaotic situation during the recovery period between 1961 and 1965. To facilitate centralized control, various regional railways administrations were merged and 12 of them were abolished.

Between 1966 and 1976, the unified railway system was soon jeopardized by the "Cultural Revolution." At that time, railway was used as the major means to transport the PLA and college students for "great exchange" (*dachuanlian*, a kind of nationwide criticizing movement). By May 1967, the railway system was under military control and normal transport was virtually paralyzed. In 1969 more and more regional governments and military units expanded their power and wanted to control a separate railway entity. As a result, the number of regional railway administrations increased from 17 to 20.

In 1976, the Gang of Four was arrested and the "Ten Years of Chaos" ended. In February 1977, another centralized campaign was put forward, namely "Railway Learns from Daqing" (*Tieluxue daqing*). Learning from Daqing was to copy the characters of the people in Daqing when they ran the state enterprises. Those role models were said to have "three honesties and four seriousness" (*sanlao siyan*); "three honesties" was to be an honest people, speak honestly, and work honestly, while "four seriousness" was to be serious in setting standards, organizing work, adjusting attitude, and maintaining discipline. This political campaign once again centralized Chinese railway administration ideologically, though people may not really have changed their behavior practically. By 1978, some of the small-scale railway administrations were merged with other railway administrations and the whole system ended up with 14 railway administrations.

The reform period (1978–2003)

Through a series of political campaigns which had resulted in waves of decentralization and re-centralization, the Chinese railway sector became a highly centralized government body under the State Council. The MOR was charged with the responsibility of formulating central objectives, maintaining a nationwide railroad network, organizing daily operations, coordinating 14 regional railway administrations, monitoring 13 academic, educational, and medical institutes, and supervising numerous spin-off enterprises.[41] With a total of 3.4 million employees, the railway regime also provided the workforce with cradle-to-grave social welfare such as housing, education, medical, and recreational facilities. The MOR stressed the importance of "ten thousand things guaranteed within" (*wanshi bu qiuren*), and the work unit (*danwei*) was designed to eliminate market coordination.

In addition to the problem of vertical integration, mammoth size, and inertia to change, which apply to the railway industry in general, China's railway was further plagued by its centralized and bureaucratic coordination.

Administratively, aside from the vertical reporting line (the *"tiao-tiao"* system) between the central headquarters of the MOR and the regional offices of railway authorities, each regional railway administration was horizontally tied with the respective local party committee (the *"kuai-kuai"* system). Financially, regional railway administrations were required to generate and turn in revenues to the MOR annually and submit their budgets to the finance department of the MOR for approval. The railway sector was, therefore, a gigantic monopolistic sector, with a criss-crossing hierarchical structure and state-owned and centrally administered property rights arrangements.

Explaining hypotheses of China's railway reform

According to the economic theory of property rights arrangements, the Chinese railway sector inherited the organizational defects of state and communal property rights arrangements, which inevitably rendered the sector inefficient. China's leadership was well aware of the problem and adopted a series of strategies with a view to enhancing railway efficiency. However, the reform policies were implemented unevenly across different units and different regions within the railway sector. The efficiency-driven model adopts a statist view and contends that such variations were a result of the state's intent to balance between different economic, political, and social imperatives. Accordingly, the more prominent the economic imperatives, the more the state would choose to adopt the best railway model through de-politicization and disintegration.

The recent twist in the railway reform policy casts doubt on the above-mentioned hypothesis. The first hypothesis (H1) is that economic imperatives do not necessarily lead to decentralization and facilitation of market competition. In fact, sometimes economic imperatives led to reform policies of re-centralization. The following evolutionary review of various decentralization and re-centralization policies in the railway sector—including the responsibility contracts, the dual-track system, and the corporatization strategies—further casts doubt on the assumption that the initial decentralization policy was aimed at privatization, and led to the formulation of the remaining hypotheses.

The second hypothesis (H2) anticipates that decentralization does not necessarily lead to privatization. Although decentralization is a very common way for policy makers to initiate the transition from state ownership to private ownership, it is not always true that a policy of decentralization will inevitably lead to a final stage of privatization. This is especially true when the cadres or government officials are half-hearted in the process of transformation, or when they actually have their own hidden agenda.

The third hypothesis (H3) examines the assets discovery mechanism in China, and assumes that decentralization is instrumental in identifying idle assets, i.e., to "pick the right assets" for transformation, but not necessarily to "pick the right owners" for privatization. This hypothesis provides a new point of view for explaining the cyclical process of decentralization and re-centralization in China's railway sector. If the process of decentralization is to pick the right owners, it is likely that, in the long run, decentralization will follow by further decentralization and result in privatization. However, what happened in China's railway sector is the continuous reinstatement of state control after a significant amount of idle assets are exposed and put into the best possible ownership—sometimes private, sometimes state-owned.

The fourth hypothesis (H4) deals with the assets recovery mechanism and expects that whether the newly discovered "assets" would be privatized depends on whether they are perceived to be strategically important or not. For productive assets relating to those industries of strategic importance or in which market competition alone could not improve the efficiency, the Chinese government would maintain the state's ownership in order to re-regulate and re-arrange the respective property rights. These industries usually have some common characteristics which would lead to the problem of market failure, and therefore required strategic efforts from the state. As a result, the more likely is market failure, the more strategically important are the newly identified assets, and the more likely it is that they will be centralized by the state.

Decentralization and re-centralization railway policies

Responsibility contracts

The property rights arrangements of the railway sector before 1978 were highly centralized. After the Third Plenum of the 11th Central Committee of the CCP, the MOR undertook a series of decentralizations, both between the central government and the MOR, and between the MOR and its subordinate railway administrations and enterprises.

Before 1981, the MOR paid a 15 percent sales tax on gross revenue, and then turned over all net profits to the government. In return, the government provided all the investment and operation costs to the MOR. Between 1981 and 1985, the MOR continued to pay the tax, but only turned over part of its profits to the central government, and the state gradually ceased to invest in the rail sector. From 1986 onwards, the MOR paid 5.3 percent of revenue as its business tax and retained all other income tax and profits as railway investment funds. The central government stopped granting any funds for railroad construction and all existing debts were written off. The MOR had to seek loans from domestic and international sources to top-up the railway investment fund. The MOR was also charged with the responsibilities of constructing and upgrading new and existing lines, and providing designated passenger and freight services. The central government still controlled prices, but promised to give a high priority to increased rail prices during the contract term, which lasted from 1986 to 1990. Such an incentive system was in place to link the total wage payment of rail staff with the traffic units that the MOR carried.[42]

While the central government was decentralizing part of its income rights and control rights to the MOR, the ministry was trying to create similar arrangements with its regional railway administrations and subsidiary railway enterprises. Starting from the early 1980s, various internal responsibility systems were put in place, all designed to allow regional railway administrations and railway enterprises to retain shares of the targeted and above-target revenues.[43] In addition, regional entities were granted the autonomy to make use of the retained profits for rehabilitation, upgrading, and minor construction of railways (large-scale construction projects were still centrally controlled), as well as to make decisions regarding production schedules, resources allocation, and lower-level personnel reshuffles.[44]

Between 1981 and 1993, various responsibility contracts between the MOR and its subsidiaries were in place.[45] To avoid asset stripping, a more stringent responsibility system was put in place, namely the Responsibility System of Assets Management. This put the responsibility of managing railway assets on the shoulders of the chiefs of the regional railways administrations and enterprises. The state assets were first audited by an external audit team, and the chief had to sign a responsibility contract to guarantee, in addition to other production targets, a fixed rate of return on state assets.

In 1996, the system was first implemented in the China Railway Locomotive and Rolling Stock Industry Corporation. Between 1997 and 1998, this pioneering project was extended to the Guangzhou Railway (Group) Corporation, the five railway related enterprises, and the other four railway administrations, namely the Hohhot, Nanchang, Liuzhou, and Kunming Railway Administrations. At the end of 1998, the MOR issued the "Implementation Method of Railway Responsibility System of Assets Management," and on 5 April 1999, all 14 regional railway administrations and the corporation signed the contracts for the Responsibility System of Assets Management with the MOR.[46]

However, the Asset Management System was criticized as being "old wine in a new bottle," with no material change as regards the property rights arrangements.[47] In fact, an in-depth analysis of the emergence of different phases of the responsibility system across the country casts doubt on the state's intent to decentralize benevolently more and more income and control rights and to enhance efficiency. Focusing on the transport sub-sectors of the MOR, Chapter 4 will examine the overall railway reform policy and validate the hypothesis (H1) that there is indeed no direct relationship between the economic imperatives and the degree of decentralization.

Dual-track system

In 1984 the Chinese government implemented the "dual-track system" ("*shuang-guizhi*"). Under the system, state-owned enterprises were allowed to maintain an additional capacity for production and sell the extra planned quantity of goods at market price in a two-tiered pricing system.[48]

Before the implementation of the system, state-owned sectors had been assigned compulsory production targets, and goods or services were sold at compulsory planned prices. Since loss-makers expected financial assistance from the state, they were spared from any disciplinary consequences of inefficient operation. As such, price responsiveness declined, entrepreneurial innovations dissipated, and excessive demand for inputs led to what Kornai refers to as a "shortage economy."[49] In view of the insufficient budgetary fund to support government functions, the Chinese government allowed local cadres to set up economic entities for self-financed purposes.[50]

In the railway sector, local cadres started to diversify the scope of business to other transport and non-transport services from 1985 onwards. For example, the regional railway administrations were situated across the country and used this advantage to adapt to regional economic developments. The Liuzhou Railway Administration was located at the end node of the railway network and was a natural point of origin or destination. As a result, local railway cadres made use of their existing connections with those shippers and forwarders, and negotiated with local governments to establish and develop a large-scale logistic center.

Other examples were Lanzhou and Hohhot Railway Administrations, which were in regions with plenty of mineral, coal, and petroleum deposits. Since they had previously helped local government transport such natural resources from the mines, they could use the links with local governments to develop the mining industries jointly.[51] Such sideline businesses also included non-transport services. Nanchang Railway Administration developed a piece of wasteland of 8,000 hectares next to the railroad at Huangtugang, into a farmland, animal farms, fish ponds, and food processing factories.[52]

Besides these region-specific connections and diversification, regional railway cadres also used the connections established in their core transport business and engaged in businesses which provided more value-added services to the passengers. For example, they rented out laser VCD players to passengers at RMB 10 per hour for entertainment.[53] Cadres started to operate restaurants, travel services, hotels, entertainment centers, car rental services, and advertising services, and to develop residential and commercial properties, and to integrate all businesses within their jurisdiction into a corporate-like entity.

Such diversified business development within the regional railway adminis-trations was similar to the development of township and village enterprises in China. During the fiscal reform of the dual-track system, "leakage" of authority from central government to regional agents encouraged village cadres to integ-rate public firms and coordinate extra-budgetary economic activities within their jurisdictions into corporation-like fiefs.[54] As a result, large numbers of small-scale enterprises evolved into multi-tiered and regionally based systems, referred to as "local state corporatism."[55] Consequently, the local economy was shaped by market-oriented decisions, albeit it was still under socialist regulation within the local state jurisdiction.[56]

The leakage and delegation of authority and decentralization of bundles of property rights from the central government to its territorial administration sub-system (the horizontal *kuai kuai* system) in China has spawned an entire branch of research into the regional economic development in China studies.[57] This current study of China's railway reform delineates a similar decentralization process which took place within the functional administrative sub-system (the vertical *tiao tiao* system) and which I refer to as "sectoral corporatism."

While "local state corporatism" eventually led to large-scale privatization of rural enterprises, "sectoral corporatism" evolved differently. As such, it is too soon to conclude that state-initiated decentralization will inevitably lead to pri-vatization. The second hypothesis (H2) thus focuses on this important, but easily confused, transformation mechanism and anticipates that there is no direct rela-tionship between decentralization and privatization.

By comparing the transport sub-sector of the railway system with other modes of transport, and reviewing the overall top-down reform policies, Chapter 5 will argue that various decentralization policies do not necessarily lead to pri-vatization arrangements. Rather, it was part of the state's strategic move to, on the one hand, mimic the Western capitalist model selectively, and, on the other hand, discover the idle production assets.[58]

Chapter 6 will continue to focus on the MOR's transport sub-sector and zoom in on local cadres' survival strategies to examine the third hypothesis (H3), the assets discovery mechanism, which assumes that the MOR's leakage of author-ity and the dual-track policy unexpectedly enabled local cadres to discover idle productive resources, i.e., to "pick the right assets," not to "pick the right winners."

Organizational changes: moving toward privatization, mimicking privatization, or re-centralization?

In addition to the fiscal reforms ranging from the various versions of responsib-ility contract to the dual-track system, the MOR also re-arranged the organiza-tional structure.

In 1983, with the State Council's permission, the MOR started to corporatize the Guangzhou–Shenzhen Railway Corporation. Apart from turning over the fixed sum of RMB 20 million to the state annually, the corporation retained full autonomy in operational services, financial control, and management of other sideline businesses such as touring, catering, entertaining, and advertising services. In the same year, the MOR established four railway-related units under the direct supervision of the ministry headquarters: the Rolling Stock Corporation; the Communication and Signaling Corporation; the Railway Construction Corporation; and the Foreign Services Corporation. The Rolling Stock Corporation was in charge of the manufacturing of the locomotives and rail cars; the Communication and Signaling Corporation was in charge of the provision of transport signals and internal communication within the railway system; the Railway Construction Corporation built and repaired railroads, tunnels and bridges; and the Foreign Services Corporation was in charge of cooperative projects with foreign partners.

In February 1993 the Guangzhou Railway Administration was corporatized to form the Guangzhou Railway (Group) Corporation.[59] The enterprise group was formed with core enterprises at the first tier, surrounded by a second tier of closely connected enterprises, a third tier of semi-closely connected enterprises, and a last tier of loosely connected enterprises.[60] Three years later, one of its sub-administrations, the Shenzhen Railway Sub-Administration, was successfully listed on the New York Stock Exchange and Hong Kong Stock Exchange, as the Guangshen Railway Company Limited.

In 1995, several transport and infrastructure services units were also turned into limited liability companies; they include the Dalian Sub-Administration, the Datong–Qinhuangdao Railway, the Nanning Railway Company, the Fuzhou Railway Sub-Administration, the China Railway Locomotive and Rolling Stock Industry Corporation, the Qiqihar Rolling Stock Works, the Second Railway Engineering Bureau, and the Twelfth Railway Engineering Bureau.[61] However, the formation of such corporations and limited companies was half-hearted and the MOR leadership were soon soft-pedaling it. As a result, not all regional railway administrations were corporatized, and even for those which had been corporatized or turned into limited liability companies, the underlying governance remained the same as their predecessors. In other words, different railway corporations were made to mimic the appearance of Western companies only, not the underlying modus operandi.

In 1998, following Zhu Rongji's policy of cutting the number of state employees, the MOR changed to focus on streamlining its administrative structure and rationalizing the staff levels. The administrative structure of the MOR headquarters was decreased from 809 to 400 persons.[62] In 2000, the five railway-related enterprises—the China Railway Engineering Corporation, the China Railway Construction Corporation, the China Railway Rolling Stock Plant Inc., the China Civil Engineering Group, and the China Railway Signal Communication Corporation—were also spun-off from the MOR headquarters and put under the jurisdiction of the State Assets Management Commission (SAMC) of the State Council. In addition, ten colleges and a group of high schools were detached from the MOR, and the Central Government Enterprise Affairs Commission, the Ministry of Education, and the local governments assumed their management.[63] By 2000, the total number of employees was reduced from 3.4 million to 2.5 million.

Beginning in 2001, the MOR officially adopted another structural reform policy—the vertical separation policy, which separated the freight and passenger transport systems from the railroad network construction and management. The goal was to break up the existing integrated management of the railway network and transportation services and to deploy resources according to market demand.

The first step set-up five passenger companies in four different railway administrations and one railway corporation, namely the Kunming, Hohhot, Liuzhou, and Nanchang Railway Administrations, as well as the Guangzhou Railway (Group) Corporation. Strictly speaking, these passenger companies did not have the status of legal persons. There were a few limitations preventing these passenger companies evolving into real market-oriented enterprises.

First, they were simply mock-up legal persons with no material changes in personnel. The same group of people who had worked in the passenger division later worked in these newly named passenger companies. The only changes were their job titles; for example, it was general practice that the party secretary became the director, the division chief became the general manager, etc.

Second, these passenger companies had to integrate into the whole railway system; they were required to cooperate and coordinate with other passenger divisions within the system and thus were restrained from innovating market-oriented methods of operation and management.

Third, these passenger companies were not able to make profits from the market directly and therefore failed to respond like market-oriented enterprises, though they were asked to maintain independent accounts of their transport income and operating costs. While they had to negotiate for an agreed internal cost with their respective railway administrations for getting different support services such as the provision of rolling stocks, water supply and ticketing services,[64] they still had to eventually pool their profits with other divisions of the same railway administrations. Such transactions simply transferred the money from the left pocket to the right, and was a matter of accounting manipulation. There was no incentive to make a profit or work hard.

It was originally thought that the experience gained in these test sites would be extended to other railway administrations. But in 2003, the new railway minister, Liu Zhijun, decided to re-centralize power into the hands of the ministerial leadership, so he called off the entire reform of vertical disintegration. Interestingly, the five passenger companies were returned to the passenger division with few difficulties because all they needed to do was change the name on the corporate signboards and name cards. As there was no material change in personnel and modus operandi, the only changes were the top leaders' job titles and company names.

In 2005, Minister Liu removed all 41 railway sub-administrations within a few days. He also recombined some railway administrations, which eventually resulted in 16 railway administrations and two railway corporations. Liu explained that this was to resolve the unclear rights and responsibilities between the railway administrations and the respective railway sub-administrations over the same geographical area. Liu also believed that such structural reform would reduce the redundant administrative reporting lines, improve transport services organization, reduce operational costs, and enhance efficiency.[65] However, such a re-demarcation of the boundary of the railway administrative units was not based on thorough research of the existing pattern of passenger and/or freight transport. As a result, the re-organization would not pave the way for the future corporation or privatization of the railway administrative units. Many media reports suggested that such a drastic re-organization of the railway administrative structure was too complicated to complete over a short period of time. Regional railway cadres were very confused as to how to conduct the separation, streamline staffing, settle the finances, and, most importantly, ensure safe allocation of the command center from railway sub-administration units to railway administration units.[66]

Research hypotheses

The railway's structural changes have never led to ownership reform. The hurdles could partly be attributed to local resistance and bargaining, and partly to the fact that the central or ministerial leadership soft-pedaled the reform initiatives and undertook re-centralization policies from time to time. After all, corporatization, spinning off, and separation did not alter the state ownership.

For example, the Guangzhou Railway Group Corporation, the Guangshen Railway Company Ltd., the China Railway Engineering Corporation, the China Railway Construction Corporation, the China Railway Rolling Stock Plant Inc., the China Civil Engineering Group, and the China Railway Signal Communication Corporation were all still operated under state ownership. They mimicked Western company structures by forming boards of directors, but the key managers, such as directors and general managers, were actually the party secretary and division chief of the same company before the reform. As a result, the corporate governance remained the same as before.

The various initiatives to adopt modern company structures were simply mimicry. Chapters 6–8 study the transport, construction, and signaling sub-sectors of the MOR and show that besides mimicry, three types of re-centralization were occurring.

First, the MOR separated the sideline sub-sectors from the core sector so that the respective productive resources were independent of each other. Second, the MOR spun-off some non-transport-related sub-sectors, which were then subsumed under different state agents according to their business functions. This was aimed at re-organizing the state assets according to their functional values, not administrative concerns. Third, the MOR re-centralized some of the newly discovered productive assets and put them under close scrutiny. These re-centralized assets were usually found to be strategically important to the national economic development and therefore required special, state-led efforts to control and phase the development.

The three kinds of restructuring involved different levels of state intervention in their business operations and did not necessarily lead to privatization. The first involved some kind of decentralization as regards the sideline businesses into which the MOR separated them after removing them from the core businesses, allowing more autonomy in their operation. The last two restructurings involved decentralization and re-centralization through which the MOR retained or regained its control after the restructuring.

Chapters 6–8 further substantiate the assets discovery hypothesis (H3), and also provide evidence to examine the last hypothesis of "assets recovery mechanism" (H4) that whether the newly discovered "assets" would be privatized depends on whether they are perceived to be strategically important or not. The more strategically important the newly identified assets, the more they will be centralized by the state.

In general, the above comprehensive review of the history of China's railway reform casts doubt on the economic explanation of reform in terms of enhancing productivity and efficiency. Although national leaders claimed to be aware of the inefficient property rights arrangements, they did not give up their power and facilitate the concentration of the truncated property rights. Rather, the decentralization policy was designed to mimic the Western model, and at the same time to allow enough room for local cadres to discover idle state assets.

To recap, this chapter describes China's railway development in context, and from which various intellectual curiosities lead to the four major hypotheses put forward in this book. Each hypothesis will be discussed in detail in the subsequent chapters focusing on three important sub-sectors of the railway regime: transport, construction, and signaling:

H1 Economic imperatives do not necessarily lead to decentralization.
H2 Decentralization does not necessarily lead to privatization.
H3 Decentralization identifies idle assets, i.e., "picks the right assets," but not "picks the winners."
H4 The more strategically important the newly identified assets, the more they will be centralized by the state.

Based on these research hypotheses, this book explains the non-economic imperatives of decentralization within the railway regime, the reform policy of decentralization without privatization, the local cadres' survival strategies of picking the right assets, and the state recovery of the newly discovered state assets.

Notes

1 Karen Barkey and Sunita Parikh, "Comparative Perspectives on the State," *Annual Review of Sociology*, vol. 17 (1991): 525–536.
2 Barry Naughton, "The Decline of Central Control over Investment in Post-Mao China," in David Lampton, ed., *Policy Implementation in Post-Mao China* (Berkeley, CA: University of California Press, 1987), pp. 51–80.

3 David Zweig, "Context and Content in Policy Implementation: Household Contracts and Decollectivizaton, 1977–1983," in David Lampton, ed., *Policy Implementation in Post-Mao China* (Berkeley, CA: University of California Press, 1987), pp. 255–283.

4 David M. Lampton, "Water: Challenge to a Fragmented Political System," in David Lampton, ed., *Policy Implementation in Post-Mao China* (Berkeley, CA: University of California Press, 1987), pp. 157–189; Lieberthal and Oksenberg also have a chapter on the policy of the Three Gorges Dam project in China during the early 1960s. See Kenneth Lieberthal and Michel Oksenberg, *Policy Making in China: Leaders, Structures, and Processes* (Princeton, NJ: Princeton University Press, 1988), pp. 269–330.

5 Thomas Fingar, "Implementing Energy Policy: The Rise and Demise of the State Energy Commission" in David Lampton, ed., *Policy Implementation in Post-Mao China* (Berkeley, CA: University of California Press, 1987), pp. 190–224; see Lieberthal and Oksenberg for another discussion on the policy of the petroleum and coal industries in China: Lieberthal and Oksenberg, *Policy Making in China*, pp. 169–258, 339–389.

6 Lester Ross, "Obligatory Tree Planting: The Role of Campaigns in Policy Implementation in Post-Mao China" in David Lampton, ed., *Policy Implementation in Post-Mao China* (Berkeley, CA: University of California Press, 1987), pp. 225–254.

7 Stanley Rosen, "Restoring Key Secondary Schools in Post-Mao China: The Politics of Competition and Educational Quality," in David Lampton, ed., *Policy Implementation in Post-Mao China* (Berkeley, CA: University of California Press, 1987), pp. 321–353.

8 Tyrene White, "Implementing the 'One-Child-per-Couple' Population Program in Rural China: National Goals and Local Politics," in David Lampton, ed., *Policy Implementation in Post-Mao China* (Berkeley, CA: University of California Press, 1987), pp. 284–320.

9 Denis Fred Simon, "Implementing China's S & T Modernization Program," in David Lampton, ed., *Policy Implementation in Post-Mao China* (Berkeley, CA: University of California Press, 1987), pp. 354–382.

10 The public services that were identified by the Chinese official foreign-language newspaper as those in need of reform include urban transportation, power delivery, education, and environment protection. See "Public Services Due for Private Business," *China Daily* (North America edition), 26 July 2000, p. 4. http://proquest.umi.com/ (accessed 16 April 2015). On 25 March 2001, Wang Qishan, then Director of Economic Restructuring Office of the State Council, gave a speech in the "China Development Forum" and said that China would "take bold steps to end the monopolies in some sectors, such as electricity, railways, civil aviation and telecommunications." See "Airfares to Float," *Shenzhen Daily*, 28 March 2001, Wisenews (accessed 16 April 2015); see also "Rail Reforms to Continue," *China Daily*, 19 October 2002, Wisenews (accessed 16 April 2015).

11 OECD, "Railway Reform in China: Promoting Competition," Summary and Recommendations of an OECD/DRC Seminar on Rail Reform, Beijing, 28–29 January 2002, www.oecd.org/regreform/sectors/34566769.pdf (accessed 16 April 2015).

12 Louis S. Thompson, "Railway Reform in China: the Great Railway Challenge," Presentation to Railway Minister Fu Zhihuan Beijing, March 2000, http://siteresources.worldbank.org/INTRAILWAYS/Resources/ch_article.pdf (accessed 16 April 2015).

13 Zhongnanhai Reform and Development Research Center, "Weilai wu-shi nian zhongguo jingji gaige zhongdian," ("China's Major Economic Reform in the Future 5–10 Years"), *Ta Kung Pao*, 22 November 2000, p. C1; and "Wangyun fenli tielaoda zhaichi tixu" ("Separation Between Rail Road and Transport Service: Railway to Increase the Speed Again") *China Enterprise News*, 14 April 2001, Wisenews.

14 Li Wai-ching, "The Reform Programme of the Ministry of Railways and its Impact on Rail Development in China" (MA Dissertation, University of Hong Kong, 2001).

15 "Wangyun fenli tielaoda zhaichi tixu," *China Enterprise News*.

16 See "Tielu gaige zhou huitoulu" ("The Railway Reform Turn Around") *People's Daily*, 2 September 2002, www.people.com.cn/BIG5/jingji/1038/2066629.html (accessed 6 March 2007).

17 Evan Osnos, "Boss Rail: Letter from China," *The New Yorker*, vol. 88, no. 33, 22 October 2012, p. 44.

18 R. Bordie, S. Wilson, and J. Kuang, "The Importance, Development and Reform Challenges of China's Rail Sector," in L. Song, R. Garnaut, and C. Fang, eds., *Deepening Reform for China's Long-term Growth and Development* (Canberra: ANU Press, 2014).

19 "Important High-Speed Railway Lines in China," www.chinahighlights.com/travelguide/transportation/china-high-speed-rail.htm (accessed 17 April 2015).

20 S.P. Guo and N. Macfie, "China Train Crash Kills 70 and Injures Hundreds," *Reuters*, 28 April 2008, www.reuters.com/article/2008/04/28/us-china-train-idUSPEK3496 7020080428 (accessed 17 April 2015).

21 "Three Killed in Passenger Train Collision in China," Xinhua News Agency, 27 July 2009, http://news.xinhuanet.com/english/2009-06/29/content_11616476.htm (accessed 17 April 2015).

22 "Chinese Questions Remain Over Wenzhou Rail Crash," 11 August 2011, BBC News, www.bbc.com/news/world-asia-pacific-14494534 (accessed 10 July 2015).

23 Briginshaw, David, "China Confirms Plans to Abolish Ministry of Railways," *International Railway Journal*, 11 March 2013, www.railjournal.com/index.php/policy/china-confirms-plans-to-abolish-ministry-of-railways.html?channel=542 (accessed 18 April 2015).

24 Alfred D. Chandler, *The Visible Hand: The Managerial Revolution in American Business* (London: The Belknap Press of Harvard University Press, 1977).

25 The historical fact is based mostly on a publication by the Zhongguo Tielu Chubanshe unless otherwise specified. Zhongguo Tielu Chubanshe, ed., *Xin zhongguo tielu wushinian* (Fifty-year Review of the New China Railway; Beijing: Zhongguo Tielu Chubanshe, 1999).

26 X. Xue, F. Schmid, and R. Smith, "An Introduction to China's Rail Transport Part 1: History, Present and Future of China's Railways," in *Proceedings of the Institution of Mechanical Engineers: Part F, Journal of Rail and Rapid Transit*, vol. 216, no. 1 (2002), pp. 153–163.

27 Lida Ferguson Junghans, "Workers in Transit: Chinese Railway Workers and the Journey from Plan to Market" (PhD thesis, Harvard University, May 1999), p. 69.

28 Wang Whing-Chun, "Why the Chinese Oppose Foreign Railway Loans?" *The American Political Science Review*, vol. 4, no. 3 (1910): 365–373.

29 Junghans, "Workers in Transit," p. 72; Wei Yingtao, *Sichuan baolu yundong shi* (Railway Recovery Campaign in Sichuan; Chengdu: Sichuan People's Publisher, 1981).

30 E-Tu Zen Sun, "The Pattern of Railway Development in China," *The Far Eastern Quarterly*, vol. 14, no. 2 (1955): 179–199.

31 Sun, "The Pattern of Railway Development in China."

32 Xue *et al.*, "An Introduction to China's Rail Transport."

33 Junghans, "Workers in Transit," p. 77.

34 Xue *et al.*, "An Introduction to China's Rail Transport," p. 157.

35 Karl Marx and Friedrich Engels, *The Communist Manifesto* (Harmondsworth: Penguin, 1967), p. 96.

36 Junghans, "Workers in Transit," p. 77.

37 Sun, "The Pattern of Railway Development in China."

38 Yu Jun, *Tielu chongzu de lilun yu shijian* (Theory and Implementation of Railway Restructuring; Beijing: Jingji kexue chubanshe, 2003), p. 176.

39 Yu Chuan, ed., *Zhongguo tielu caiwu kuaiji* (Finance and Account of China's Railways; Beijing: Zhongguo tielu chubanshe, 1999), pp. 106–108.

40 Junghans, "Workers in Transit," p. 81.

41 These railway-related enterprises provide services in five areas: construction of infrastructure industry; production of rolling stocks and locomotives; provision of materials and supplies; signaling and communication; and engineering.

42 Jian Hong Wu and Chris Nash, "Railway Reform in China," *Transport Reviews*, vol. 20, no. 1 (2000): 25–48.

43 *Dangdai zhongguo congshu bianjibu*, ed., *Dangdai zhongguo de tiedao shiye* (The Contemporary Railway Business in China; Beijing: Zhongguo shehui kexue chubanshe, 1990), pp. 90–100.

44 Jian and Nash, "Railway Reform in China."

45 *Dangdai zhongguo congshu bianjibu*, *Dangdai zhongguo de tiedao shiye*, pp. 97–98.

46 "The Brilliant 50 Years History of China's Railway Development," *China Railway Monthly*, vol. 2, no. 13 (1999): 3–14.

47 "Luotuo tiaowu," ("Camel Dances") *Zhongguo gaige bao* (*China Reform Newspaper*), 26 February 2001, p. 7.

48 Naughton quotes from Collected Economic System Reform Documents that five documents were officially issued, specifying that "enterprises selected for expanded autonomy would have the right to retain a share of profits, enjoy accelerated depreciation, and have the right to sell above-plan output." See Barry Naughton, *Growing out of the Plan: Chinese Economic Reform 1978–1983* (Cambridge: Cambridge University Press, 1995).

49 Kornai distinguishes four basic forms of coordination: bureaucratic coordination, market coordination, ethical coordination, and aggressive coordination. He also argues that "over-regulation ultimately makes regulation illusory. If only one or two market diversions from the original profit were applied, it might be effective. But a combination of a thousand different considerations is ineffective." See Janos Kornai, *Vision and Reality, Market and State: Contradictions and Dilemmas Revisited* (New York: Routledge, 1990), pp. 2–4, 69.

50 Duckett christens this arrangement as state entrepreneurialism in her study of the case in Tianjin and concludes that "departments in the state administration, aside from carrying out the designated duties, have begun to engage in a wide range of business or commercial activities in the new market environment." See Jane Duckett, *The Entrepreneurial State in China* (New York: Routledge, 1998), pp. 1–20. See also Lin and Zhang for a detailed review of the emergence of such spin-off enterprises. Lin Yi-min and Zhang Zhanxin, "Backyard Profit Centers: The Private Assets of Public Agencies," in Jean Oi and Andrew Walder, ed., *Property Rights and Economic Reform in China* (Stanford, CA: Stanford University Press, 1999), pp. 203–225.

51 *Dang dai zhongguo congshu bianji bu*, *Dangdai zhongguo de tiedao shiye*, pp. 323.

52 "*Nanchang tieluju huangtogang bianqian xilie*" ("The Series on the Change of Huangtugang at the Nangchang Railway Administrations"), *People's Railway Daily*, 1 November 2000, p. 1.

53 "Chinese Railway has New Image," *People's Daily*, 12 December 2001, http://english.peopledaily.com.cn/other/archive.html (accessed 30 May 2004).

54 Anthony Downs, *Inside Bureaucracy* (Boston, MA: Little, Brown, 1967).

55 Jean Oi, *Rural China Takes Off: Institutional Foundations of Economic Reform* (Berkeley, CA: University of California Press, 1999), p. 12 and 97.

56 Christine Wong, "Between Plan and Market: The Role of the Local Sector in Post-Mao China," *Journal of Comparative Economics*, vol. 11 (1987): 385–398.

57 See Andrew Walder, *Zouping in Transition: The Process of Reform in Rural North China* (Cambridge, MA: Harvard University Press, 1997); Gu Chaolin, Shen Jianfa, Wong Kwan-yiu, and Zhen Feng, "Regional Polarization under the Socialist-Market System since 1978: A Case Study of Guangdong Province in South China," *Environment and Planning*, vol. 33, no. 1 (2001): 97–119; Fong Shiaw-Chian, "The Shareholding System in a Shandong Township: Practice and Impact," *Issues & Studies*, vol. 35, no. 4 (1999): 33–54.

58 Guthrie believes that, despite the mimicry, China will not convert to the Western capitalist system. He argues in his study of state-owned enterprises in general that the spread of Western practices is not a drive for efficiency, but for legitimacy to comply with the national reform directives and to attract foreign investors. See Doug Guthrie, *Dragon in a Three-Piece Suit: The Emergence of Capitalism in China* (Princeton, NJ: Princeton University Press, 1999).

59 Wu Jianzhong, *Tielu yunshu jiye shichanghua guanli* (Management of Railway Transport Enterprises during the Transition towards Market Economy; Beijing: Zhongguo tiedao chubanshe, 1998), p. 77.

60 "Chinese Institutions in Detail: GRC," Intercity Services Department, Kowloon-Canton Railway Corporation, September 2001.

61 Sheng Guangzu (Vice Minister of Railways of China), "*Guanyu tielu de gaige yu fazhan wenti*" ("Problems in Railway Reform and Development") *Zhongguo tielu*, vol. 7, no. 2 (1999), pp. 1–3.

62 Jiang Shijie, "*Yu wushengchu ting jingle: tiel xitong gaige shaomiao*," ("A Quiet Surprise: To Scan through the Railway Reform"), People.com.cn, 17 January 2001, www.people.com.cn/BIG5/jinji/32/180/20010117/380412.html (accessed 30 October 2007).

63 Wei Heping, "*Fu Zhihuan: tielu xitong de jianshe, tiaozheng yu fazhang*," China.com.cn, 18 December 2002, http://big5.china.com.cn/chinese/2002/Oct/219610.htm (accessed 30 October 2007).

64 "*Wangyun fenli tielaoda zaici tixu.*"

65 "*Tiedao buzhang liu zhijun tan chexiao tielu fenju yuanyin*," ("Railway Minister Liu Zhijun Discuss the Reasons of the Removal of Railway Sub-administration") *People Daily*, 19 March 2005, http://news.sina.com.cn/c/2005-03-19/03595400438s.shtml (accessed 27 April 2015); also see Zheng Wan and Xiang Liu, "Chinese Railway Transportation: Opportunity and Challenge," Transportation Research Board Annual Meeting 2009 Paper #09-2279, http://trid.trb.org/view.aspx?id=881652 (accessed 27 April 2015).

66 "*Po chulai de chexiaolin: yichang 'caosui' de tielu gaige*," ("A Forced Order of Removal: An Arbitrary Railway Reform") *Shangwu zhoukan (Commercial Weekly)*, 14 April 2005, http://media.163.com/05/0414/16/1HAGM8IS00141EJF.html (accessed 27 April 2015).

4 (De)centralization policies

Overview

As mentioned in Chapter 2, both OECD and the World Bank suggested that China should decentralize the interlocking sectors within the national railway system. In 2001, the State Council approved, and the Ministry of Railways (MOR) rolled out the master plan of vertical separation. Although such a reform strategy had been projected as theoretically sound and practically feasible for the sector to move further toward the best railway model, Liu Zhijun, the new railway minister, called off the whole plan in 2003. The MOR's organizational structure remained the same—the vertically and horizontally integrated model. In 2013, Liu Zhijun was imprisoned and sentenced to death for corruption. In the same year, the MOR was dissolved, with its administrative functions subsumed under the Ministry of Transport and its operational functions taken up by the newly established China Railway Corporation.

The so-called newly established China Railway Corporation was nothing more than putting up a new corporation plate on the front gate of the original railway headquarters in Beijing. The head of this new railway corporation was the last railway minister, Sheng Guangzhu. The corporatization of the operational arm of the railway regime was therefore not a result of privatization, marketization, or decentralization; it was actually a result of the re-centralization of the administrative arm under stricter state control. Sheng used be a minister and now he reports to the Minister of Transport, which means the chief of the China Railway Corporation is one rank lower than ministerial level. With all the planning and regulating functions centered at the State Railway Administration under the Ministry of Transport, the Chinese government was actually re-centralizing its control over the railway sector.

Such a policy twist raised doubts about the economic explanation, or more precisely the efficiency model, of railway reform. Campos and Cantos argue that any discrepancy from the best reform model can be explained by the fact that the leadership has other non-economic reform imperatives.[1] Although this approach explains why China's railway reform was slow—because the railway leadership has to take into consideration political and social factors—it does not explain how political and social factors shaped railway reform, nor does it clarify why re-centralization took place when there were strong economic imperatives.

Focusing on the limitation of the efficiency model, this chapter validates the hypothesis (H1) that economic imperatives do not necessarily lead to decentralization, and (H2) that decentralization does not necessarily lead to clarification of property rights and privatization. The first section of this chapter dissects the three-dimensional integration of China's railway sector: (1) the functional integration of the upper components which provided transport services, and the lower components which supported the railway network; (2) the social integration of the core components which involved profit-making transport businesses and ancillary components which involved non-profit making sectors, such as universities, hospitals, publishing houses, and recreational associations; and (3) the administrative integration between the vertical reporting lines with the MOR headquarters (the "*tiao tiao*" system) and the horizontal reporting lines (the "*kuai kuai*" system) with the respective local governments.

The second section reviews the efficiency model and argues that the rational choice of the best model of railway reform focuses only on the problems of functional integration and undermines the social and administrative integrations. This is especially critical in explaining railway reform in China. The efficiency model considers social imperatives as the government's concern in social obligations or social goods. The heritage of social administrative integrations in the state sector in China, however, imposed a much stronger hindrance in the process of decentralization. The result was a more complicated reform outcome. While the efficiency model provides a normative analysis of how to restructure a state-owned and integrated railway system, this section provides a positive explanation on how the transformation of the railway system in China really took place.

The third section zooms in on the transport components and examines the relations between the economic imperatives and the property rights arrangements under various reform strategies, and proves that the efficiency model failed to explain many of the top-down reform policies, including those related to decentralization and others related to re-centralization.

China's railway: a three-dimensional integrated structure

The railway sector has been playing an important role in China since 1949. Economically, it is vital for the transport of natural resources, people, and goods across the territory. Socially, it is important for regional development, troop delivery, military supply, and disaster relief. Politically, it was put under state ownership under one ministry in the name of the people to reinforce national pride and communist ideology. In view of such unique significance, the Chinese railway has long been functionally, administratively, and socially integrated.

Functional integration

Stressing the importance of scale economy and self-sufficiency, China's railway regime integrated all functional components together, including the transport, manufacturing, engineering, construction, material and supply, and signaling components. Transport studies refer to such functional integration as vertical integration and they categorize functional components of a railway system into the upper part and the lower part (see Figure 2.2). The upper part provides transport services, which take place on the rail track, such as the passenger and freight services. The lower part provides all-round infrastructure services which take place off the rail tracks, such as construction, engineering, signaling, and manufacturing services. Together these two parts were responsible for providing services related to the railway's core businesses (see Figure 4.1).

In China, the planned regime had divided the entire railway system into numerous regional sub-administrations. With a view to demarcating the boundary of the sub-units so that each one of them was taking up more or less the same quantity of work, the boundaries of railway sub-administrations did not follow the provincial boundaries. As a result, one railway administration might span across one or more provinces, and one province might be cut through two railway administrations. By 1999, there were 14 railway administrations.[2] These railway administrations and sub-administrations comprised some small-scale units which were capable of offering ad-hoc rail track repair and maintenance services, and they were mainly responsible for providing transport services and are considered as the transport services component.

The major infrastructure services for the railway system were shared among six corporations: China Railway Engineering Corporation; China Railway Construction Corporation; China Railway Locomotive & Rolling Stock Industry Corporation; China Railway Signal & Communication Corporation; China Civil

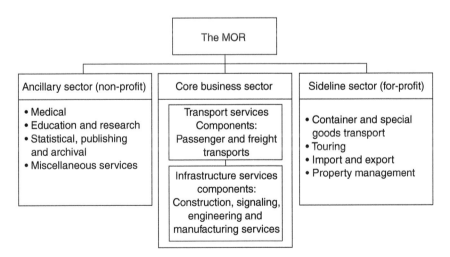

Figure 4.1 Functional and social integration of the MOR.

Engineering Construction Corporation; and China Railway Materials & Supplies Corporation.[3] The headquarters of these corporations were located in Beijing, with subsidiaries covering the whole country.

Social integration

The second dimension of integration originated from the communist ideology of "ten thousand things guaranteed within" (*wanshi buqiuren*). The railway regime integrated not only the up-stream and down-stream functional sectors, but also many other loosely related non-profit-making sectors such as universities, hospitals, research institutes, statistical institute, publishing houses, news agencies, and arts and recreational associations.[4] These institutes were responsible for what the MOR referred to as ancillary businesses (*fuye*).

In 1984, because of insufficient funds to support these social responsibilities, the Chinese government allowed state sectors to set up sideline economic entities.[5] By 1999, there were 12 such sideline corporations attached to the MOR headquarters. The original logic was that while social institutions, such as universities and hospitals, were draining the state's financial resources, these sideline firms could pump in money. Unfortunately, it was unclear whether they pumped in resources from the market or from the state. Such a social integration of the core, the ancillary, and the sideline sectors inevitably complicated the property rights arrangements and re-arrangements:

Such an all-in-one and gigantic organizational structure and interlocking bureaucratic coordination made the railway regime inefficient. The oft quoted "soft budget constraint" well describes such regulatory adjustment between expenditure and earnings and the problematic heritage of inefficiency. Since loss-makers always expect external financial assistance from the state, in terms of subsidies, tax exemptions, generous credits, mandatory prices, or other preferential policies, they are spared from the disciplinary consequences of inefficient operations. As such, price responsiveness declines, entrepreneurial innovations dissipate and excessive demand for inputs leads to what Kornai refers to as "shortage economy"[6] (see Table 4.1 and Figure 4.1).

By diversifying the nature of businesses, railway cadres were exposed to enormous opportunities aside from providing passenger and freight transport services. The competition for more financial rewards from the market inevitably undermined the traditional ideology of equal distribution of wealth and enhanced the legitimacy of material incentives. The widespread "fever to get rich first" spawned hundreds of diversified businesses, such as catering, advertising, farming, mining, etc., at the regional level.

Administrative integration

Aside from functional and social integrations, another type of integration was administrative in nature, and was commonly known as the criss-cross reporting system: the vertical (*tiao tiao*) and the horizontal (*kuai kuai*) system. Under the

Table 4.1 For-profit enterprises and offices in the sideline sector of the MOR 1999

Transport related
China Railway's Center for Special Goods Transport of China's Railways
China Railway's Center of Container Transport
Special Transport Office

Non-transport related
China Huayun Travel Agency
China Railway Foreign Service Company
China Railway Import and Export Company
China Railway Property Management Company
China Railway Service (Hong Kong) Holding Co.
China Railway's Center for Communication
China Railway's Center of Construction and Development
Communication Office
House Property Office

Source: Zhongguo Tielu Chubanshe, ed., *Xin zhongguo tielu wushinian* (Fifty-year Review of the New China Railway; Beijing: Zhongguo Tielu Chubanshe, 1999), pp. 358–359.

vertical administrative system, all regional railway subsidiaries, both in the core and the ancillary sectors, were linked to the respective supervisory bodies at the MOR headquarters. At the same time, each regional subsidiary was also tied horizontally to their respective local governments and party committees (the "*kuai kuai*" system).

Administrative integration was not unique for the railway system. The development of "local state corporatism" was an unexpected cooperation between local government and regional state-owned enterprises or township and village enterprises (TVEs). The railway system was more complicated because each regional railway subsidiary was connected to form the entire national network and such interlocking characteristics enhanced bureaucratic inertia.

Economic explanation of railway reform

As mentioned in Chapter 2, Kopicki and Thompson, the railway experts of the World Bank, suggested that China's railway system should undertake the reform of disintegration and de-politicization.[7] In theory, they believed, disintegration separates the transport service sector and the infrastructure service sector, breaks the myth of economy of scale and natural monopoly, and introduces market competition. At the same time, de-politicization shields railway operations from state intervention, enhances entrepreneurial autonomy, facilitates ownership concentration, encourages various incentive designs, and, finally, paves the way for partial or outright privatization. To put such reform proposals into practice, it is necessary to demarcate the boundaries of the units along which the monopolistic railway giant should be disintegrated and determine the extent to which the planned railway regime should be shielded from government intervention.

The history of the US railway, which moved from dispersed private ownership to collective ownership, and from deregulated operation to more regulated coordination, shows the difficulties in determining how small in scale a railway enterprise should be and the optimal degree of disintegration.[8] The lesson learned is that, having been integrated and centralized for decades, it is unwise for the Chinese railway to pursue the objectives of outright privatization and full-fledged deregulation, if eventually that may not be the optimal organizational setting.[9]

The restructuring of the railway sector in China was more problematic, for the system was not only functionally integrated, but also socially and administratively integrated.

Limitation of the efficiency model

While economic theory provides a useful discussion on the network characteristics and functional integration of the railway industry, it ignores other aspects of China railway's three-dimensional integrated regime. The particularistic ties embedded in the administratively and socially integrated regime constituted the overriding constraint on the property rights arrangements and organizational changes in China's railway sector.

Before the reform era, Chinese state leaders tried to keep the state's planned logic intact and coherent by multi-stranded and overlapping integration and regulation. It was complicated to regularize and integrate the system, and to deregularize and disintegrate it. Since the railway system was meant to be self-sufficient with different administrative and social supporting sub-systems, railway reform meant addressing the difficult task of disentangling each and every regulatory knot, and the resulting property rights re-arrangements and organizational changes were never the same as those predicted by economic theories. Very often, railway reform polices unfolded as the leadership sought legitimacy. Efficiency did play a role, but not a determinative one.

Economic imperatives, decentralization, and property rights arrangements

Big bang theorists argue that socialist economies should undertake immediate commitments to mass privatization in a transparent and legal way.[10] Accordingly, the best way to restructure state assets, including the railways, is to delineate the ownership of its property rights clearly and concentrate the control, income, and transfer rights into the hands of private owner(s).

But the experience of economic reform in Eastern European suggested that various ways of property rights partitioning, such as spontaneous privatization, management buyout, mass privatization, franchise/leasing, and management contract emerged in place of direct sale arrangements.[11] It was thus not surprising that China would grope for its own way in terms of property rights arrangements and re-arrangements.

Economists explain such variation of property rights arrangements by assuming that the policy makers have made a trade-off between efficiency and other non-economic factors, and subsequently tilted toward different degrees of privatization of property rights. The efficiency-driven theory adopts a statist view and contends that it is the state's intent to balance among different economic, political, and social imperatives. The more prominent the economic imperatives, the more likely the state will give away its control, income, and transfer rights.[12]

According to this logic, if the ruling elites in China put more weight on the economic imperatives, they would push for a subsequent wave of decentralization, as predicted by economic theory.[13] On the other hand, if they are concerned more about non-economic imperatives, they would retain the state ownership, or compromise by adopting a partial concentration of the property rights of the physical assets

However, the efficiency model is problematic as it cannot explain the following. First, the MOR undertook a spiral pattern of decentralization and re-centralization over years when they have continuously stressed the importance of economic concerns of the railway sector. Second, consider the period when the MOR administered decentralization and de-politicization policies, such as various profit-sharing and responsibility contracts; these were not real changes in the control and income rights. The hypothesis put forward in this regard is as follows:

H1 Economic imperatives do not necessarily lead to decentralization.
H2 Decentralization does not necessarily lead to privatization.

Economic imperatives and degree of decentralization

Testing the relations between economic imperatives and the degree of decentralization in terms of property rights re-arrangements, this section studies the transport services sub-sector of the MOR and focuses on the regional railway administrations.

According to the three-bundle property rights theory, the transfer rights refer to the right to sell the ownership of productive assets such as the railway track, the rolling stocks and other supporting equipment. The control right refers to the right to allocate the use of different assets such as to schedule train movements, and to price transport services. The income right refers to the right to retain the profits earned through passenger and freight transport services. After the Third Plenum of the 11th Central Committee of the CCP in 1978, the MOR put forward a series of profit-sharing reform strategies. The efficiency model explained such reform as a state-led strategy of increasing decentralization in view of economic imperatives, and as a gradual convergence to the best model.[14]

Putting such a statist hypothesis to the test and reviewing the variations of control and income rights over years, it is worthwhile to note that there was no observable correlation between economic imperatives and implementation of decentralization of income and control rights. The MOR did have increasing economic imperatives, but it administered a spiral pattern of decentralization and re-centralization policies. At the time of decentralization, regional railway administrations did not enjoy more income and control rights in reality.

Continuous economic imperatives for reform over years

In order to show that there were continuous economic imperatives for the MOR reform over years, this section operationalizes the measurement of economic imperatives by a set of comprehensive indices, including the reported net profits, passenger and freight transport market share, and labor productivity. All indexes suggest that the MOR has been facing and realizing increasing economic pressure to introduce further reform.

Railway net profit

The railway sector suffered from a drastic fall in profits from RMB 11.31 billion in 1990 to RMB 1.27 billion in 1993. The situation became worse as it failed to make a profit after 1993. In 1994, the deficit was RMB 2.87 billion. The losses increased to RMB 6.4 billion in 1995, and gradually dropped to RMB 1.38 and 2.6 billion in 1996 and 1997, respectively. Although a small surplus of RMB 30 million was recorded in 1998, and the profit gradually increased to about RMB 2–3 billion between 1999 and 2003, it was still far less than the profits the railway sector had gained before (Figure 4.2).

Rail passenger and freight transport market share

Besides the drastic drop of net receipts, the railway sector has been facing fierce competition from other modes of transport. According to China's official statistics, the railway passenger and freight shares of the total transport market have

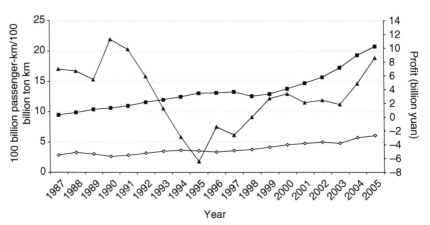

−◇−100 billion passenger-km −■−100 billion ton-km −▲−Annual net profit/loss in billion yuan

Figure 4.2 Annual handling volume and net profit/loss, railway sector, 1987–2005 (source: Financial Indicators of National Railway Transport, National Bureau of Statistics in China (1998, 2000, 2005, 2006, www.stats.gov.cn) and *China Statistical Yearbook* (Beijing: China Statistics Press, 1995, 1998, 2000, 2002).

been declining from 63 percent in 1978 to 35 percent in 2005, and from 54 percent in 1978 to 26 percent in 2005 (Figures 4.3 and 4.4). The rapid development of expressways in China since the late 1970s has lured millions of passengers into buses and away from trains.[15] The railway freight transport, on the other hand, was losing its competitive edge to both highway and waterway transport. Although railway freightage was comparatively low, cargo trucks and ships together offered more flexible and door-to-door logistics services. Such statistical reports on the declining trends of railway performance posed severe economic problems to the central leadership of the MOR.

Productivity

Railway's labor productivity can be calculated by various methods. Some transport analysts undertake multivariate measures of total factor productivity, or more complicated mathematical models of frontier econometric measures or data envelopment analysis. While these models take into consideration the aggregate effects of various inputs on railway performance, their accuracy depends on the availability of a comprehensive set of input measurements such as liters of fuel

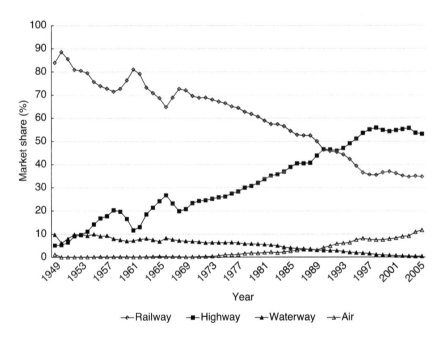

Figure 4.3 Passenger transport market share, 1949–2005 (source: passenger kilometers 1978, 1980, 1985, 1989–2005, National Bureau of Statistics of China, www.stats.gov.cn/tjsj/ndsj/2006/html/P1607E.HTM (accessed 19 April 2007); passenger-kilometers 1952, 1957, 1962, 1965, 1970, 1975, 1978, 1986–1988, National Bureau of Statistics of China, www.stats.gov.cn/ndsj/information/zh1/n071a (accessed 19 April 2007)).

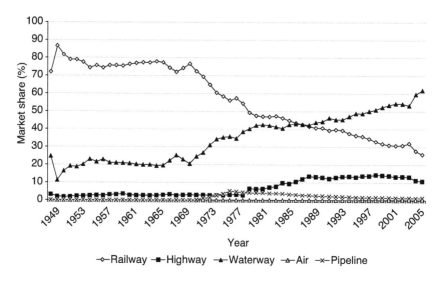

Figure 4.4 Freight transport market share, 1949–2005 (source: freight ton kilometers 1978, 1980, 1985, 1989–2005, National Bureau of Statistics of China, www. stats.gov.cn/tjsj/ndsj/2006/html/P1609E.HTM (accessed 19 April 2007); freight ton kilometers 1952, 1957, 1962, 1965, 1970, 1975, 1978, 1986–1988, National Bureau of Statistics of China, www.stats.gov.cn/ndsj/information/zh1/n091a (accessed 19 April 2007)).

consumed, employees' working hours, and capital investment. Given that the actual figures are simply unavailable in China and proxies are not reliable, this study computes the ratio of traffic units to labor size (traffic units is the summation between passenger turnover, person kilometers, and freight turnover, ton kilometers). These partial productivity factors are intuitively easy to interpret. Louis Thompson, the railways advisor of the World Bank, also used the same index to brief Fu Zhihuan, China's railway minister in Beijing in 2000 and 2002, on the relative railway productivity among various countries. It is therefore a good and reliable index for China's railway leadership to comprehend the railway performance, and thus contributed to the economic drive for railway reform.[16]

China's railway labor productivity in terms of traffic units per staff member, i.e., (passenger kilometers + ton kilometers)/number of staff members, improved by 150 percent between 1991 and 2005, while the highway and waterway sectors demonstrated a huge leap of 470 percent and 842 percent, respectively, over the same period of time. Wu and Nash measure China's railway labor productivity by another indicator: train units per number of staff members, i.e., train car kilometers/number of staff members, and conclude that the average labor productivity of Western European railways in 1990 was 490% higher than China's railways.[17] The difference was huge, but we should take into consideration that labor productivity projected by train unit per staff member was worse than that of traffic units per staff member in China. China's railways have been enjoying very favorable market demand as passenger and freight trains are overloaded all the time; the traffic unit has been growing faster than the train unit.

However, since the sector failed to produce enough train units and services to satisfy market demand, labor productivity measured by train units per staff member tend to underestimate the real labor productivity (Figure 4.5).

All these poor performance indicators posed continuous economic problems for China's leadership. The central leadership also declared that the MOR was to embark on a series of structural overhauls to curb inefficiency. However, various reform policies implemented among regional railway administrations show that nominal changes in the demarcation of the property rights bundles did not result in decentralization of the income, control, and transfer rights, not to mention the expected separation of transport services sub-sectors from the functional integrated railway structure.

Nominal changes in control and income rights over years

Between 1978 and 2003, four major reform polices of profit sharing were put in place: responsibility contracts; full-scale and integrated contracting responsibility system; responsibility system of assets management; and corporatization of transport enterprises. The MOR proclaimed that these reforms represented a degree of decentralization and would allow regional railway administrations to assume increasing shares of the targeted and above-target profit, and to make decisions about production schedules, resources allocation, and lower-level, personnel reshuffle.[18] But these rights were granted with many supplementary conditions and were subject to negotiations. The bundles of property rights were not as clearly partitioned and decentralized as expected.[19] The regional railway administrations, therefore, did not really enjoy more income and control rights than before. My informants criticized these top-down reform policies as being "old wine in a new bottle," with no material change regarding income and control rights.[20]

Responsibility contracts

Between the 1960s and the end of the 1970s, the MOR centralized the income rights by maintaining two separate lines of income and expenditure (*shouzhi liang tiaoxian*) the MOR planned both the passenger and freight transport volume and drew up a budget for each regional railway administration. Although there was a bonus mechanism to reward the railway administration if it eventually generated more revenue and/or incurred fewer expenses than the estimates, the regional railway administrations did not have much autonomy within the national plan because regional railway administrations could not produce traffic units without the cooperation of other regional railway administrations. Their revenues depended largely on the state-planned schedule for freight and

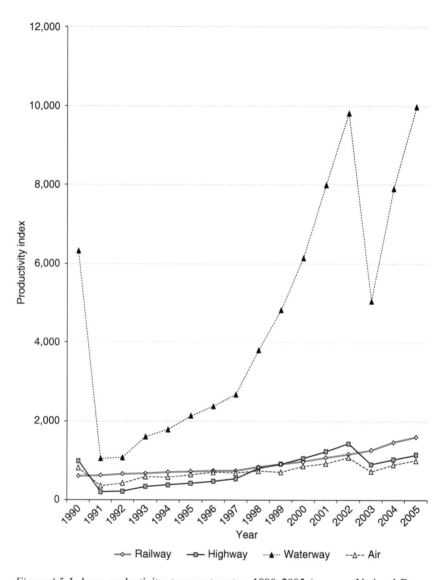

Figure 4.5 Labour productivity, transport sector, 1990–2005 (sources: National Bureau of Statistics of China, www.stats.gov.cn; financial indicators of national railway transport, National Bureau of Statistics of China, (1998, 2000, 2005, 2006 www.stats.gov.cn) and *China Statistical Yearbook* (Beijing: China Statistics Press, 1995, 1998, 2000, 2002)).

Note
Productivity index = (100 billion passenger kilometers + 100 billion ton kilometers)/number of staff members.

passenger transport services. As a result, the railway administrations tried to maximize the expenditure. Railway cadres had the following saying at that time:

> It makes no difference to spend more or less, because all expenditures were reimbursed; it makes no difference to earn more or less from the transport services, because we have to remit all revenue. (*Hua duoshao, bao duoshao, hauduo haushao yigeyang; yunshu shouru shou duoshao, jiao duosho, shouduo shoushao yigeyang*).[21]

The MOR was not alone in maintaining the planned heritage. The rebuilding of the centralized regime after the end of the Cultural Revolution and the death of Mao Zedong led to problems of over-spending and over-investment in many sectors. When the state's collected income could no longer sustain its expenditure, the bubble of the shortage economy burst, and the government realized that it was impossible for the planning apparatus to control the entire state sector.

After the Third Plenum of the 11th Central Committee of the Chinese Communist Party in 1979, the central leadership was aware of the pressing need to recast the development strategy. Having no blueprint for the reform agenda, efforts were made to expand enterprise autonomy and combine the plan and the market.[22] The efficiency model would explain this as the state's benevolent effort to truncate property rights, decentralize part of it, and pave the way for the best property rights arrangements. However, China's railway reform unfolded in a more complicated way and cast doubt on such an explanation.

Following the general reform directives for the state sector to expand enterprise autonomy, the MOR announced its first attempt to introduce a responsibility system and allow profit retention. But since the MOR had separated the lines of income and expenditure before, it was necessary for each railway administration to factor in the cost structures (operating cost$_i$) and calculate its net profit (profit$_i$). For example, railway administrations situated in mountainous areas would negotiate for a higher operating cost than those situated in less mountainous area because the operating cost of moving the same amount of goods over the same distance would be different in different geographic regions. Taking into consideration the share of the total planned passenger and freight transport volume and different operating costs incurred along the en-route railway administrations, the MOR assigned a specified target in terms of annual estimated profit (profit$_i$) to each railway administration.

$$\text{Profit}_i = (\text{share of total handling volume}_i) / (\text{total revenue}) - (\text{operating cost}_i)$$

Theoretically, if a railway administration could materialize a larger actual profit, either by handling more transport volume or by cutting its actual operating cost, it would receive a fixed percentage of the above-target profit as a bonus for staff welfare and various awards.[23] The rest of the actual profit would then be remitted to the MOR, which would centralize and re-allocate the funding for infrastructure construction and other expenses. Between 1978 and 1985, the retention rate of the above-target profit varied from time to time. There were at least three major changes of the calculation method within the eight years.[24] The general idea was to link the bonus with the efforts to increase the actual transport revenue and/or reduce the actual operating cost.

However, such incentives were impeded by the top-down planned and integrated schedule as a whole. Since most railway transport took place across the jurisdictions of two or more regional railway administrations, it was very hard for those regional railway administrations along the route to design, produce, and market their railway services to increase the transport revenue.[25] Even if they did put forward such initiation, the revenue had to be shared with other relevant railway administrations.

On the other hand, since regional railway administrations received the funds from the MOR for their operating expenditure, and the amount was far more than the bonus, it would be against their interests if they reported a drop of the operating cost. Since regional cadres did not care about the national operational expenditure, they would convince the MOR headquarters that the cost of providing the designated railway services was high owing to different external factors, such as geographic environment, local economic endowment, and the state's capital investment and preferential treatment. As a result, it became a common practice that regional railway administrations tended to falsify the operating costs and the reported operating cost was much higher than the real cost. Such practice guaranteed the operating funds, and at the same time justified lower targets which would be much easier for the railway administrations to accomplish.

According to the property rights theory, profit sharing signified a reform initiative to clarify the demarcation of the boundaries of the property rights by decentralizing partial control and income rights to the local railway administrations. However, the MOR's responsibility contracts designed to specify the conditions for gaining more of the income rights unexpectedly created much room for bureaucratic negotiation and increased the fuzziness of the property rights arrangements. In addition, since the MOR would retain part of the profits as a reserve to balance any serious inequality in actual profits gained among regional railway administrations, there was huge room for negotiation and the calculation method was subject to arbitrary adjustments. Since the MOR still dictated the overall redistribution of funds, the responsibility contract did not really lead to decentralization of property rights.

As a result, in 1979, there were 12 different clearance formulae for 20 regional railway administrations to calculate their operating costs, and by 1983, each railway administration had developed its own unique way to calculate the amount of operating costs it had borne and the subsequent profits made.

In April 1983, following the general reform directive of "tax for profit" ("*ligaishui*"), each railway administration and enterprise was required to remit 55 percent of the actual profit as tax to the MOR.[26] However, as long as the operating costs were negotiable, there was no incentive for local cadres to work hard to increase the retainable profits.

What was worse was that, starting from 1986, any increase in handling capacity over the previous year would bring in an extra bonus. This further induced shirking, since all railway cadres tended not to work too hard so that it would be easier to exceed the previous year's record and thus guarantee the respective bonus.[27]

Full-scale and integrated contracting responsibility system

China started to open up the country in 1978, and the state had to increase its capital investment in railway construction because of the pressing need for mass transportation. Starting from 1985, the state allocated capital into the railway system in the form of a national loan, instead of a direct cash allocation, which was known as "*bogaitai*" ("reform of loan for funding"). But the difference between state funding and state loans was not clear because the MOR and its subsidiaries did not pay back the loans and interest.[28]

The railway was deeply in debt and the concept of "loan for funding" did not help recover the state's investment. In 1986, the state leadership put forward a more extensive responsibility system, namely the full-scale and integrated contracting responsibility system (*dabaogan*). Instead of focusing only on the provision of transport services, this time the state also contracted out the railway construction work to the MOR. The five stipulated responsibilities were: provision of railway transport services; production of rolling stocks; construction of railroad; investment in infrastructure and rolling stock; and paying taxes.

The ministry then sub-contracted these businesses to its regional railway administrations and enterprises. Since *dabaogan* covered aspects of construction, the railway subsidiaries had to take into consideration both the operating cost and the sunk cost in railroad construction. This was meant to move further toward a clearer demarcation of bundles of property rights because not only the transport services sub-sector, but also the infrastructure services sub-sectors, were forced to make good use of their respective railway assets to provide the obliged railway services in lieu of the rights to retain part of the profit after tax. There was a saying at that time: "*bao touru, bao chanchu, bao yi lu jian lu*," i.e., the railway sector had to use its own profits to guarantee investment, production, and railroad construction.[29]

In 1987, the MOR started to allow the Guangzhou, Liuzhou, and Urumqi Railway Administrations to retain part of the profit to construct regional rail road. These three railway administrations were selected as test sites because they were situated at the end node of the railway network and were the places of origin and destination for freight and passenger transport, and thus handled more freight and passenger transport and received much more cash revenue than their inland counterparts. Before this arrangement, they had to return 55 percent of the profits to the MOR, and the ministry centralized and reallocated funds for railway construction if necessary. With this new arrangement, they were allowed to estimate and negotiate for a different remittance rate so that they could retain part of the profits for local railway construction within their jurisdictions.

By extending the scope of the responsibility contract to cover both the transport operation and rail track construction, the three railway administrations enjoyed more room to maneuver because they had a larger budgetary base which included not only the operating cost, but also the construction cost. While the operating costs could vary among different railway administrations, so could the construction costs. The three administrations were therefore able to negotiate separately for a lower rate of profit remittance.

As a result, between 1987 and 1990, these three administrations did not need to remit profit made to the MOR at the usual rate. For example, the Guangzhou Railway Administration undertook responsibility for the construction of the specified railroad and railway operations, and had to generate a minimum transport profit of RMB 8.04 billion and deliver 12 percent of the planned target and 32 percent of the above-planned target to the MOR; the Liuzhou Railway Administration undertook similar responsibility and was required to produce a minimum transport profit of RMB 3.5 billion, and deliver a net amount of RMB 1.05 billion and an additional of 30 percent of the above-target profit, if any; the Urumqi Railway Administration would have to produce a minimum transport profit of RMB 2.06 billion and deliver a net amount of RMB 0.412 billion and an additional 20 percent of the above-target profit, if any. The rest of the budgetary and extra-budgetary profit was meant to cover the cost of railway construction.[30]

Besides income rights, such profit-sharing reform was thought to decentralize part of the control rights. On the surface, regional entities were granted the autonomy to use the retained profits for worker rehabilitation, upgrading and minor construction of railway lines (large-scale construction projects were still centrally controlled), and to make decisions as regards production schedule, allocation of train cars as well as lower-level personnel reshuffling.[31] However, because railway assets were integrated and their services coordinated, decentralization of such a tiny part of the control rights was like dealing with just the tip of the iceberg. The control rights that regional cadres were granted were conditional upon whether the regional plan of railway services was in agreement with the overall national plan. Such attenuation of rights again rendered local cadres' control rights nominal:

> We have to follow the big picture painted by the MOR. Of course the MOR leadership is unable to extend their jurisdiction down to the regional nitty-gritty. But we did enjoy the same de facto control rights even before the reform. There is no real change in this regard.[32]

In fact, since the state still maintained an iron grip on the national plan for railroad network construction, the provision of railway transport services, and the railway fare for both freight and passenger transport,[33] the full-scale responsibility system did not involve full-scale autonomy, but rather full-scale negotiation with the MOR over everything from transport services to construction services.

Responsibility system of assets management

The full-scale and integrated contracting responsibility system was not very successful because the construction of some railway in the remote areas could hardly be decentralized and undertaken by regional railway administrations without the central funds.[34] A few years later, in 1996, the MOR put forward a seemingly more stringent type of responsibility contract, the responsibility system of assets management. Under the new system, the state sent out an audit team to evaluate the value of the assets and then signed a contract with the heads of all the regional railway administrations. This time the state put the responsibility of managing railway assets on the shoulders of the leadership of the railway subsidiary administrations and enterprises.

All director-general-level officials and their deputies were requested to turn into the MOR a personal stake of RMB 10,000 and RMB 8,000, respectively, as a pledge to achieve certain targets within the statutory period. They would later be audited and appraised against the assigned targets. The yardsticks of evaluation were the rate of depreciation of fixed assets, the rate of return on operational assets, and the rate of return on investment. If the responsible local cadres failed the evaluation, their personal stake would be forfeited. A failure for the first year would warrant a "yellow card" to the parties concerned, and a repeated failure for the second year would render the officials unfit to carry out their jobs. On the other hand, outstanding performers would be awarded double or triple the amount of the deposit.

The responsibility system of assets management was further implemented between each level of cadres and their respective subordinates. A widespread slogan was "to set production targets down to individual level, to audit performance down to production teams, and to conduct appraisal for each and every post" ("*zhibiao dao rendou, hexuan dao banzhu, kaohe dao gangwei*"). By way of pinning down the scope of responsibilities and fixing the production targets, the system claimed to decentralize further the control and income rights so as to strengthen the link between performance and rewards.

The concept of "*bao*" or "responsibility system" was borrowed from the rural reform under which the government contracted out the output responsibility to the group (*baocan daozhu*) and eventually evolved into total responsibility to the household (*baogan daohu*). Such responsibility contracts were signed between households and the government, and the farmers were free to sell their surplus in the free market after fulfilling the quota stipulated by the state and the local authorities. For the farmer, such a responsibility system significantly clarified the property rights and enhanced productivity.

However, since production relations in railway transport were far more complicated than in the rural areas, the formulations of time rate or piece rate calculation for the railway sector were so complicated that the organization of different work teams involved tedious description of working methods. For example, the time rate systems of a railway unit which manufactured rail cars stipulated every single hand movement of the workers sitting along the production line in order to make sure that the railway workers performed exactly the way they were designed and planned, and facilitated the calculation of the responsibility system.[35] As a result, what had happened in the rural sector regarding the evolution of property rights arrangements did not work well in the railway sector.[36] Railway cadres did not find the responsibility system, in particular the time rate system, useful in streamlining the production activities:

> The time rate system within the railway sector was more of a nominal arrangement because the production process of railway transport services was much more complicated. Although we had established different production groups and designed various ways to measure performance, it was not easy to separate the finished product between each group and calculate the relevant cost structures. Moreover, the production process of one group depended very much on the up-stream and down-stream production groups.[37]

After all, the entire responsibility system failed to effectively link performance with reward. First, the calculation of the profit and retainable reward was negotiated between the ministerial headquarters and regional railway administrations, and efforts were wasted as local administrations negotiated with the MOR for larger recognized costs and thus more allocated funding for expenditure, rather than tried to improve the efficiency and thus increase the profit. That was why many rail-borne freight transports were not organized as the shortest train route—because local cadres wanted to increase the railway handling volume (passenger kilometers and ton kilometers), not really the productivity.[38] Between 1990 and 1995, as a result of such distorted incentives, the railway sector's net profit has been dropping dramatically, despite the continuous increase in transport volume in terms of the total amount of passenger kilometers and ton kilometers (Figure 4.2).

The MOR did not know the real operating cost of its transport services. In 1995, the ministry had sought financial assistance from the World Bank to facilitate its institutional reform, and part of the US$3.3 million of the World Bank loan to China's railway was allocated to improve areas such as the railway tariff system, railway costing methodology, and railway accounting system, etc.[39] Finally, in 2001, the MOR announced the operating cost for running passenger train no. K67 between Beijing and Nanchang was RMB 142,900. This was the first time in the 50 years since 1949 that the MOR was able to ascertain the true operating cost of its transport services.[40] The cost calculation was even more difficult for freight cars because there was no fixed train route for freight transport—loaded train cars were scheduled according to their assigned places of destination and empty cars would be transported away for loading at the nearest railway station.[41]

Railway reform: the search beyond efficiency

When the railway minister announced the abandonment of the policy of vertical separation and put forward a centralized policy of Great-Leap-style railway development, the MOR had been facing continuous and severe economic reform issues. Moreover, the central and ministerial leadership had proclaimed that the profit-sharing policies would grant more control and income rights to local cadres. Hence these various responsibility systems seemed to imply a positive correlation between economic imperatives and the increased decentralization. However, an in-depth dissection of the reform process in the transport service sub-sector proved that only nominal changes in property rights arrangements had occurred. There was no significant correlation between variations in economic imperatives and the degree of decentralization and clarification of control and income rights. On the contrary, these profit sharing arrangements encouraged arbitrary negotiation between localities and the central government, resulting in more fuzzy property rights arrangements.

If the state leaders did not want to streamline the property rights bundles, why would they address the issue of profit sharing in line with property rights theory and Western railway experts' expectations? Why bother to mimic the convergence phenomenon?

International recognition and domestic legitimization

The superficial compromise was aimed at convincing Western powers, especially organizations such as the World Bank, that China's railway sector was integrating into the Western standards—the idea of decentralization and de-politicization were exactly what the MOR had been told to do by the World Bank's railway expert. The Western communities were willing to influence the developing countries to move in the directions they preferred, and by moving in the desired directions, albeit only superficially, the MOR received financial and technological assistance from Western organizations such as the World Bank, the Japan Bank for International Cooperation, and the Asian Development Bank (ADB).[42]

For example, between 1979 and 2005, the Japan Bank for International Cooperation provided China with a total loan of RMB 558 billion for 15 railway projects to increase transportation capacity; between 1984 and 2005, the World Bank provided ten loans of about US$2.4 billion for nine national railway projects to expand the capacity, improve the technology, and strengthen the institutional capabilities. The ADB, focusing on poverty reduction, has also provided 13 loans of US$2.64 billion to finance the construction of railways and to coordinate among the ADB, MOR, National Development and Reform Commission (NDRC) and the Ministry of Finance (MOF) to stimulate economic growth in poor areas. In addition to monetary assistance, the MOR has, since 1989, received 11 TAs (technical assistance) from the ADB in various aspects such as policy reforms, institutional development, commercial and business operations, marketing and business development, tariff setting, cost recovery, human resources, financial management, and accounting systems.[43]

In addition to maintaining international recognition, the three major initiatives of profit sharing that took place in 1979 (the responsibility system), 1987 (the *dabaogan*), and 1999 (the responsibility system of assets management) also fitted into the overall ideological theme of the open policy that China had adopted since 1978. The name of the responsibility system and profit sharing were borrowed from the previous rural reform, and it was always politically safe to follow what had been proven successful and acceptable by the leadership.

Each time the MOR leadership also chose to test the reform in one or a few railway subsidiaries. Although the MOR claimed that reforms would enhance railway efficiency and improve profitability, it did not start with the subsidiaries which were economically worst off. The logic in pacing the reform agenda suggested that railway reform was indeed moving beyond the search for efficiency.

The first round of the responsibility system started with the locomotive section in the Shanghai Railway Administration in 1979, after which the reform extended to the entire Shanghai Railway Administration in 1982.[44] The second round of the *dabaogan* system started with the Guangzhou Railway Administration in 1987. The last round of the responsibility system of assets management was first implemented in the China Railway Locomotive and Rolling Stock Industry Corporation in 1996, and then extended to the Guangzhou Railway (Group) Corporation, six infrastructure-support enterprises (the China Railway Engineering Corporation, the China Railway Construction Corporation, the China National Railway Signal & Communication Corporation, the China Civil Engineering Construction Corporation, and the China National Railway Materials & Supplies Corporation), and the four other railway administrations, Hohhot, Nanchang, Liuzhou, and Kunming in 1997 and 1998.[45]

Shanghai and Guangzhou railway administrations were situated in economically well-off provinces that had well-developed railroad networks. In view of their potentially enormous demand for railway transport and minimal need for railroad construction, these two railway administrations were expected to generate a promising result under the new responsibility system. This was important because it legitimized the initiatives of responsibility contracts and proved that such reform solved the problems of separated lines of revenue and expenditure.

Later, the Hohhot, Nanchang, Liuzhou, and Kunming Railway Administrations were chosen as test sites for the responsibility system of assets management, because these four were the only administrations without sub-administrations.[46] It was very difficult to calculate the total transport receipts and total operating cost incurred within different railway administrations, and the responsibility system of assets management involved even further specification of the calculation methods of the time rate and piece rate system among different work teams. Since these four railway administrations were smaller in scale and simpler in organizational structure, they were picked because it would be easier to administer and obtain promising results.

Revitalization of idle assets

The profit-sharing and responsibility systems were administered in light of the increasing difficulties in balancing the separate lines of income and expenditure within the railway sectors.[47] As mentioned above, the operating cost of the railway involved nationwide coordination, which made it very complicated to specify the cost of operating a single trip. By contracting out both the transport and construction responsibilities to the regional railway subsidiaries, railway leaders set the targeted profit level, turned a blind eye at the "black box of closed capital circulation,"[48] and hoped that the fuzzy property rights arrangements would allow more room for the localities to maneuver and revitalize the hidden productive assets. Whether these recently discovered productive assets would be centralized or decentralized depended on their strategic importance and will be dealt in more detail in the following chapters.

Notes

1 Javier Campos and Pedro Cantos, "Rail Transport Regulation," *The World Bank Group Working Paper* (1999), p. 7, www.worldbank.org/wbi/regulation/pubs/2064rail.htm (accessed 15 October 2002).
2 The 14 railway administrations are: Harbin Railway Administration, Shenyang Railway Administration, Beijing Railway Administration, Zhengzhou Railway Administration, Jinan Railway Administration, Shanghai Railway Administration, Guangzhou Railway (Group) Corporation, Chengdu Railway Administration, Lanzhou Railway Administration, Urumqi Railway Administration, Liuzhou Railway Administration, Huhhot Railway Administration, Nanchang Railway Administration, Kunming Railway Administration.
3 Zhongguo Tielu Chubanshe, ed., *Xin zhongguo tielu wushinian* (Fifty-year Review of the New China Railway; Beijing: Zhongguo Tielu Chubanshe, 1999), pp. 358–359.
4 *Xin zhongguo tielu wushinian*, pp. 358–359.
5 In 1984, the State Council put forward the principle of *"yiye weizhu, duozhong jingying"* ("Focusing on the core business and diversifying other businesses at the same time").
6 According to Kornai, "bureaucratic coordination" is ineffective because it dictates too many administrative logics and coherence between the regulator and the subordinates. János Kornai, *Vision and Reality, Market and State: Contradictions and Dilemmas Revisited* (New York: Routledge, 1990), p. 69.
7 Ron Kopicki and Louis S. Thompson, "Best Methods of Railway Restructuring and Privatization," World Bank CFS Discussion Paper Series (November 1995).
8 Alfred D. Chandler, *The Visible Hand: The Managerial Revolution in American Business* (London: The Belknap Press of Harvard University Press, 1977).
9 Williamson's study of economic theory of organization also contends that a certain degree of vertical integration takes place in capitalist economies because of the combinatory effects of uncertainty and bounded rationality. See Oliver E. Williamson, "The Vertical Integration of Production: Market Failure Considerations," *American Economic Review*, vol. 61 (1971): 112–123.
10 Wing Thye Woo, "The Real Reasons for China's Growth," *The China Journal*, vol. 41 (1999): 8–13.
11 Eva Voszka, "Centralization, Re-Nationalization, and Redistribution: Government's Role in Changing Hungary's Ownership Structure," in Jerzy Hausner, Bob Jessop, and Klaus Nielsen, ed., *Strategic Choice and Path-Dependency in Post-Socialism:*

Institutional Dynamics in the Transformation Process (Aldershot: Edward Elgar, 1995); Morris Bornstein, "Non-standard Methods in the Privatization Strategies of the Czech Republic, Hungary, and Poland," *Economics of Transition*, vol. 5, no. 2 (1997): 323–338; Roman Frydman and Andrzej Rapaczynski, *Privatization in Eastern Europe: Is the State Withering Away* (Budapest: CEU, 1994); Philippe Aghion and Olivier J. Blanchard, "On Privatization Methods in Eastern Europe and their Implication," *Economics of Transition*, vol. 6, no. 1 (1998): 87–99.

12 Chapter 2 describes in more details the economic imperatives, which includes considerations such as fiscal and efficiency constraints.

13 Rawski suggests that "institutional changes arising from partial reform created a virtuous circle in which the growing intensity of competition not only rewarded winners and punished losers but, by slowing the growth of tax revenues, diminished the state's ability to protect losers ... and pressed for further deregulation." Thomas G. Rawski, "Implications of China's Reform Experience," *The China Quarterly*, vol. 144 (1995): 1156.

14 See Chapter 2 for detailed analysis of the efficiency model of reform.

15 This problem was most obvious in the Beijing–Tianjin–Tanggu, Shenyang–Dalian, and Nanchang–Jiujiang routes. Also, in 1995, Guangshen Railways lost more than three million passengers—a loss of 15 percent—to the Guangzhou–Shenzhen–Zhuhai Superhighway after the road entered use. See Li Wai-ching, "The Reform Programme of the Ministry of Railways and Its Impact on Rail Development in China" (MA dissertation, University of Hong Kong, 2001).

16 For more detailed analysis of various productivity measurement in railway transport, see Tae Hoon Oum, W.G. Waters II, and Chunyan Yu, "A Survey of Productivity and Efficiency Measurement in Rail Transport," *Journal of Transport Economics and Policy*, vol. 33, no. 1 (1999): 9–42. For discussion about traffic unit and railway labor productivity, see Louis Thompson and Julie Fraser, "Notes on World Bank's Railway Database," Transport No. RW-6 (October 1993), http://siteresources.worldbank.org/INTTRANSPORT/Resources/336291-1119275973157/td-rw6.pdf (accessed 19 April 2015).

17 Jian Hong Wu and Chris Nash, "Railway Reform in China," *Transport Reviews*, vol. 20, no. 1 (2000): 25–48.

18 Wu and Nash, "Railway Reform in China."

19 Interviews, WYBJ, December 2003; LHZBJ, December 2003.

20 Interview, RCHBJ, October 2003.

21 Interview, YFFSZ, October 2003.

22 Barry Naughton, *Growing out of the Plan: Chinese Economic Reform, 1978–1993* (Cambridge: Cambridge University Press, 1995), pp. 98–119.

23 Yu Chuan, ed., *Zhongguo tielu caiwu kuaiji* (Finance and Accounting for China's Railway; Beijing: China's Railway Publisher, 1999), p. 65; and *Dang dai zhongguo congshu bianjibu*, ed., *Dangdai zhongguo de tiedao shiye* (The Contemporary Railway Business in China; Beijing: Zhongguo shehui kexue chubanshe, 1990), pp. 90–100.

24 Li Xuechong, *Boyilun yu jingji chuangxin: Jianlun Zhongguo Tielu Gaige* (Game Theory and Economic Transformation: Including a Discussion on China's Railway Reform; Beijing: Shehui Kexue Wenxin Chubanshe, 1999), p. 82.

25 Wu estimates that more than 60 percent of the work of railway transport involves inter-railway administration coordination and more than 75 percent of the income of each railway administration involves inter-railway administration settlement. Wu Jianzhong, *Tielu yunshu qiye shichanghua guanli* (The Market-oriented Management of Railway Transport Enterprises; Beijing: Zhongguo ttiedao chubanshe, 1988), p. 105.

26 Chuan, *Zhongguo tielu caiwu kuaiji*, p. 114.

27 Chuan, *Zhongguo tielu caiwu kuaiji*, p. 65.

28 Chuan, *Zhongguo tielu caiwu kuaiji*, p. 199.
29 Interview, WHYWH, January 2004.
30 Chuan, *Zhongguo tielu caiwu kuaiji*, pp. 106–108.
31 Wu and Nash, "Railway Reform in China."
32 Interview, LLXGZ, October 2003.
33 Xuechong, *Boyilun yu Jingji Zhuangxin*, p. 87.
34 Interview, ZYLBJ, October 2003.
35 Liu Qinglin, ed., *Teilu qiye banzhu guanli jichu zhishi* (Basic Knowledge of Work Group Management of Railway Enterprises; Beijing: Zhongguo tielu chubanshe, 2001), p. 74.
36 See *"Luotuo Tiaowu"* ("Camel Dances"), *Zhongguo Gaige Bao* (*China Reform Daily*), 26 February 2001, p. 7.
37 Interview, CQBJ, 2003.
38 Rong Chaohe, *"Cong yunshu changpin kang tielu chongzhu de fangxiang"* ("To Study the Direction of Railway Reform in the Light of the Characteristics of Transport Product"), *China.com.cn*, www.china.org.cn/chinese/OP-c/434301.htm (accessed 26 March 2007).
39 According to the World Bank Group, the Seventh Railway Project in China was aimed at assisting the MOR to

> 1) redefine the relationship between the railway and the Government; 2) reshape the railway's organization and strengthen its internal management; 3) expand the railway's transport capacity, raise its investment efficiency, and enhance its finances; and 4) modernize the railway's technologies and bolster the efficiency and quality of its transport operations and service
> (www-wds.worldbank.org/external/default/WDSContentServer/WDSP/IB/1995/04/14/000009265_3961019100557/Rendered/PDF/multi0page.pdf (accessed 19 April 2015)).

40 Zhao Yanling, *"Zhongguo tielu xitong dapo longduan kunnan chongchong"* ("Numerous Difficulties in Breaking the Monopoly of China's Railway System,") *Cijing Shibao*, 8 June 2001, China Infobank.
41 *"2001 nian zhongguo 14 ge tielu du Jiang zhujian keyun gongshi shixian wanyun fengli"* ("In 2001 China's 14 Railway Administrations will Establish Passenger Transport Companies and Separate the Railway Network from Transport Services"), *Zhongguo Jingying Bao*, 1 May 2001, China Infobank.
42 Interview, LHCBJ, 2003. Kuen's study in Chinese firms during the reform era shows similar conclusions: "private foreign investment tends to be less focused on infrastructure and more on quick-profit earning businesses. In the meantime, many important infrastructure projects have been put on hold due to the lack of funds. The resulting bottleneck in infrastructure is one of the factors responsible for inflationary pressure and material shortages. In this light, the leadership has good reason to take a more active attitude toward foreign borrowing and revise its perception of the optimum level of indebtedness.... Also, from the point of view of policy makers, foreign borrowing might be a better choice than foreign direct investment because leaders do not have to worry about how to control the joint ventures. See Keun Lee, *Chinese Firms and the State in Transition: Property Rights and Agency Problems in the Reform Era* (London: M.E. Sharpe, 1991), p. 181.
43 "Technical Assistance: People's Republic of China—Railway Passenger and Freight Policy Reform Study," Technical Assistance Report, Asian Development Bank, Project Number 37628, November 2005, www.adb.org/Documents/TARs/PRC/37628-PRC-TAR.pdf (accessed 25 September 2007).
44 *Dangdai zhongguo congshu bianjibu*, *Dangdai zhongguo de tiedao shiye* (The Contemporary Railway Business in China; Beijing: Zhongguo shehui kexue chubanshe, 1990), pp. 97–98.

45 *Renmin Tiedao Bao* (People's Railway), 7 January 1999, 2 April 1999 and 6 April 1999; Archives and Records Centre, MOR, "The Brilliant 50 Years History of China's Railway Development," *China Railway Monthly*, vol. 2, no. 13, (1999), pp. 3–14.
46 Interview, RCHBJ, October 2003.
47 See also "*Wangyun fenli tielaoda zaici tisu*" ("Separation Between Railway Network and Transport Services: Railway to Increase the Speed Again") *China Enterprise News*, 14 April 2001, Wisenews.
48 Xuechong, *Boyilun yu jingji chuangxin*, p. 88.

5   Great-Leap-Forward approach of railway development

Overview

Chapter 4 illustrated the limitations of the efficiency model in explaining China's railway reform and that there was no direct relationship between economic imperatives and the degree of decentralization. First, the Ministry of Railways (MOR) administered various cyclical reform strategies of decentralization and re-centralization over years when there were continuous and obvious economic problems of declining railway market share and shrinking profit. Second, despite the implementation of a series of profit-sharing reforms, there were no substantial changes as regards the property rights arrangements. On the contrary, these profit-sharing arrangements encouraged arbitrary negotiation between localities and the central government and resulted in even fuzzier property rights arrangements.

Rejecting the efficiency explanation, this and the next three chapters offer an alternative explanation for railway reforms. The first research question is why the MOR bothered to design and put forward a series of complicated profit-sharing formulae, and yet was unable to achieve the "desired" property rights arrangements in the end. If searching for the most efficient model was not the primary drive for railway reform, what was the hidden agenda?

The hypothesis (H2) is that decentralization does not lead to privatization. Rather, it is part of the search for strategic and well-paced development for the centralized enterprises in China. The various decentralization and profit-sharing reforms served two purposes.

First, the profit-sharing approach was a mere mimicry of the Western model. By complying with the Western style, the Chinese government could easily be legitimized in obtaining financial and technological assistance from various international donors. But the so-called decentralization reform policies did not lead to partial or full-scale privatization.

This chapter compares the railway sector with the other modes of transport, in particular the highway sector, and argues that railways were identified as a constraint on China's further economic take-off in the early 2000s. China's railway hindered the circulation of natural resources, raw materials, manufactured goods, and people. China's accession to the WTO and its increasing role as the world's "workshop" meant that the railway sector was becoming more and more strategically important. After 2003 the central leadership tightened its grip on railway development by reversing the previous commitment to decentralize the railway, and commanding the sector to undertake a Great-Leap-Forward approach to railway development (*dakuayue shi fazhan*).

In 2013 the planning and administrative functions of the railway sector were further re-centralized at the State Railway Administration under the Ministry of Transport.

Second, the so-called reform policy of decentralization also facilitated the recovery and discovery of productive assets which had become idle during the planned era. The property rights arrangements of the reformed railway enterprises were thus not as clearly demarcated as predicted by the economic model. The decentralization provided enough gray area for policy interpretations. The fuzzy property rights boundary, on the one hand, allowed local cadres to negotiate for more operating expenditure, as discussed in Chapter 4, and, on the other hand, also allowed local cadres to discover idle assets. This chapter on the Great Leap development of the railway sector focuses on the discussion that decentralization does not necessarily lead to privatization. Chapters 6–8 further discuss the discovery hypothesis by zooming in on the transport, construction, and signaling sub-sectors of the MOR.

Before the Great-Leap-Forward approach

Twists and turns of vertical and horizontal separations

Since 1994, China's railway deficit has been putting a strain on the already stretched state resources. In 1995, the MOR started to explore possible alternatives to reforming the railway system.[1] In 1996 the MOR formed the Office for the General Reform of the Railway (*Tielu zongti gaige bangongshi*) to formulate a comprehensive MOR reform program.[2] In 1998, the State Council ordered the MOR to embark on a reform program to turn the deficit into a surplus in three years.[3] Given the fact that the cumulative losses in the railway sector had amounted to RMB 12.7 billion by 1998, the reform was under great pressure.

In June 1999, the MOR took the side of Professor Rong Chaohe of the Northern Jiaotong University, who had written a paper about vertical separation and railway reform.[4] In the second half year of 2000, the MOR organized a series of policy fora and invited railway specialists from different institutes, such as investment banks, the Public Transport Department of the Policy Research Office of the State Council, the Department of Industrial Policy of the State Economic and Trade Commission, the National Development and Planning Commission, the Ministry of Finance, the Chinese Academy of Social Sciences, and the Development Research Center of the State Council, to debate and formulate a ten-year plan for vertical separation.[5]

This reform strategy of separation implied that the transport services components, the upper parts of the functionally integrated assets, would be separated from the railway regime, and paved the way for privatization. Since privatization would involve listing on the stock market, a few investment banks, such as China International Capital Corporation Limited, Bank of China International, and UBS Warburg, were invited to participate in the initial design of the railway reform.[6] Finally, in July 2000, the State Council approved the railway reform of vertical separation and included the project in the 10th Five-Year Plan. The World Bank specialists and many other railway experts were confident that the MOR would put into practice all the reform elements.[7]

The original plan was to establish one passenger transport company under each of the 14 regional railway administrations by the end of 2001. But the MOR had only managed to put in place six passenger transport companies before the termination of this separation policy. In fact, starting from August 2001, the railway cadres were asked to keep quiet about vertical separation and passenger transport enterprises because the MOR was preparing to reverse the policy and put forward a new development strategy.[8]

In March 2002, when Premier Zhu Rongji reported on the progress of the restructuring of the monopolistic sector, he singled out the railway sector in order to make further and special efforts to formulate a reform strategy.[9] This report hinted at the top leader's intent to not support the railway's vertical separation and soon unleashed negative commentary against such a reform strategy. The newspaper commentary had once been arguing that vertical separation was the best way to reform the railway sector because the transport services companies were detached from the railway monopoly and could compete with each other by offering different railway transport services. However, seeing the changing reform direction, the editorial comments undertook an opposite view.

Two major problems were identified. First, the social demand for passenger and freight transport put a lot of strain on China's railroad capacity. Since every train route was already stretched to breaking point, it would be difficult to arrange an extra train service running in parallel with the existing transport services running across the country. As a result, even if the transport service components were separated from the entire railway system, the detached transport companies could not compete to offer comparable train services and offer customers a choice in the market. Second, while the transport services companies could be detached from the infrastructure components and pay the network company an infrastructure access fee, the network company would still be a monopolistic gatekeeper, and the problem of inefficient allocation of assets would remain unresolved.[10] So the railway reform of vertical separation was terminated before it had gone very far.[11]

In February 2003, the MOR revised the reform strategy and submitted a plan of horizontal separation to the 10th NPC annual meeting. Instead of having one single rail track operator and several transport services companies, the revised plan suggested establishing three regional network companies covering Northern, Southern, and Central China. This arrangement resembled the Japanese railway model. Each company would undertake both the construction and maintenance of the rail network, and the operation of the freight and passenger transport services. In addition, several companies would be established to specialize in the business of cargo leasing, container transport, material supply, and engineering support, and the MOR would function as an industry supervisor.[12] However, this reform of horizontal separation was not even trialed.

Why the Great-Leap-Forward approach?

Since 1949 the railway sector has been identified as a strategic sector. After the CCP took over the disjointed and fragmented rail lines from the imperialist countries after the war, the Chinese People's Revolutionary Army Railway Bureau was set up to centralize construction and repair work.[13] Thereafter, the railway sector was regarded as one of the public sectors which were strategically important and characterized by its unique institutional history, close military ties, natural monopolistic infrastructure, and low substitutability.[14] As a result, the railway services have long been centrally planned in various respects, such as scheduling, pricing, personnel, and management.

As China's economy developed, the railway sector became more and more strategic. The MOR wanted foreign financial and technical assistance to expand and upgrade the railway network. It also administered various profit-sharing and corporatization reform strategies to mimic the Western model and facilitate global integration in terms of capital, management, and technology transfer.

Since the railway sector has never really been decentralized, the recent Great-Leap-Forward approach was thus not a policy shift driven by the lack of economic imperatives, as suggested by the efficiency model. On the contrary, it was because the railway sector has become a bottleneck for China's rise to becoming an economic superpower that the top leadership decided to set the pace in the state sector reform, and put forward a more centralized and coordinated development approach. It is indeed the economic imperatives that drove the centralization policy.

Railway transport as a bottleneck

Between 1993 and 2004, China's gross domestic product (GDP) recorded a year-on-year increase of 7–14 percent.[15] With a view to maintaining such rapid economic growth, the Chinese government needed to overcome all the possible bottlenecks that might hinder the country's further development.

Zhang Jianping, head of the railway development planning section of the MOR admitted: "The mileage of the railway network has become unable to meet the requirements of the expanding population and economy."[16] Huang Min, director for the department of development and planning of the MOR, also contended that: "Strained railway transportation has created a bottleneck for the sound development of China's economy since the end of last year [2003]."[17] Wu Mingyu, chairman of the China Institute of Technical Economy also said:

We have put much emphasis on the development of highways and aviation services in recent years. We can no longer afford to sidetrack railway development.... Railway infrastructure construction has lagged other sectors in the past decade, which is the root cause of today's transportation bottleneck.[18]

In 2004, China recognized that the railway sector was a crucial bottleneck for the nation's growing economy. To catch up with the nation's rapid economic development, the State Council approved, and the MOR announced, the "Medium- to Long-term Railway Construction Plan." The scheme, spanning from 2004 to 2020, will require an investment of RMB 2 trillion (US$250 billion) to lay 16,000 km of new rail lines, which include 5,000 km of dedicated passenger lines, and increases double tracking and electrified rail roads by 2020 (Table 5.1).[19] Later, the National Development and Reform Commission (NDRC) formulated the 11th Five-Year Plan (2006–2010) (Table 5.2).

Such a "Great-Leap-Forward" (*da kuayue*) approach to railway development was a further centralization strategy aimed at concentrating all efforts to push for coordinated development in the transportation and logistics industry. This strategy was put in place largely because the railway system was causing bottlenecks in China's economic rise—its unsatisfactory handling capacity inevitably hindered the distribution of natural resources, constrained the movement of production parts and manufacturing goods, and inflicted social unrest during the peak season for passenger transport.

HINDRANCE TO CIRCULATION OF NATURAL RESOURCES

In May 2005 the State Council formed an energy task force under which Premier Wen Jiabao, Vice Premier Huang Ju, and Zeng Peiyan were appointed to lead the newly established State Energy Office (SEO) to ensure sufficient power

Table 5.1 China's Medium to Long-term Railway Construction Plan, 2004–2020

Invest RMB 2 trillion (US$250 billion) in the railway sector.

Extend the length of railways in operations by 16,000 km to 100,000 km (first to reach 85,000 km by 2010, among which 5,000 km is for a dedicated passenger line, 35,000 km for double tracks, and 35,000 km for electrified lines).

To increase the ratio of double-track railways and electric lines to 50 percent.

To upgrade major railway technology and equipment to the international standard.

To separate cargo and passenger transportation in busy trunk lines.

To construct 12,000 km of four East–West and four North–South dedicated lines for passenger trains, and three intercity express passenger transport systems in the Bohai Sea Ring, the Yangtze River Delta, and the Pearl River Delta. The target speed will be 200 km/h and the total investment will be about RMB 2,000 billion.

Source: "Introduction of China's Medium- to Long-term Railway Network Construction Plan," www.gov.cn/ztzl/2005-09/16/content_64413.htm (accessed 20 April 2015).

Table 5.2 China's railway Eleventh Five-Year Plan, 2006–2010

To add 17,000 km of new lines, of which 7,000 km will be dedicated passenger lines.

To commence construction of the Beijing–Shanghai, Beijing–Zhengzhou–Wuhan–Guangzhou–Shenzhen, Harbin–Dalian, and Tianjin–Qinhuangdao, Shanghai–Hangzhou–Ningbo, Shijiazhuan–Taiyuan, Tsinan–Qingdao, and Hsuchow–Zhengzhou–Xi'an–Baoji dedicated passenger lines.

To complete construction of the Shanghai–Wuhan–Chengdu and Ningbo–Xiamen–Shenzhen dedicated passenger express lines.

To complete construction of the Beijing–Tianjin, Shanghai–Nanjing, Nanjing–Hangzhou, Guangzhou–Zhuhai, Jiujiang–Nanchang, etc. intercity passenger line.

To complete construction of Shanghai–Hangzhou magnetism aerosol transportation.

To expedite establishment of container logistics centers and double-deck container transportation corridors in 18 places, including Shanghai, Tianjin and Guangzhou.

To continue upgrading the existing rail lines for high-speed trains, targeted to have 200 km of high-speed rail lines

---

Source: Eleventh Five-year Plan, www.china-mor.gov.cn/tllwjs/tlwgh_2.html (accessed 25 April 2007).

supply for China's blueprint of "peaceful emergence."[20] The task force included 13 top leaders from the country's major ministries and administrations, such as Ma Kai, Minister of the National Development and Reform Commission, Bo Xilai, Minister of Commerce, Li Zhaoxing, Minister of Foreign Affairs, and Zhang Yunchuan, Minister of the State Commission of Science, Technology, and Industry for National Defence.[21]

The high-level support to the SEO suggested that the government was worrying about China's growing energy consumption. China needed natural resources to power its role as "workshop of the world," and raw materials to feed the factories' manufacturing lines.[22] Although different studies have different foci and project slightly different estimates, there is a general consensus that the current energy boom in the world is driven by China's increasing demand for energy.

In 2006 the Energy Information Administration (EIA), the official energy statistician of the US government, estimated that China's oil consumption would increase from 5.6 million barrels per day in 2003 to 8.7 million barrels per day in 2010, and 15 million barrels per day in 2030, with an average annual increase of 3.8 percent, making it the top consumer in the world. In 2014 the EIA revised its estimates upwards and projected that China's oil consumption will be doubled between 2010 and 2040, and will surpass the United States as the largest oil consumer in the world by 2035.[23]

Based on China's economic growth of 9.5 percent, and the subsequent increase of oil imports by 40 percent in 2004, another estimate suggests that if China is to quadruple its economy by 2020, the country will have to increase its crude consumption by 12 percent annually until 2020.[24] Without doubt, the enormous demand for oil imports prompted Chinese leaders to try every means to ensure adequate access to crude oil. In 2004, China imported more than 40 percent of its needs from overseas countries,[25] and was criticized as foolish to invest in overseas oil wells because any political shocks could increase the price of every barrel of oil regardless of the ownership of oil assets.

On the other hand, China was also concerned about being overly dependent on external resources, of which the supply could be unstable and expensive; the country therefore has been looking into various domestic energy sources, such as liquefaction of coal, wind power, solar energy, methane power, geothermal energy, and small-scale hydroelectric power, to help close the widening gap between energy supply and demand.[26] Although liquefaction of coal leads to various problems including pollution, environmental degradation, and fatal mining accidents, coal still accounts for 70 percent of China's power supply.[27] With such a "coal rush,"[28] some experts forecast that China will be able to produce 1.2 million barrels per day of liquid oil from coal by 2015, which is one-sixth of its current demand.[29]

However, such diversification of energy sources by liquefaction of coal is clearly constrained by four factors: the availability of coal mines, an adequate supply of water, the technology of liquefaction, and the distribution of coal from coal mines to various energy generators. The MOR is charged with the responsibility to coordinate the transport of coal all over the country, and schedule dedicated freight services for the sole purpose of coal transport. But the allocated coal transport capacity has never been adequate.

For example, in 2002 China's new power generation units had placed an order for 20.46 million tons of coal for electricity generation at the Changsha Coal Ordering Conference. But the MOR barely managed to allocate the transport capacity for 12 million tons of coal.[30] In 2004 the situation became even worse when the MOR could only meet 30 percent of the demand for coal transport. Wu Yin, deputy director-general of the Energy Bureau of the NDRC warned that if the coal could not be shipped on time, piles could self-ignite. Wu went to study the situation in the coal mines in Shanxi and saw many workers busy moving coal from one place to another to prevent this self-ignition.[31]

Since most of the coal mines were situated in Shanxi, Shaanxi, and Inner Mongolia Autonomous Region, the coal simply could not be shipped out to the main consumers in the East and Southeast China. The 2005 Coal Ordering Conference in Qinghuangdao again attributed the insufficient supply of coal partly to inadequate coal production capacity, and partly to transportation bottlenecks.[32] In January 2005, the *China Daily* reported that an anonymous insider from China Coal and Coke Holding Ltd commented on the problem of lack of transport capacity in China: "China is expected to produce 2.05 billion tons of coal in 2005, meeting basic coal needs, yet inadequate transportation will largely bottleneck the country's market balance."[33]

A local railway official also said that their internal conservative estimation was that, by 2010, China's GDP would be double, and even if the increase in energy consumption rate would only be half of the current rate of increase, railway's transport capacity would have to increase by 1.8 billion tons per year.[34]

So if energy has become a bottleneck for the Chinese economy in recent years, railway capacity has become "the bottleneck of the bottleneck." Wang Qingyun, director of the NDRC's transport department admitted: "Almost 40 per cent of the nation's rail capacity is used to transport coal ... the strained capacity is a stumbling block to rapid economic growth."[35]

In addition to oil, other resources, such as steel, iron ore, nickel, copper, and aluminum are all expected to double in consumption by the end of this decade.[36] However, the transport of these goods has been suspended with a view to prioritizing the transport of coal. In 2002, 77 percent of rail-borne freight transport went to coal, and the shares increased to 88 percent the following year.[37] As a result, transportation of other goods was given less priority and such delay in transportation served as a drag on the economic development of the country.

HINDRANCE TO CIRCULATION OF MANUFACTURED GOODS

The post-1949 command economy in China resulted in a highly fragmented distribution network which inhibited the integration of logistical services. The subsequent inefficient and insufficient circulation of goods became the bottleneck for the country's further development after the initial economic take-off. Again, the rail system has proved to be the bottleneck of the bottleneck.

After 1949: centralized and yet fragmented distribution network   In the early 1950s China emphasized heavy industry, and the main concern for economic development was to adequately supply raw materials at low transport costs. At such "distribution's stone age," the Maoist regime encouraged self-sufficiency for each province and city, which led to the problem of "considerable industrial overcapacity, few logistical synergies, and a vast bureaucracy."[38] As a result, not only provincial and township governments established their own warehousing systems for the local community, but different functional sectors, such as the raw material (*wuzi*), commercial (*shangye*), supply and sale (*gongxiao*), foreign trade (*weimao*), transport (*jiaotong*), and food (*shipin*), also built and operated their own warehouse and storage facilities.[39] Such independent warehousing systems were conducive to a fractured and inefficient distribution network.

What made the logistic synergies worse was the state's iron grip on resource allocation, and the rigid, unified, and command-oriented distribution system. Such a vertical distribution system comprised three tiers: the first tier was the state distributors located in Beijing, Shanghai, Tianjin, and Guangzhou; the second tier was the wholesalers situated in provincial capitals and middle-range cities; and the third tier was the wholesalers in small cities and towns.[40] Following the state's central directives, state-owned enterprises shipped their products from one tier to another until they arrived at the targeted cities or towns, and each layer increased the product price by adding 5–17 percent operating margins.[41] At that time, only foreign trade corporations were endowed with the rights to import goods. But once the imports arrived in China, they had to go through the rigid distribution channels.

From 1978 to the 1990s: slow increase in handling capacity After 1978, China shifted its focus to light industries and required fast and flexible transportation services.[42] The opening of the country and the rapid development of the economy gradually shaped the pattern of transportation within China. For example, the Chinese government tried to get around the lack of railway capacity by restricting short-distance (normally 5,100 km) journeys and thus diverted freight transport from railway to highway and waterway. At the same time, the global supply chain became popular and the new logistics concept of just-in-time (JIT) or zero inventory system also favored the more flexible and door-to-door highway and water transport services. The result was that the railway sector quickly lost its monopoly position.[43]

In the mid-1980s, provinces and municipalities were allowed to establish their own trading companies. By the late 1980s, domestic enterprises which had met specified trade volumes were permitted to import and export goods directly.[44] However, foreign firms could only import parts or components of the goods to China through an authorized Chinese trading company, and they could not sell and distribute the finished products by themselves.[45] Later, China granted limited trading rights to foreign firms within free trade zones (FTZs), such as Dalian, Shanghai, Fujian, and Guangdong. To attract more foreign investment, the Chinese government allowed foreign firms to establish their own distribution centers to circulate their raw materials and production supplies. These firms could also carry out third-party distribution services for other foreign or Chinese firms in FTZs. Between 1988 and 1998, the Chinese government offered preferential tax rates to foreign firms who promised to seek manufacturing components from local sources rather than imports. As a result, there was a growing demand for reliable distribution networks to ensure production supplies and market penetration in China.[46]

At the beginning, some logistics firms and non-competing multinational companies in China worked together and shared their distribution networks. Later, the Li & Fung Group developed the concept of "Distri-Centre" which consolidated warehousing, wholesale, and distribution functions.[47] Soon a few multinational companies (MNCs), such as Wal-Mart and Carrefour, were also allowed to establish their own distribution centers, import manufacturing components directly from abroad, and sell the products at branch offices in other FTZs.[48]

The demand across China for better transport services and a seamless logistics system further increased, as many companies consolidated to attain economies of scale.[49] In addition, the emergence of large chain stores, such as Guomei, also enhanced market competition and was conducive to declining profit margins. Foreign firms were forced to further cut costs by optimizing and streamlining their distribution chains.[50]

During the first two decades of economic reform, China realized the limitations of the centralized material allocation system. The original focus was to mobilize and liberalize the trucking system to provide more flexible logistical services for the transport of raw materials and final products. The first stage of reform indeed endangered the railway system, which was still highly centralized for transport of strategic resources. The result of such a tilt to the trucking system was rapid development of road infrastructure as compared with the far less vigorous development in the railway sector.

Between 1985 and 2013, national allocation of fixed assets investment in railways increased from RMB 10.7 billion per year to RMB 669.07 billion per year. Over the same period, annual investment in the highway sector increased from RMB 3.4 billion per year to RMB 2050.29 billion per year (Figure 5.1). Investment in railway obviously lagged behind highway. Before identifying railway as a bottleneck for national economic development, China's leadership thought highway and water transport would be able to meet increased demand for freight and passenger transports. As a result, national investment in railways was low as compared with highway and waterway transport, and the increase in the length of rail track was far too little.

As a result of the allocation of national fixed assets investment, between 1978 and 1987, the length of highways increased by 10.3 percent while the length of railways increased by 14.8 percent; between 1988 and 1997, the length of highways increased more rapidly by 22.7 percent while the railway increased by only 17.7 percent; the situation went to an extreme between 1998 and 2007 when the highway increased by 180.30 percent and the railway increased by a mere 17.5 percent (Figure 5.2). Similarly, between 1985 and 1994, the number of civilian motor trucks increased by 151 percent while the number of railway freight cars increased by 38.2 percent only; the gap decreases in the next decades, yet the number of motor trucks still recorded an increase of 52.5 percent while railway freight cars increased only 20.20 percent (see Table 5.5 and Figure 5.3). In fact,

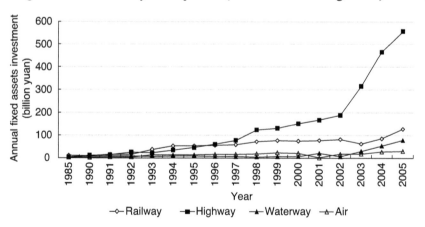

Figure 5.1 State allocation of fixed assets investment in the transport sector, 1985–2005 (source: *China Railway Yearbook*, 1999, 2001, 2002, 2003, 2004, 2005 and 2006; National data 2014, National Bureau of Statistics of China, http://data. stats.gov.cn/workspace/index?m=hgnd (accessed 20 April 2015)).

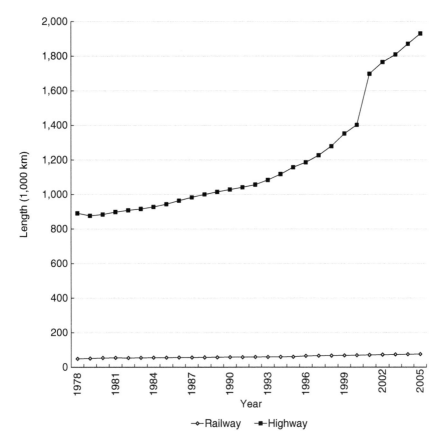

Figure 5.2 Length of China's railways vs. highways, 1978–2005 (source: *Chinese Statistical Year Book*, 2001, 2006, and 2014; National Bureau of Statistics of China, http://data.stats.gov.cn/workspace/index?m=hgnd (accessed 20 April 2015)).

the change of the trend of the market share of China's freight transport sectors clearly illustrated that around the late 1980s and early 1990s, China's freight transport "migrated" from railway transport to highway and waterway (see Figure 4.4).[51]

In comparison with the railway system in India, the United Kingdom, United States, and Japan, the Chinese railway had very low network density in the mid-1990s. In terms of kilometers per $1,000\,m^2$, China was three times less dense than India. The situation was much worse when comparing with other railway systems in developed countries. However, the demand for railway transport in China was exceptionally high. Interestingly, China had the highest traffic density among the six countries, twice that of Japan, and more than ten times that of the United Kingdom (Table 5.3).

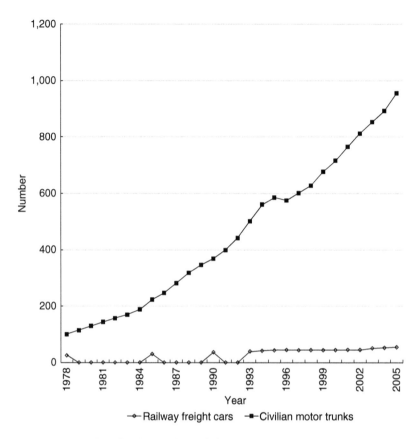

Figure 5.3 Number of China's railway freight cars vs. motor trucks, 1978–2005 (source: *Statistical Year Book*, 1997, 1998, 2000, 2001, 2002, 2004, 2005, and 2014, National Bureau of Statistic of China, http://data.stats.gov.cn/workspace/index?m=hgnd (accessed 20 April 2015)).

After 2000: Great-Leap-Forward for intermodal and containerized transport
With China's booming economy, trucking alone could no longer handle the demand for distribution services. First, the liberalization of trucking led to serious coordination problems and skyrocketing logistics costs. Second, the worldwide trend in globalization urged for a more comprehensive and seamless logistics service.

The Chinese government's iron grip on the distribution services rendered the system rigid and inefficient. During the 1980s and 1990s, the Chinese government deregularized the system, and allowed manufacturers to transport and sell their finished goods directly to any retailers. As a result, the traditional three tiers began to compete against each other and against the newly established and privately owned companies.[52]

Table 5.3 Railway statistics, China, India, Britain, the United States and Japan, 1994 and 1995

	China (1995)	India (1994)	United Kingdom (1994)	USA freight (1995)	Japan (1994)
Length (km)	54,616	62,461	16,536	174,619	20,255
Percentage of double-track railway (%)	31.0	24.1	70.1	N.A.	40.6
Percentage of electrified railway (%)	17.8	18.3	30.7	N.A.	58.6
Freight traffic units (million ton kilometers)	1,283,600	252,411	12,292	1,911,023	24,100
Passenger transport volume (million passengers)	1,021	3,915	702	N.A.	8,813
Passenger traffic units (passenger kilometers)	354,300	319,365	28,656	N.A.	244,375
Traffic density (million traffic units/km)	30	9	2.5	11	13
Number of staff	3,372,000	1,623,158	106,748	188,215	193,145

Source: Adapted from Jian Hong Wu and Chris Nash, "Railway Reform in China," *Transport Reviews*, vol. 20, no. 1 (2000), p. 26.

The original plan was to facilitate more flexible and tailor-made logistics services. But the overwhelming competition and the regional protectionism led to an even more fragmented system. The result was that local logistics providers recorded a maximum market share of only 2 percent. The scale of business was simply too small to build a modern logistics industry.[53] In 2005 there were some 2.3 million small haulage companies, mostly "one man and a truck" operations competing for short-haul routes.[54]

In addition, local rulings in logistics were frustratingly complicated—a trucking service provider would have to comply with different local regulations, such as applying for a national truck operation license from the Ministry of Transportation, a provincial operation license from the provincial government at the place of origin, and a city operation license from the local police authority. For example, Shanghai required trucking service providers to obtain an additional local truck title from the city transportation bureau for truck purchasing and registration. Many logistics practitioners, freight forwarders, and port handling executives were frustrated with these perplexingly negotiable situations which resulted from the problem of local protectionism.

In 2001 the McKinsey & Company's Greater China Office studied the impact of China's entry into the World Trade Organization on the country's transportation and logistics sector. By interviewing a few joint venture freight forwarding executives, port handling executives, and trucking executives, the report shows the serious problem of local protectionism:

> Many cities will not allow trucks to enter without a tedious registration process. Did you know a Tianjin truck cannot enter Beijing without waiting hours in line to register for a temporary delivery permit?

> If your truck is not a local truck, local authorities will often go out of their way to fine and detain you.

> Even with permission at the national level, local regulations prevent us from operating in many regions.

> We like the bonded trucking business because no one will dare to touch a customs truck. Otherwise, you would need a Gong An escort to travel to places like Northeast China.[55]

As a result, local logistics firms were dominated by entrepreneurs who had good connections with local "power brokers" and knew how to handle the red tape at various levels. That was why many consultancy reports came out for Western logistics practitioners to learn more about the industry in China:

> According to Richard Armstrong, president of Armstrong & Associates, getting the go-ahead for any logistics project in China still depends on the strength of a company's contacts within the Chinese bureaucracy. The

necessary relationships with local power brokers—a city mayor or a regional business titan—can often hinge on cultural nuances. At a business dinner, for example, a person's status determines how high he or she can raise a glass during a toast.[56]

Since local logistics firms were busy getting around the tangle of local regulations, they did not pay much attention to the business operation, such as developing appropriate equipment, advanced technology, and efficient management.[57] It was reported that these companies have the mentality toward preventive maintenance that states: "if it isn't broke, don't fix it."[58]

Consequently, foreign companies have often complained that China's low labor costs are offset by its high logistics costs.[59] In the late 1990s and early 2000s, logistics costs in China were prohibitively high at about 20 percent of China's GDP, 20 percent of the total revenue, and 30–40 percent of the total production cost and wholesale price. In the United States, the average logistics costs were about 10–12 percent of GDP and 5–20 percent of the wholesale price. In Europe it was about 6–14 percent of total revenue, and in Asia it was 12 percent of total revenue (Table 5.4). Ou Xinqian, vice-minister of the NDRC, also pointed out that, in 2004, China's total expenses on logistics were RMB 2.9 trillion (US$350 billion), rising 16.6 percent year-on-year, but the industry's added value was RMB 846 billion (US$102 billion), rising only 8.4 percent year-on-year.[60]

It was not surprising that the Chinese government wanted to reduce logistics costs. Research on the logistics industry in India shows that the lower the logistics costs, the higher the trade volume.[61] Logistics services are becoming more and more important because the organization of production nowadays involves global division of labor in terms of design, planning, manufacturing, assembly, and packing. The result is the development of the new logistics concept, JIT or the zero inventory system.

The basic idea is to further cut costs and increase economic gains by better synchronizing the process of sourcing, purchasing, production, storing, and delivery, and reducing and eventually eliminating inventories at all. Such an innovative concept, however, requires a seamless movement of goods.[62] It is therefore a worldwide trend to streamline the logistics process by third-party logistics companies, which will coordinate among different sectors, unitize the cargo handling standard, usually by containerization, lower the transaction costs of shifting from one sector to another, and provide all-in-one and door-to-door intermodal logistics services.

The problem with moving containers in China was that there were no standards at all for tracking, height of bridges, turnaround time, routing, surcharges, etc. Many consigners complained that railway officials had a "take-it-or-leave-it" attitude. Before 1998, shippers had to place shipment orders one month or more in advance. The consigning procedures were very complicated, and yet they could never track down the goods. The goods were often traveling into a "black hole," damaged, lost, or stolen, and companies were always confronted by illegal surcharges.[63]

Table 5.4 Comparative cost of logistics as a percentage of GDP, wholesale price, total revenue, and total cost, 1987–2005.

	Percentage of GDP	Percentage of wholesale prices	Percentage of total revenue	Percentage of total cost	Damage rate (%)
China	20 (red tape adding another 15) (2005)[a]	30–40 (2001)[b]	20 (2005)[c]	30–40 (manufactured goods); >60 (food and livestock); 70–80 (chemical products) (2001)[d] 40 (2002)[e]	5 (1999)[f]
United States	10–12 (2005)[a]	5–20 (2001)[g]	N.A.	N.A.	<1 (1999)[f]
Europe	N.A.	N.A.	6.2–14.3 (1987–97)[h] 10.4 (2001)[i] 10–12 (2005)[a]	N.A.	<1 (1999)[f]
Asia	N.A.	N.A.	13.7[i]	N.A.	N.A.

Notes

a Helen Atkinson quoting APL Logistics in "China's New Logistics Choices."

b Andrew Tanzer quoting Stephen Shaw, Director of McKinsey & Co. in "Chinese Walls," *Forbes Global*, 12 November 2001, www.forbes.com/global/2001/1112/091.html (accessed 12 April 2007).

c John Kerr, "10 Key Challenges for the Chinese Logistics Industry."

d Hertzell, "China's Evolving Logistics Landscape."

e Hong Kong Trade Development Council, "China's WTO Accession: Enhancing Supply Chain Efficiency: Transportation and Logistics" (2002), www.tdctrade.com/econforum/tdc/tdc020501.htm# (accessed 12 April 2007).

f Economist Intelligence Unit, *China Hand* (London: EIU, 1999), chapter 12, section 1.

g Tanzer quoting Stephen Shaw in "Chinese Walls."

h Luo and Findlay, "Logistics in China."

i Ken Gibson, "Analysing the Trends: Predicting the Future of Logistics in Asia," presentation to the conference "Toward the Final Frontier: Logistics and the Efficient Supply Chain," 27 September 2001 (quoted in Luo and Findlay, "Logistics in China.")

Also, there was little integration between the railway and the entire transport network. Rail systems were originally designed for bulk transport of natural raw materials, such as coal and iron ore, and were not suitable to carry finished goods or components in a timely manner. The most obvious problems for moving manufactured, perishable, and urgent goods were the long advance-booking schedule, slow delivery time, poor tracking system, and high damage rate.[64]

For example, William O'Brien, the vice president and regional director for Greater China of HAVI Food Services, which was responsible for the distribution for all 521 McDonald's restaurants in China, had been thinking of using China's railway due to its fixed schedules and low prices. But since food must be refrigerated and frozen, and China's railways have poor refrigeration units and cannot guarantee low temperatures throughout the cars, HAVI continued to use refrigerated truck fleets to distribute goods from its warehouses. Later, refrigerated rail container services were available on a limited scale, but the "inexplicably high prices" rendered the service economically infeasible.[65]

To facilitate the provision of intermodal services within China and across the border, China needed to bring railways into play as a transport mode and comply with the international standard use of containers. For example, they should ensure the integration of rail track with similar gauges, the sufficient supply of flat cars for moving containers, the appropriate craning facilities to handle the loading and unloading process, etc. In general, railways are considered as a mode of transport that incurs a lower cost per ton kilometer.[66] Shippers, of course, prefer to use rail lines whenever possible. In addition, rail is also favored as it is generally less congested and more environmental friendly than trucking.[67] The trend of containerization dramatically increases the need for railways.

A RECAP OF THE SITUATION BEFORE 2005: INSUFFICIENT, SLOW, AND NOT YET CONTAINERIZED

For the following reasons, China needed to enhance its logistics infrastructure, in particular the railway sector. Thus the MOR put forward a concerted effort to administer the great leap approach to railway reform because the railway was identified as the bottleneck of the bottleneck for China's movement of goods.

First, as mentioned before, because of the lack of capital investment, the increases in the length of China's railways and the number of railway freight cars were far lower than those of China's highways and motor trucks, respectively. However, the railway handling capacity was far above that of the highways. Between 1978 and 2005, although the total length of railways has dropped from about 6 percent to 4 percent of that of highways, and the total amount of freight traffic units produced (ton kilometers) by railways had decreased dramatically from about 20 times to two times that by highways, China's railways still produced far more freight traffic units than highways (Table 5.5).

Table 5.5 Highway vs. railway: length and freight transport product, 1952–2005

Year	Length (in '000 km)		Railway/highway (%)	Total amount of freight traffic units produced (billion ton kilometers)		Railway/highway (%)
	Railway	Highway		Railway	Highway	
1952	N.A.	N.A.	N.A.	60.16	1.45	4,148.97
1957	N.A.	N.A.	N.A.	134.59	4.80	2,803.96
1962	N.A.	N.A.	N.A.	172.11	6.21	2,771.50
1965	N.A.	N.A.	N.A.	269.87	9.51	2,837.75
1970	N.A.	N.A.	N.A.	349.60	13.81	2,531.50
1975	N.A.	N.A.	N.A.	425.57	20.27	2,099.51
1978	48.60	890.20	5.46	534.52	27.41	1,950.09
1979	49.80	875.80	5.69	559.87	74.50	751.50
1980	53.30	883.30	6.03	571.69	76.40	748.29
1981	53.90	897.50	6.01	571.20	78.00	732.31
1982	52.90	907.00	5.83	611.99	94.90	644.88
1983	54.10	915.10	5.91	664.65	108.40	613.15
1984	54.50	926.70	5.88	724.76	153.60	471.85
1985	55.00	942.40	5.84	812.57	190.32	426.95
1986	55.70	962.80	5.79	876.48	211.80	413.82
1987	55.80	982.20	5.68	947.15	266.04	356.02

1988	56.10	999.60	5.61	987.76	322.04	306.72
1989	56.90	1,014.30	5.61	1,039.42	337.48	307.99
1990	57.80	1,028.30	5.62	1,062.24	335.81	316.32
1991	57.80	1,041.10	5.55	1,097.20	342.80	320.07
1992	58.10	1,056.70	5.50	1,157.56	375.54	308.24
1993	58.60	1,083.50	5.41	1,195.46	407.05	293.69
1994	59.00	1,117.80	5.28	1,245.75	448.63	277.68
1995	59.70	1,157.00	5.16	1,287.03	469.49	274.13
1996	64.90	1,185.80	5.47	1,304.44	501.12	260.30
1997	66.00	1,226.40	5.38	1,325.33	527.15	251.41
1998	66.40	1,278.50	5.19	1,251.71	548.34	228.27
1999	67.40	1,351.70	4.99	1,283.84	572.43	224.28
2000	68.70	1,402.70	4.90	1,390.21	612.94	226.81
2001	70.06	1,698.00	4.13	1,469.41	633.04	232.12
2002	71.90	1,765.20	4.07	1,565.84	678.25	230.86
2003	73.00	1,809.80	4.03	1,724.67	709.95	242.93
2004	74.40	1,870.66	3.98	1,928.88	784.09	246.00
2005	75.40	1,930.50	3.91	2,072.60	869.32	238.42

Source: *Statistical Year Book*, 2001 and 2006; National Bureau of Statistics of China, www.stats.gov.cn (accessed 16 April 2007).

In 2004, Sun Rongfu, the vice railway minister, admitted that the daily request for rail cars for break-bulk (loose cargo) freight transport in China was about 200,000 to 250,000, but that the MOR could guaranteed a supply of only 100,000.[68] This suggests that the railway's productivity in terms of freight traffic units was actually highly constrained by its insufficient handling capacity, and such a bottleneck could be broken by increasing its handling capacity.

Second, railway transport was slow for various reasons. The mixing of passenger trains with cargo trains meant that the freight trains would have to give way to the passenger trains and increase the turnaround time. The turnaround time for freight railway cars in China increased from 4.2 days in 1991 to 5.48 days in 1999, and dropped to 4.92 days in 2005; the handling time in freight stations increased from 17.3 hours in 1991 to 23.8 hours in 1999, and dropped to 15.2 in 2005; the speed of freight trains recorded a minimal improvement from 29.5 km per hour in 1999 to 32.1 km per hour in 2005 (see Table 5.6).

What worsened the situation was the low percentage of double lines and electrified lines, and the fact that less than 20 percent of freight trucks could carry containers.[69] As a result, rail transport from the port of Shanghai to the northern provinces took 15–45 days, and to northeastern regions took up to 60 days. It is estimated that China's railcars traveled about 250 km per day.[70]

Third, as discussed earlier, China's railway system was not equipped with the infrastructural facilities for container transport—there were not enough compatible container cars and craning facilities. As a result, between 1990 and 2005, about 80 percent of the goods moved by the railway were bulk goods (Table 5.7). The percentage of bulk goods moved by the Indian and British railways

Table 5.6 Turnaround time, handling time and speed of railway freight cars, 1991–2005

Year	Turnaround time of freight cars θ (day)	Handling time of freight in freight station T (hour)	Commercial speed of freight trains V (km/h)
1991	4.20	17.3	29.5
1992	4.15	17.1	29.9
1993	4.18	17.3	30.3
1994	4.48	17.9	29.9
1995	4.50	17.9	30.2
1996	4.48	17.8	30.4
1997	4.57	18.1	31.4
1998	5.48	22.8	31.8
1999	5.48	23.3	32.4
2000	5.39	23.1	32.6
2001	5.09	22.0	32.1
2002	5.07	21.2	32.4
2003	5.05	20.9	32.8
2004	4.94	17.2	32.2
2005	4.92	15.2	32.1

Source: For data 1991–1998: Ruhe Xie, "Migration of Railway Freight Transport from Command Economy to Market Economy: The Case of China," *Transport Reviews*, vol. 22, no. 2 (2002): 170; For data 1999–2005: *China Railway Yearbook* 1999, 2000, 2002, 2003, 2004, and 2005.

Table 5.7 Distribution of goods lifted by China's railway, 1990–2005

Item	1990	1991	1992	1993	1994	1995	1996	1997	1998	1999	2000	2001	2002	2003	2004	2005
Total (million tonnes)	146	147	152	156	157	159	161	161	153	157	165	179	187	199	217	231
Bulk goods (%)	80.00	77.00	79.00	82.00	81.00	81.00	82.00	82.00	82.00	80.00	80.00	81.00	81.00	81.00	81.00	82.43
Coal	44.72	42.34	42.10	41.71	41.96	42.25	44.55	43.51	41.83	41.38	41.42	42.91	43.80	44.27	45.72	46.35
Petroleum	4.47	4.43	4.40	4.69	4.40	4.63	4.52	4.78	5.14	5.55	5.67	5.52	5.51	5.41	5.50	5.48
Coke	–	–	1.65	1.97	2.34	2.36	2.37	2.47	2.61	2.48	2.86	2.79	3.00	3.58	3.31	3.42
Metal ores	5.93	6.00	6.14	6.27	6.48	6.70	6.95	7.25	7.77	7.83	7.87	8.39	8.98	9.08	8.90	9.61
Steel and iron	5.67	5.62	5.58	6.29	6.20	5.89	5.87	6.12	6.58	6.66	6.97	7.22	7.56	7.68	7.41	7.59
Non-metal ores	5.38	5.28	5.36	6.28	6.00	5.90	5.86	5.54	5.48	5.20	4.92	4.76	4.37	3.99	3.71	3.57
Phosphorus ores	–	–	0.94	0.75	0.90	1.06	0.97	0.89	0.98	0.00	0.00	0.00	0.00	0.00	0.00	0.00
Mineral building material	8.53	8.09	7.83	8.25	7.16	6.60	6.11	6.19	6.61	6.59	5.84	5.49	4.60	3.85	3.59	3.39
Cement	2.83	2.51	2.68	3.10	3.10	3.00	2.63	2.41	2.42	2.46	2.36	2.20	1.92	1.83	1.71	1.50
Timber	2.50	2.35	2.23	2.25	2.20	2.50	2.44	2.39	2.31	2.14	2.08	1.88	1.68	1.53	1.49	1.52
Break-bulk goods (%)	20.42	23.38	21.09	18.44	19.26	19.11	17.73	18.45	18.27	19.71	19.91	18.84	18.57	18.78	18.65	17.53
Grain	3.72	4.20	4.21	4.22	4.80	4.21	3.73	4.38	3.62	4.12	4.79	3.97	4.43	5.09	5.03	4.80
Cotton	–	–	0.10	0.08	0.07	0.08	0.08	0.09	0.10	0.14	0.14	0.09	0.13	0.11	0.12	0.12
Chemical fertilizer	2.30	2.54	2.51	1.87	2.35	2.65	2.56	2.59	3.20	3.45	3.14	3.14	3.18	2.84	2.94	3.10
Salt	0.80	0.75	0.73	0.79	0.64	0.63	0.72	0.68	0.71	0.74	0.75	0.68	0.67	0.63	0.59	0.56
Others	13.60	15.89	13.54	11.48	11.40	11.54	10.64	10.71	10.64	11.25	11.09	10.97	10.16	10.10	9.96	8.95

Source: *Statistical Year Book*, 1997, 1999, 2001, 2003 and 2005; National Bureau of Statistics of China, www.stats.gov.cn (accessed 13 April 2007).

were even greater than that by the Chinese railways—95 percent of the goods moved by railway in India were bulk goods. The share of bulk goods moved in Sweden, Spain, and France accounted for only one-fifth to one-third of the total transport goods (Table 5.8).

HINDRANCE TO THE CIRCULATION OF PEOPLE

Although the Great-Leap approach to railway reform focused on freight transport, China's railway was also a bottleneck for passenger transport. And such bottlenecks in turn took up the railway transport capacity and affected the circulation of goods. In the mid-1990s, the number of railway passengers in China was as low as eight times less than that of Japan, and three times less than that of India. However, in terms of total passenger product (passenger kilometers), the Chinese railways were the highest among India, Britain, and Japan (see Table 5.3).

In 2004, Sun Rongfu, China's vice railway minister, admitted that, on average, China's railway was loaded with 2.7 million passengers per day while only 2.42 million seats per day were available. The situation becomes worse each year during the Spring Festival season, when migrant workers rush back to their hometowns for family reunion and festival celebration. In 2004 and 2005, the maximum number of passenger transported during the Spring Festival was between 3.6 and 4.4 million per day.[71]

As a matter of fact, it was very common for migrant workers to get up at 4–5 a.m. in the morning and join the queue with other early risers at the railway ticketing office to buy a ticket to go home for a family reunion during the Lunar New Year. It was also very common for them to fail to secure a seat on the train. In this case, they had to pay a scalper 10–20 percent over the normal rate.[72] In the spring of 2005, the media widely reported that one passenger was so desperate that he kneeled down in front of a policeman and begged for a train ticket to travel to his home town from Guangzhou.[73] During these festive seasons, the MOR has no choice but to deploy its already insufficient freight trains to carry passengers between provinces like Guangdong and the inland provinces.[74]

Table 5.8 Distribution of goods lifted by railways in China, India, United Kingdom, Sweden, Spain, and France, 1994 and 1995

Country	Bulk goods (including coal, if any)	Coal	Non-bulk Goods
China (1994)	73.1	42.3	26.9
India (1994)	95.5		4.5
United Kingdom (1995)	76.0	22.0	24.0
Sweden (1995)	22.0		68.0
Spain (1995)	34.0		66.0
France (1995)	38.0		62.0

Source: adapted from Wu and Nash, "Railway Reform in China," p. 28.

The Great-Leap approach

Chapter 4 argued that the efficient theory failed to explain China's railway reform. Different kinds of profit sharing and responsibility systems were mere mimicries of Western property rights arrangements. On the surface, the MOR followed the efficiency theory and gradually re-partitioned the property rights bundles according to the best railway reform model. But the top-down reform policy was never really intended to clarify the property rights nor to privatize the existing railway assets. In fact, there were traces of an iron grip along with the seemingly decentralizing policies.

Traces of iron grip behind the reform policies

Despite the implementation of various profit-sharing and responsibility reforms, local railway operators were not given the rights to set the price for passenger and freight transport services. Although local railway cadres were gradually allowed to set up sideline businesses under the dual-track system, various traces of the MOR's iron grip on the pricing mechanism show that the ministerial leadership has been keeping a close eye on its core business of transport services.

The first trace of centralization was that, besides regularizing the pricing procedures, the MOR also dictated the ad hoc and seasonal pricing mechanism. For example, the MOR used to increase the price of passenger train fare by 20–30 percent around the Lunar New Year to drive down market demand and divert passenger overflows during the peak times because migrant workers were traveling back to their home town for family reunions every year. Although the MOR started to organize public hearings for the price hike from 2002 onwards, it was criticized that the price hearing was a mere formality.[75]

Second, the MOR also dictated the terms on regional pricing policies. For example, after the Guangshen Railway Corporation Limited (GSRL) had been listed on the stock market in 1996, the MOR had allowed the company to set a minimum service charge at the level equivalent to the price of freight transport of 100 kilometers. Such a preferential pricing structure was meant to guarantee GSRL's freight revenue. However, in June 1998 the MOR suddenly ordered GSRL to cancel the policy of minimum charges, with retrospective effect on 1 January of the same year.[76]

Consequently, GSRL had to refund the surcharge to shippers, and such administrative policies created a lot of hassle for the accounting departments of GSRL. As a result, the interim annual report of 1998 of GSRL embarrassingly stated that the data regarding the revenue was not accurate because of the changing pricing strategy, and that the company expected to erase 10 percent of revenue in its freight business, which in turn contributed 40 percent to the company's total revenue.[77]

In fact, all other major logistics players in China, such as China Ocean Shipping Company (COSCO), which provided water-borne transportation services,

China Material Storage and Transportation Company (CMST), which provided warehousing and trucking services, China National Foreign Trade Transportation Corporation (Sinotrans), which provided air-borne freight forwarding and shipping services, and China Post, which provided mailing and parcel posting services, were also state-controlled and near monopolies. Such centralized logistics system and tough policies prevent local firms or foreign–local joint ventures from gaining "true operating control of critical assets."[78]

High-key centralization policy of Great Leap reform

In 2003 the MOR did not mimic the Western model of decentralization or disintegration; instead it put forward the "Great Leap" approach to railway development (*dakuayueshi fazhan*) to get around the bottleneck of the railway's capacity, which would otherwise constrain China's general economic development. On 7 January 2004, Prime Minister Wen Jiabao convened the State Council's general meeting and approved in principal the "Medium- to Long-Term Planning for Railway Network" (see Table 5.1). Later, the NDRC formulated the Eleventh Five-Year Plan (2006–2010) (see Table 5.2).[79] The overall target was to extend the length of the railway from 16,000 km to 100,000 km by 2020.

In 2005, all 41 railway sub-administrations were removed to flatten the organizational structure and facilitate the centralization of planning and decision making. They were replaced by 16 railway administrations and two railway corporations. The 16 railway administrations and two railway corporations were not based on thorough research of the existing pattern of passenger and/or freight transports, but on arbitrary decision making to centralize ministerial control and achieve the Great Leap railway development target.[80] (See Table 5.9 for the railway administrations after 2005.)

China wanted to overcome the incapacity problem because of the ever-accelerating demand for rail transport as a result of rapid economic growth. The "Great Leap" approach was intended to concentrate efforts in pursuing such a national goal: "Although western organizations always push us for decentralization and de-politicization, they in fact are more willing to arrange financial loans and technology transfer if they believe that what they have offered is under a strong state control."[81]

Foreign investment and technology transfer

Compared with other foreign countries, China's railway network has enormous room for development. China's railway density (length of railway network per total land area) was one-fortieth of England's and one-twenty-fifth of Japan's.[82] But the big plans to expand the railway network required huge capital investment. The Medium- to Long-term Railway Network Construction Plan estimated a total investment of RMB 2 trillion (US$240 billion) through 2020. In other words, at least RMB 100 billion (US$12 billion) will have to be spent annually. The Great-Leap approach thus pushed railway officials to look for multiple

Table 5.9 Railway administrations and sub-administrations in the transport services sub-sector, the MOR, 1999 and 2005

1999	2005
Harbin Railway Administration Sub-administrations: Harbin, Qiqihar, Mudan Jiang, Jiamusi, Hailar	Harbin Railway Administration
Shenyang Railway Administration Sub-administrations: Shenyang, Changchun, Dalian, Jinzhou, Tongliao, Jilin, Tonghua, Tumen	Shenyang Railway Administration
Beijing Railway Administration Sub-administrations: Beijing, Tianjin, Shijiazhuang, Taiyuan, Daton	Beijing Railway Administration Taiyuan Railway Administration*
Zhengzhou Railway Administration Sub-administrations: Chengzhou, Wuhan, Ankang, Xiangfan, Luoyang, Xi'an	Zhengzhou Railway Administration Xi'an Railway Administration* Wuhan Railway Administration*
Jinan Railway Administration Sub-administrations: Jinan, Qingdao, Xuzhou	Jinan Railway Administration
Shanghai Railway Administration Sub-administrations: Shanghai, Bengbu, Nanjing, Hangzhou, Fuzhou	Shanghai Railway Administration
Guangzhou Railway (Group) Corporation Subsidiary enterprises: Yangcheng, Changsha, Huaihua, Guangshen	Guangzhou Railway (Group) Corporation Subsidiary enterprise: Guangshen
Chengdu Railway Administration Sub-administrations: Chengdu, Xichang, Kaiyuan, Chongqing, Guiyang	Chengdu Railway Administration
Lanzhou Railway Administration Sub-administrations: Lanzhou, Wuwei, Yinchuan, Xining	Lanzhou Railway Administration
Urumqi Railway Administration Sub-administrations: Urumqi, Hami, Northern Territories	Urumqi Railway Administration
Liuzhou Railway Administration Sub-administrations: Liuzhou, Nanning Huhhot Railway Administration	Naning Railway Administration** Huhhot Railway Administratio
Nanchang Railway Administration	Nanchang Railway Administration
Kunming Railway Administration	Kunming Railway Administration Qinghai–Tibet Railway Company

Notes
* Became a separate railway administration in 2005.
** Renamed from Liuzhou Railway Administration to Naning Railway Administration in 2007.

financing mechanisms. Liu Zhijun, the railway minister, Wang Min, director-general of the planning department, and Zhang Jianping, head of the railway development planning section, all encouraged multiple investment entities to take part in the railway construction and operation:

> Multiple investment entities, including private and foreign capital, is being encouraged into the rail construction and operation sector on a market-oriented basis.... Market access will be widened to enterprises to encourage them to invest their capital into the railway projects.[83]

In September 2004 the Institute of Comprehensive Transportation of NDRC drafted a blueprint for the MOR to allow private capital, including foreign funds, to invest in railway construction.[84] But in December, Dong Yan, director of the institute, admitted to Xinhua News Agency that China Datang Group, an electric power company, and Inner Mongolia Yitai Coal Company Limited had proposed to build railways themselves before but were rejected by the MOR. Dong also contended that the MOR has signed agreements with ten provincial governments to build railways together, but he believed that the ministry would prefer to centralize and coordinate the national rail networks. By financing the railway project, local governments were able to negotiate the construction of the rail tracks to the benefit of their local economic developments or transportation needs, but they would not be able to run the railway themselves and assume the profits.[85]

In February 2005, Wang Min, director of the MOR's planning department, announced the first private investment in the construction of the Quzhou–Changshan railway in Zhejiang Province, which would be constructed with a total budget of RMB 775 million (US$93.7 million). The Changshan Cement Co. Ltd held a 32.5 percent stake in the project, the MOR held 35 percent, and the Changshan County Government 32.5 percent.[86]

Experts are cautiously optimistic about such a key move in the financing arrangements of this railway sector. Paul French of Access Asia, a market intelligence and consultancy firm on business development in China and Southeast Asia, criticized private ownership in China's railway as just a rhetorical arrangement: "How do you get a return?"[87] The problem for China's railway was that investors would not be able to control the pricing of freight transport, and thus would not have guaranteed profits.[88]

The paradoxical situation was that the Chinese government wanted to attract foreign investment and yet did not want to decentralize freight transport. The government needed to keep freight transport under control so it could continue to transport coal at a very low price. Otherwise, thousands of Chinese enterprises which needed coal as their fuel or raw material would become non-viable and millions of workers would be thrown onto the street; such mass unemployment would put the state's legitimacy at risk. While Paul French, the Access Asia consultant, concluded that "Coal itself is a crisis industry, but now it's totally messed up the rail industry,"[89] China's railway cadres commented that:

We understand their concern, but since railway transport serves many strategic purposes, we wanted to keep it centralized. In fact, we believe that investing in a sector with a strong authority behind the scene is better than investing in a sector with a fragmented and disjointed system.[90]

The New Silk Road

The centralized and ambitious approach to developing the railway network has resulted in 17,000 km of high-speed rail supporting high-speed trains running at an average speed of 200 km/h or higher by 2012.[91] In 2011, China had put in place the second-largest rail network supporting the third busiest railway system in the world in terms of combined passenger and freight traffic density.[92] However, such a Great-Leap approach was hit by the tragic accidents in Shandong and Hunan in 2008 and 2009, respectively.[93] In 2011, in the middle of these railway accidents, the then minister of railways, Liu Zhijun was dismissed and imprisoned for taking bribes and gifts with a total amount of 64.6 million yuan between 1986 and 2011. In July 2013, he was sentenced to death with a two-year reprieve. In the same year, another accident in relation to the high-speed train accident which took place in Wenzhou in 2013 killed 40 people.

In view of these incidents, the Ministry of Railways was dissolved and the China Railway Corporation was established to operate the national railway. Such a political move was to further centralize the administrative functions of the railway sector and put it under the control of the State Railway Administration under the Ministry of Transport.[94]

The central leadership may have been surprised by the corrupt activities undertaken by Liu during the Great-Leap period of railway development, but President Xi Jinping was well prepared to step in and take control of the entire regime. The well-paced coordination and centralization of the sector has always been the planned strategy to advance China's economy. As a result, President Xi acted quickly on railway development and scaled up the Great-Leap development to a national scale, involving trans-regional networking in Central Asia.

In September 2013, during his visit to Kazakhstan, President Xi Jinping introduced the concept of the Silk Road Economic Belt.[95] In the next month, Xi further proposed building a Maritime Silk Road to promote maritime cooperation. With a view to financing infrastructure construction and regional integration, Xi also proposed to establish the Asian Infrastructure Investment Bank (AIIB) to finance infrastructure construction and promote regional interconnectivity and economic integration. In 2014, China commissioned a study on the international railway between Kashgar in the Xinjiang Uygur autonomous region and Pakistan's deep-sea Gwadar Port, as part of the Silk Road Economic Belt.[96] In March 2015, China announced the framework of its Belt and Road Initiative, which ran through the continents of Asia, Europe, and Africa. According to Xinhua News Agency, the initiative is to "enhance regional connectivity and embrace a brighter future together."[97] The *Asian Wall Street Journal* explained this move from another perspective: "Beijing is looking westward precisely because the view out toward the Pacific is filled with peril"[98]

Such a centralized strategy of the construction of the Railroad Economic Belt (*"yilu yidai"*) exemplifies the government's iron grip on the railway sector, especially when the railway network can be used as a strategic asset for enhancing international relationship building and expanding China's influence in regional economic development in Central Asia. This time, the Chinese government centralized every effort to break the bottleneck of connectivity.

A peep into the railway sub-sectors

This chapter demonstrates that the search for strategic development drives the whole railway reform agenda in China. Since profit-sharing policies merely mimicked the Western model, the apparent decentralization policies did not necessarily lead to privatization arrangements. In fact, when the railway system was seen as the bottleneck of the bottleneck of China's economic take-off, the government focused its efforts and put forward the Great-Leap approach of railway development, and disregarded the integrated contracting responsibility system (*dabaogan*) which requested that regional railway administrations allow their own profits to guarantee investment, production, and railroad construction (*yilu jianlu*).

Chapters 7 and 8 will study two infrastructure-support services and argue that these sectors, which originated from the same railway regime, experienced similar reform policy, albeit at different pace, because of their strategic importance to the national economic development. Before that, in the next chapter, we will deal with the asset discovery strategies in the transport sub-sector, and show that the so-called decentralization polices were administered with a view to "pick the right assets," not to "pick the right owner."

Notes

1 Li Wai-ching, "The Reform Programme of the Ministry of Railways and Its Impact on Rail Development in China" (MA dissertation, University of Hong Kong, 2001), p. 68.
2 Xiao Yilin, *"Teilu gaige de miju: 'hengqie' yu 'shuqie' liunian zhizheng"* ("The Myth of the Railway Reform: The Six Year Fight between 'Horizontal Separation' and 'Vertical Separation'"), People.com.cn, 23 October 2002, www.people.com.cn/GB/ji nji/222/9285/9287/20021023/849272.html (accessed 20 April 2015).
3 Jiang Shijie, *"Yu wushengchu tingjinglei: tielu xitong gaige shaomiao"* ("A Quiet Surprise: To Scan through the Railway Reform"), People.com.cn, 17 January 2001, www. people.com.cn/GB/jinji/32/180/20010117/380412.html (accessed 20 April 2015).
4 Rong Caohe, *"Shilun 'shangxia fenli' yu tielu zongzu de guanxi"* ("An Attempt to Discuss the Relationship between 'Vertical Separation' and Railway Reform"), *Journal of Northern Jiatong University*, vol. 1.24, no. 3 (2000): 35–40. Rong's paper was widely cited on Chinese newspapers and magazines, such as Bo Jingwei, *"Zhongguo tielu zhongzu: hengqie? haishishuqie?"* ("The Restructuring of China's Railway: Horizontal Separation? Or Vertical Separation?"), People.com.cn, 17 July 2001, www.people.com.cn/BIG5/jinji/36/20010719/515398.html (accessed 20 April 2015).

5 Wan Xiaobing, *"Tielu xiang zhiji huiqi shoushudao"* ("Railway Undertook Operations Itself"), *Caijing Magazine*, vol. 4 (2001), www.chinanews.com.cn/zhonghua-wenzhai/2001-06-01/txt/16.htm (accessed 20 April 2015).
6 Xiaobing, *"Tielu Xiang Zhiji Huiqi Shoushudao."*
7 Yangqin *"Zhongguo tielu gaige dati queding: gaoceng qingxiang congqie luwang"* ("China's Railway Reform Largely Confirmed: Leadership Inclined to Vertically Separate the Network"), *Caijing shibao*, 6 December 2002, http://finance.sina.com.cn/b/20021206/1626287174.shtml (accessed 20 April 2015); and *"Zhongguo teilu gaige congxing tisu"* ("Speeding up China's Railway Reform Again"), *Caijing shibao*, 18 October 2002, http://finance.sina.com.cn/roll/20021018/1002268255.html (accessed 20 April 2015).
8 *"Tielu gaige xianru kunjing"* ("Railway Reform in Difficulties"), *China Economic Information Network*, 27 August 2002, Wisenews, http://libwisenews.wisers.net, Document ID: 200208273760025 (accessed 20 April 2015).
9 The Government Work Report delivered by Premier Zhu Rongji at the 5th Meeting of the 9th National People's Congress, 5 March 2002, http://focus.hustonline.net/html/2005-12-7/25454_4.shtml (accessed 25 June 2007).
10 Zhaoyun *"Zhongguo tielu gaige fang'an geqian,"* ("The Termination of China's Railway Reform"), *The Economic Observer*, 30 September 2005, www.chinainfobank.com (accessed 7 August 2005); and Wang Lingfeng *"Zhongguo tielu gaige de zongdian"* ("The Main Points of China's Railway Reform"), *21st Century Business Herald*, 16 January 2003, www.chinainfobank.com (accessed 7 August 2005).
11 Wang Chenbo and Lin Yingli, *"Tielu gaige 'huigui' tubian"* ("The Railway Reform Back to Square One") *China's News Week*, vol. 32 (2003), www.chinanewsweek.com.cn/2003-09-05/1/2160.html (accessed 7 August 2005); and Zhao Anying, *"Teilaoda kumi gaige luxiantu"* ("The Railway Big Brother is Endeavoring to Look for the Reform Strategy") *China Economic Net*, 12 April 2004, www.ce.cn/ztpd/hqmt/gnmt/cjj/more/200504/12/t20050412_3585578.shtml (accessed 8 April 2007).
12 Zeng Qingkai, "Three Regional Firms to Deal with Railway Business," *China Daily HK Edition*, 18 February 2003, www.chinadaily.com.cn (accessed 14 April 2004).
13 Lida Ferguson Junghans, "Workers in Transit: Chinese Railway Workers and the Journey from Plan to Market" (PhD thesis, Harvard University, May 1999), p. 77.
14 Jae Ho Chung, "The Political Economy of Industrial Restructuring in China: The Case of Civil Aviation," *The China Journal*, vol. 50 (2003): 61–82. Chung also ranked the railway sector as having low receptivity to structural reform. The least receptive sectors were the sector of national defense, water, and electricity.
15 China has revised its GDP growth rates. However, if we take the original statistics, the year-on-year increase in GDP between 1993 and 2004 was between 7.1 and 13.5 percent. See "Country Risk? Chinese Historical GDP Growth Rates Revised." Economic Intelligence Unit, 12 January 2006, www.riskcenter.com/story.php?id=12085 (accessed 24 September 2007).
16 Li Shi, "Time to Stoke up Railway Reform," *China Daily* (North American ed.), 7 February 2005, p. 6, Wisenews, http://libwisenews.wisers.net/, Document ID: 2005 02072260020 (accessed 21 May 2007).
17 Lu Haoding, "Railway Financing Plan Chugging Along," *China Daily*, 8 August 2005, www.chinadaily.com.cn/english/doc/2004-08/08/content_363168.htm (accessed 13 April 2007).
18 Li, "Time to Stoke up Railway Reform."
19 "Introduction of China's Medium- to Long-term Railway Network Construction Plan," Central People's Government of the People Republic of China, www.gov.cn/ztzl/2005-09/16/content_64413.htm (accessed 20 April 2014). See also "Bombardier Transportation in China," 12 May 2005, www.bombardier.com/en/0_0/0_0_1_7/0_0_1_7_8/pdf/20050512_China_Tour_Scotia_en.pdf (accessed 4 May 2007); Central People's

Government of the People Republic of China, www.gov.cn/jrzg/2006–04/07/content_248455.htm (accessed 20 April 2015).

20 Qiu Xin, "China Overhauls Energy Bureaucracy," *Asia Times Online*, 3 June 2005, www.atimes.com/atimes/China/GF03Ad01.html (accessed 13 April 2007).

21 "Premier Wen Heads New Energy Group," *China Daily*, 27 May 2005, www.chinadaily.com.cn/english/doc/2005-05/27/content_446253.htm (accessed 20 April 2015).

22 David Zweig and Jianhai Bi, "China's Global Hunt for Energy," *Foreign Affairs*, (September/October 2005), p. 25. See also Andy Rothman, "China Eats the World: Sustainability of Chinese Commodities," Credit Lyonnais Securities Agency, Asia-Pacific Markets, 2005, www.cctr.ust.hk/articles/pdf/China%20Eats%20the%20World%20Spring%202005.pdf (accessed 24 September 2007).

23 Energy Information Administration, *Annual Energy Outlook 2006* (2006), www.eia.gov/forecasts/archive/ieo06/pdf/0484(2006).pdf (accessed 20 April 2015); and Energy Information Administration, *Annual Energy Outlook 2014*, (2014) www.eia.gov/forecasts/ieo/pdf/0484(2014).pdf (accessed 20 April 2015).

24 Wenran Jiang, "Fueling the Dragon: China's Quest for Energy Security and Canada's Opportunities," Working paper of the Canada in Asia Series, Asia Pacific Foundation of Canada, May 2005, www.asiapacific.ca/sites/default/files/cia_fueling_dragon.pdf (accessed 20 April 2015).

25 "China Looks to Coal to Oil the Wheels of Industry," *Asia Times*, 27 May 2005, www.atimes.com/atimes/China/GE27Ad03.html (accessed 20 April 2015).

26 "Call for China to Develop Multiple Energy Sources," *ABC News*, 18 April 2005, www.abc.net.au/news/newsitems/200504/s1347165.htm (accessed 13 April 2007).

27 "Call for China to Develop Multiple Energy Sources."

28 Qiu Xin, "China Overhauls Energy Bureaucracy."

29 "China Looks to Coal to Oil the Wheels of Industry."

30 *"Zhongguo tielu zongzu wangyun fengli taolun gao chulong"* ("The Announcement of the Discussion Paper of the Separation between Network and Transport in China's Railway Reform"), *Zhongguo Dianli Bao*, 1 April 2003, China Infobank, http://210.177.11.50/gate/big5/www.chinainfobank.com/ifbase643-L0lyaXNCaW4~/-VGV4dC5kbGw~?-ZGI9SEsmbm89MTk5NzI5MCZjcz0yMTg5NDEmc3RyPdbQufrM+sK3K9bY1+krzfjUy7fWwOsrzNbC2w~~ (accessed 25 June 2007).

31 "Ministry's Control on Railways Questioned," *China Daily*, 5 December 2004, www.chinadaily.com.cn/english/doc/2004-12/05/content_397425.htm (accessed 20 April 2015).

32 Wang Ying, "Shortfall in Coal Supply to Remain," *China Daily*, 4 January 2005, www.chinadaily.com.cn/english/doc/2005-01/04/content_405663.htm (accessed 20 April 2015).

33 Ying, "Shortfall in Coal Supply to Remain."

34 Interview, LHCBJ, 2002.

35 Cao Desheng, "Transport to Focus on Moving Key Goods."

36 Rothman, "China Eats the World: Sustainability of Chinese Commodities."

37 "Ministry's Control on Railways Questioned."

38 Patrick Powers, "Distribution in China: The End of the Beginning," *The China Business Review*, July–August (2001): 9–12, www.chinabusinessreview.com/public/0107/powers.html (accessed 10 April 2007).

39 Luo Wenping and Christopher Findlay, "Logistics in China: Implications of Accession to the WTO," December 2002, http://siteresources.worldbank.org/INTRANET-TRADE/Resources/WenpingFindlay_logistics.pdf (accessed 20 April 2014).

40 Powers, "Distribution in China."

41 Bin Jiang and Edmund Prater, "Distribution and Logistics Development in China: The Revolution has Begun," *International Journal of Physical Distribution and Logistics Management*, vol. 32, no. 9 (2002): 783–798.

42 Luo and Findlay, "Logistics in China."

43 Ruhe Xie, Haibo Chen, and Chris Nash, "Migration of Railway Freight Transport from Command Economy to Market Economy: The Case of China," *Transport Reviews*, vol. 22, no. 2 (2002): 159–177.

44 Jiang and Prater, "Distribution and Logistics Development in China."

45 Pamelar Baldinger, "Secrets of the Supply Chains," *The China Business Review*, September–October (1998): 8–14.

46 Jiang and Prater, "Distribution and Logistics Development in China."

47 Huu-Phuong Ta, Hwee-Ling Choo, and Chee-Chuong Sun, "Transportation Concerns of Foreign Firms in China," *International Journal of Physical Distribution & Logistics Management*, vol. 30, no. 1 (2000): 35.

48 Jiang and Prater, "Distribution and Logistics Development in China."

49 Business consolidation took place in many sectors, such as manufacturers of colored television sets and air conditioners, as well as beer brewers. For example, the number of manufacturers producing air conditioners has fallen from over 400 in 1996 to 90 by 2000, refrigerators from nearly 200 to fewer than 40. See Staffan Hertzell, "China's Evolving Logistics Landscape," McKinsey & Company, Greater China Office, 30 August 2001, p. 10.

50 Hertzell, "China's Evolving Logistics Landscape."

51 Xie *et al.*, "Migration of Railway Freight Transport from Command Economy to Market Economy."

52 Pamelar Baldinger, "Secrets of the Supply Chains."

53 John Kerr, "10 Key Challenges for the Chinese Logistics Industry," *Logistics Management*, vol. 44, no.. 2 (2005): S64–68.

54 Michael Mackey, "China Integrates into Global Supply Chain," *Asia Times*, 28 April 2005, www.atimes.com/atimes/China/GD28Ad02.html (accessed 10 April 2007).

55 Hertzell, "China's Evolving Logistics Landscape."

56 Quoted in John Kerr, "10 Key Challenges for the Chinese Logistics Industry."

57 Interview, WDHHK, September 2003.

58 Ainsley Mann, "Dry Packaged Goods: Overcoming Logistical Hurdles," *The Chinese Business Review*, July–August (2001): 24–29.

59 Atkinson quoted Koay Peng Yen, president for the Greater China Region at APL Logistics, headquartered in Oakland, CA. See Helen Atkinson, "China's New Logistics Choices," *Traffic World*, 9 May (2005).

60 Dai Yan, "Logistics Industry Moving Forward," *China Daily*, 19 May 2005, www.chinadaily.com.cn/english/doc/2005-05/19/content_443922.htm# (accessed 12 April 2007).

61 Limao and Venables studied the logistics industry in India and estimated that a reduction of 35 percent of logistics costs led to an increase of 250 percent of trade volume. See Nuno Limao and Anthony Venables, "Infrastructure, Geographical Disadvantage, and Transport Costs," World Bank Policy Research Working Paper no. 2257 (December 1999), http://ssrn.com/abstract=629195 (accessed 12 April 2007).

62 D.J. Kasarda, "Transportation Infrastructure for Competitive Success," *Transportation Quarterly*, vol. 50, no. 1 (1996): 35–50.

63 Hertzell, "China's Evolving Logistics Landscape."

64 Kerr, "10 Key Challenges for the Chinese Logistics Industry."

65 See Robert Gates, "Beyond Sinotrans: China's Distribution Infrastructure," *The China Business Review*, July–August (2001): 14–17.

66 Claude Comtois, "The Integration of China's Port System into Global Container Shipping," *GeoJournal*, vol. 48, no. 1 (1999): 35–42.

67 Xie *et al.*, "Migration of Railway Freight Transport from Command Economy to Market Economy."

68 "*Zhufu fengli, tielu gaige de zhuyao moshi*," ("Separation Between the Core and the Ancillary Businesses: The Major Model for the Railway Reform") *Zhongguo Jingyingbao*, 19 March 2004, http://news1.jrj.com.cn/news/2004-03-22/000000775268.html (accessed 12 April 2007).

69 Luo and Findlay, "Logistics in China."
70 Gates, "Beyond Sinotrans."
71 Gates, "Beyond Sinotrans," and Li Shi, "Time to Stoke up Railway Reform," *China Daily* (North American edition), 7 February 2005, p. 6.
72 Interview, MGXGZ, October 2003.
73 "*30 cai cunyun*" ("Thirty Years of Spring Transport"), *China News Digest*, 15 March 2005, http://my.cnd.org/modules/wfsection/article.php?articleid=9593 (accessed 23 March 2005).
74 Li Wai-ching, "The Reform Programme of the Ministry of Railways."
75 "Opinion: Public Rail Price Hearing a Good Start," *China Daily*, 15 January 2002.
76 Interview, YFFSZ, October 2003.
77 *GSRL Annual Report*, 1998.
78 Hertzell, "China's Evolving Logistics Landscape."
79 Cao Desheng, "Transport to Focus on Moving Key Goods," *China Daily*, 10 August 2005, www.chinadaily.com.cn/english/doc/2005-08/10/content_467771.htm (accessed 20 April 2015).
80 "*Liu Zhijun shiqi: chefenju, yong fazhen huan gaige*," ("The Era of Liu Zhijun: Removing Railway Sub-administration and Slowing Down the Reform in Exchange for railway Development"), Caijing.com.cn, 25 January 2015, http://economy.caijing.com.cn/2013-01-25/112463210.html (27 April 2015).
81 Interview, LBRQBJ, December 2003.
82 "*Zhongguo shixian tielu kuayueshi fazhan shuoyao jiejue de zhuyao maodun shi yunli duanque wenti*," ("The Major Problem for China's Great Leap Approach in Railway Development is to Solve the Transport Incapacity") *Wuliu Shidai* (*Logistics Times*), 3 September 2003.
83 Michael Mackey, "Privatizing the 'Iron Rooster,'" *Asia Times*, 18 June 2005, at www.atimes.com/atimes/China/GF18Ad03.html (20 April 2015).
84 Lu, "Railway Financing Plan Chugging Along."
85 "Ministry of Railways' Control on Railways Questioned," *Xingua News Agency*, 5 December 2004, www.chinadaily.com.cn/english/doc/2004-12/05/content_397425.htm (accessed 20 April 2015).
86 "Private Cash to Help Build Railway Line," *China Daily*, 23 February 2005.
87 Mackey, "Privatizing the 'Iron Rooster.'"
88 Yu Jun, CITIC Securities in Guangdong, quoted in Michael Mackey, "Privatizing the 'Iron Rooster.'"
89 Michael Mackey, "China's Working on the Railroad," *Asia Times*, 17 June 2005, http://atimes01.atimes.com/atimes/China/GF17Ad02.html (accessed 12 August 2005).
90 Interview, LBRBJ, December 2003.
91 "Important High-Speed Railway Lines in China," www.chinahighlights.com/travelguide/transportation/china-high-speed-rail.htm (accessed 17 April 2015).
92 R. Bordie, S. Wilson, and J. Kuang, "The Importance, Development and Reform Challenges of China's Rail Sector," in L. Song, R. Garnaut, and C. Fang, eds., *Deepening Reform for China's Long-term Growth and Development* (Canberra: ANU Press, 2014).
93 "Three Killed in Passenger Train Collision in China," Xinhua News Agency, 27 July 2009, http://news.xinhuanet.com/english/2009-06/29/content_11616476.htm (accessed 17 April 2015).
94 David Briginshaw, "China Confirms Plans to Abolish Ministry of Railways," *International Railway Journal*, 11 March 2013, www.railjournal.com/index.php/policy/china-confirms-plans-to-abolish-ministry-of-railways.html?channel=542 (accessed 18 April 2015).
95 Wu Jiao, "Xi 'Travels in Time' Along the Ancient Trade Route," *China Daily*, 10 September 2013, http://usa.chinadaily.com.cn/china/2013-09/10/content_16959249.htm (accessed 21 April 2015).

96 Cui Jia, "China Studying New Silk Road Rail Link to Pakistan," *China Daily*, 28 June 2014 http://usa.chinadaily.com.cn/business/2014-06/28/content_17621848.htm (accessed 21 April 2015).

97 "Chronology of China's Belt and Road Initiative," Xinhua.net, 28 March 2015, http://news.xinhuanet.com/english/2015-03/28/c_134105435.htm (accessed 21 April 2015).

98 Andrew Browne, "Beijing Revives Silk Road Over Fears of Perilous Seas," *The Wall Street Journal Asia*, 4 March 2015: 1, 16.

6 The railway's transport sub-sector

Top-down re-centralization and local cadres' survival strategies

Overview

Chapter 5 argued that decentralization does not necessarily lead to privatization—the resulting property rights arrangements of the reformed railway enterprises after a series of profit-sharing reforms were not as clearly demarcated as predicted by the economic model. Rather, it was part of the search for strategic and well-paced development for the centralized enterprises and the economy in general in China. Hence, in 2003, when railway transportation was identified as the bottleneck of the bottleneck for China's economic development, the Ministry of Railways (MOR) tightened its grip and introduced a Great-Leap-Forward approach to railway development. In 2013, when China wanted to seize the opportunity to develop its economic influence in Central Asia, the government dissolved the MOR and regained state control over the planning and administration of the sector.

This chapter deals with the hypothesis (H3) that decentralization creates the fuzzy property rights arrangements which in turn encourage local cadres to discover idle state assets. The central leadership tried to resolve the fiscal problems of budgetary constraints within the state sector by administering the dual-track system and allowing local cadres to diversify into non-core businesses. This problem-solving approach resulted in an unexpected "assets discovery mechanism."

During the exploratory process of decentralization, local railway cadres were aware of the fuzzy property rights boundaries and negotiable fiscal arrangements, and began to make use of their political position as de facto gatekeepers of state resources, and engaged in short-sighted profiteering activities. However, in view of the increasingly important role of transportation in global and domestic economies, local railway cadres adapted differently—instead of focusing only on their political capital, they soon learned to apply their technocratic and managerial ability to explore diversified entrepreneurial businesses and maximize profit.

The result was that while the formal property rights arrangements of the existing productive assets in the transport services sub-sector remained intact, local railway cadres turned idle resources into new productive assets and boosted the extra-budgetary production capacities under the dual-track system. Although the

MOR required local subsidiaries to submit budgetary plans for these diversified businesses, in addition to that of the traditional railway businesses, local cadres could manipulate their reports and retain more profit. As long as local cadres could meet the agreed-upon transport targets, the railway leadership kept one eye closed, allowing local cadres to exhaust their local production capabilities. Consequently, local cadres made very good use of the retainable revenue. They got rich themselves, and at the same time brought business opportunities and extra revenue to their staff.

The central leadership later realized the value of the hidden productive resources. When the MOR decided to streamline the entire establishment, the railway leadership separated the non-core, diversified businesses from the core businesses, and expected these sideline businesses to sustain the excessive personnel in the sector. Such sideline businesses were decentralized in the sense that they had separate institutional, financial, and personnel arrangements, and were independent from the core businesses. However, not all newly discovered productive assets were decentralized; the last hypothesis (H4) predicts that if the newly discovered assets were involved in industries in which market competition alone could not improve efficiency, or if the Chinese government considered it to be strategically important, the assets would remain under the state's ownership in order to re-regulate and re-arrange the respective property rights. As such, the more likely the result of market failure, the more strategically important the newly identified assets, and the more likely that they will be centralized by the state.

By discussing how local cadres of the transport sub-sector survived and adapted to the reform policies, this chapter demonstrates that decentralization did not clarify property rights arrangements, which could have helped the central leadership to gradually identify the right person to inherit the state's assets. This is a process I call "picking the right owner." Rather, during the initial phase of reform, decentralization led to fuzzy property rights boundaries, which allowed the state leadership to pick the right assets which could later be privatized or "statized." This is a process I called "picking the right assets."

Such an assets discovery mechanism was not confined to the railway sector. In fact, it was the general state strategy to reform the core, state-owned sector at what they called the "critical stage" (*gongjian jieduan*). In 2006, Li Bao, Associate Director of the Economic Research Center of the SASAC, realized that the fixed assets of the state-owned centralized enterprises were worth RMB 10 trillion, one-third of which generated a total profit of RMB 600 billion in 2005; one-third did not report their profits; and the remaining one-third were idle assets:

> Our major efforts are to rejuvenate the idle assets.... In a nutshell, we are short of money and where can we get more money? We get it from rejuvenating the idle assets; we have abundant personnel and how can we settle the cadres? We allocate them to the new assets that they rejuvenated.... In this process, we diversify the property rights arrangements, and energize the system.[1]

Based on the conceptualization of hidden production resources discussed in Chapter 1, this chapter illustrates the productive assets within the transport sub-sector which are intangible, individually based, floating in nature, and informal. The discussion turns to the topic as regards the process through which these idle assets were discovered by the local cadres and recovered by the state leadership. The discussion of the re-centralization of the newly discovered production assets will pave the way for the next two chapters about railway construction and signaling sub-sectors, which will further illustrate the pattern of restructuring of state assets.

Reviewing the concept of extra-budgetary productive resources

As mentioned in Chapter 1, orthodox property rights theory considers only the production assets which are tangible, fixed, and in operation. However, property rights actually take various forms. This is particularly true during the reform era, when the latent productive resources are being identified and discovered for potential production. Some of these hidden resources are idle machinery; others are intangible resources which have never been listed as fixed assets of the company.

During the reform era, decentralization brings out the latent potential of these hidden resources, which manifest themselves in a series of production activities.

These hidden assets are embedded in the state firms and do not come to the attention of the supervising body, mostly because of their fluidity. On some occasions, the cadres in charge of those assets may not be aware of these latent productive assets because they are so used to depending on the state's soft budget constraints and they themselves became idle productive resources. On other occasion, the cadres were well aware of the potential production capacity, but they deliberately ignore them because of the lack of incentive. They knew that they could be more productive, but they chose not to be.

All these hidden productive resources were in the process of taking shape and being discovered. Their property rights cannot possibly be demarcated, at least during the stage when these hidden assets are taking shape and being recovered. Usually, such "extra-budgetary production capacities" involved the application of intangible resources, such as local cadres' human and political capital. As a result, these newly identified capacities are based on individual cadres, who can channel and coordinate the production capacities among different positions regardless of what they really own. These "floating" resources were embedded within the state sector and required special attention from local cadres to discover their value. During the transformation era, the property rights of these intangible, individually based, and floating resources are "informal"—they were not legally, explicitly, or formally recognized, and yet individuals in the right position could benefit from these resources. The property rights arrangements of such newly discovered productive assets may eventually be formalized and converged to the Western property rights system—at that point the economic theory of property rights may become more useful in explaining economic behavior; or the property rights arrangements may emerge into a different kind of property rights arrangement with Chinese characteristics.

Local railway cadres' survival strategies

Chapter 4 discussed how various forms of decentralized and profit-sharing reforms failed to provide sufficient incentives for local railway cadres to utilize fully the productive assets and maximize the potential profits. Instead, local cadres competed for more operating costs and worsened the efficiency level. Chapter 5 showed that, starting from 2003, China's leadership put forward the Great-Leap style of railway development. Obviously, the MOR's decentralization policies did not clarify property rights, nor did it lead to privatization. On the contrary, the MOR leaders would re-centralize the sector when they felt pressure to eradicate the problem of railway incapacity.

With the conceptualization of the extra-budgetary production resources, this section will discuss how local railway cadres survived the seemingly conflicting top-down reform policies—some of them engaged in short-term profiteering activities; some were involved in entrepreneurial deployment; some quickly started small-scale sideline businesses; others developed into nationwide group corporations.

The emergence of extra-budgetary production resources

The Chinese railway sector had been highly centralized under the State Council and was mandated by the Railway Law of China from 1949. The MOR administered two separate lines of income and expenditure and mandated monthly production and budgetary plans for all regional railway administrations, such as the plans on freight and passenger services, locomotive utilization, train scheduling, and car organizing. Although the railway sector had long been highly centralized for various strategic purposes, the economic reform in China since 1978 brought changes to cadres' ideological thinking and made room for the emergence of intangible property rights in the following decades.

The ideology of egalitarianism wore off

After 1978, China's economic reform undermined the ideology of equal distribution of wealth and legitimized material incentives. The widespread fever for getting rich emphasized material gain, and as they watched the rapid development of the private sector, local state cadres were lured to trade their political power for economic benefits.

After the Third Plenum of the 11th Central Committee of the Chinese Communist Party, the open policy rolled over different sectors across the country.[2] The MOR also implemented a series of decentralization reforms, including a few versions of the profit-sharing reforms, the dual-track system, and the corporatization reform. While superficial, profit-sharing and corporatization did provide local cadres with the ideological justification for entrepreneurial endeavors.

Many local cadres admitted that there was no material change in the organizational structure and modus operandi before and after the reform, but they still think it was a good start for them to follow the structure of a modern company, such as to set up a board of directors and appoint general managers. One railway cadre who has been working at the transport bureau of a regional railway administration for ten years said that his *danwei* had been turned into a so-called "transport service company" for about nine months, but was later asked by the MOR to revert back to the original unit:

> The reform seemed to be superficial. But at least we had a framework to follow. Some cadres might not want to change the old practice because they had accumulated resources from it and could be better off under the planned regime. But they gradually recognized the opportunities offered by business diversification, the new organizational structure served as a platform under which they could set up numerous subsidiaries with different ownership forms, such as joint ventures, joint stock, or limited liability companies.[3]

Business diversifications

The continuous drain on the state's financial resources by ever-increasing railway operating costs forced the MOR to follow other sectors in China and put forward the dual-track system. In 1978, one year before the MOR started the responsibility system, the operating cost for the railway sector was RMB 5.01 billion and it increased by more than threefold to reach RMB 18.46 billion in 1988. In 1998, when the MOR began to downsize the sector, its operating cost hit RMB 84.84 billion. On the other hand, the profits increased slowly from RMB 5.45 billion in 1989 to RMB 11.31 billion in 1990, dropped to RMB 1.27 billion in 1993, and recorded a net loss of RMB 6.41 billion in 1995 (Figure 6.1). Without doubt, there was a pressing need to solve the problem of a shrinking state budget in order to help the state sectors to survive the competitive domestic and global market.

In 1984, as in many other state-owned enterprises, the Chinese government allowed local railway cadres to set up sidelines because of insufficient funds to support their social responsibilities.[4] In 1985, local railway cadres started to diversify into different non-transport services (*duozhong jingying*).[5] The Guangshen Railway Company, which had been corporatized in December 1984, served as a test case to operate various sideline businesses, such as shopping malls, restaurants, advertising agencies, touring agencies, and intermodal freight transport agencies, etc.[6] The dual-track system soon proliferated throughout the whole railway sector. In 1990, the revenue generated from business diversification was

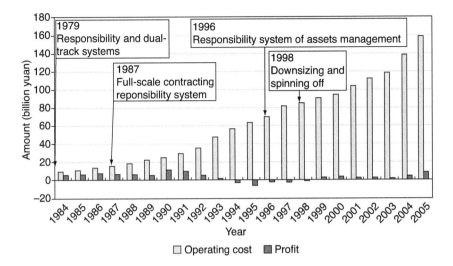

Figure 6.1 Operating cost and net profit/loss, Chinese railway, 1984–2005 (source: data for 1952–1980, *Zhongguo tiedao; 1949–2001* (Chinese Railway: 1949–2001; Beijing: Zhongguo); data for 1984–1993, *China Statistical Year Book*, 1986, 1987, 1988, 1993, 1994 (Beijing: China Statistics Press); data for 1994–2005, *China Yearly Statistical Data*, 1998, 2000, 2003, 2004, 2005; National Bureau of Statistics of China, www.stats.gov.cn (accessed 28 April 2007)).

nearly RMB 6.3 billion, 15.3 percent of the total railway revenue, and the profit was about RMB 1.3 billion, 11.4 percent of the total (Table 6.1).[7]

In 1992 the vice premier, Zhu Rongji, requested the railway sector to focus on three major businesses: transport services, railway construction, and business diversification. The railway leadership thus urged local railway cadres to explore as many ways as possible to make a profit. In 1993, the MOR put forward a directive on business diversification, namely *"Tielu 'bawu' ji liangqiannian duozhong jingying fazhan guihua"* ("The 2000 year plan and the Eighth Five-Year Plan for railway's business diversification").[8] In 1994 the MOR established the Center for Collective Development on Business Diversification (*Duozhong jingying jiti jingji fazhan zhongxin*) to coordinate different diversified businesses.

The railway sector in China was designed and planned in a way that regional railway subsidiaries were all equipped with abundant staff members and a wide variety of production assets. The system, being "large and self-sufficient," ("*daerquan*") was endowed with a wide variety of production assets to support the core railway services and many other social functions. As a result, local cadres could easily re-organize and revitalize the assets, which had not been fully utilized, to diversify into different business activities other than the core transport services. Local cadres were very excited in the mid-1990s when they first got involved in diversified business:

Table 6.1 No. of enterprises, no. of staff members, revenue and profit: diversified business of the MOR's transport sub-sector vs. the MOR, 1990–2005

Year	Diversified business of the MOR's transport sub-sector (A-D)				The MOR (E-G)			B/E (%)	C/F (%)	D/G (%)
	(A) Number of enterprises	(B) Number of staff members	(C) Revenue (RMB billion)	(D) Profit (RMB billion)	(E) Number of staff members ('000 people)	(F) Revenue (RMB billion)	(G) Profit (RMB billion)			
1990	3,438	N.A.	6.28	1.29	3,380	41.11	11.31	N.A.	15.28	11.41
8th Five-Year Plan										
1991	4,054	237,000	6.03	0.91	3,420	44.45	9.86	6.93	13.57	9.28
1992	N.A.	291,115	11.87	1.61	3,414	47.80	5.92	8.53	24.83	27.14
1993	N.A.	333,925	23.72	3.10	3,409	57.43	1.27	9.80	41.30	243.95
1994	5,894	342,969	23.87	3.16	3,396	58.28	-2.91	10.10	40.96	∞
1995	6,243	354,277	29.93	3.42	3,372	63.21	-6.41	10.51	47.35	∞
9th Five-Year Plan										
1996	9,743	366,770	34.74	3.43	3,355	75.61	-1.38	10.93	45.95	∞
1997	9,259	397,121	37.76	3.31	3,342	84.21	-2.61	11.88	44.84	∞
1998	9,078	401,032	31.93	1.88	3,179	92.21	0.25	12.62	34.62	750.56
1999	9,345	428,176	35.65	2.32	3,191	99.89	2.72	13.42	35.69	85.26
2000	8,644	462,035	44.44	2.66	2,486	109.74	3.38	18.59	40.50	78.70
10th Five-Year Plan										
2001	7,654	403,691	49.84	2.44	2,485	134.57	2.12	16.25	37.03	115.32
2002	7,433	416,271	58.62	2.73	2,484	142.05	2.47	16.76	41.26	110.83
2003	6,603	407,106	66.48	1.98	2,254	148.34	1.85	18.06	44.82	107.26
2004	5,805	373,621	82.79	2.51	2,165	179.44	4.85	17.25	46.14	51.72
2005	4,941	347,207	100.00	2.78	2,137	201.91	8.58	16.25	49.53	32.40

Source: data for transport sub-sector: *Zhongguo tiedao nianjian, 1999–2005*; data for the MOR: *Zhongguo jiaotong nianjian, 1992–1994, 1999, 2003, 2005; zhongguo tongji nianjian, 1997; zhongguo tiedao nianjian, 2001, 2004.*

Seeing the green light go on, everyone wanted to start sideline businesses, to *xiahai*, and to get rich. We mobilized what we had on hand, our staff members, our production assets, our knowledge, our information and our relations. This is what we call *zai shan chi shan, zai shui chi shui* (making use of the resources on the mountain when one is next to the mountain; and making use of the resources of the sea when one is close to the sea).[9]

Arbitrarily charged services

In the early stage of business diversification, local railway cadres quickly staked claims on those idle assets which had been incorporated into the railway regime during the planned era. One of the easiest ways was to provide "value-added services" on top of the basic transport service. For example, in 1993 the train between Nanjing and Shanghai started to provide a song-dedication service for RMB 5. Passengers could also rent computer games and purchase food and drink from train attendants.[10] Also, many train cars and stations began to rent out wall space for advertisements for all kinds of products, ranging from food and drinks to hotels and touring services.

The original idea was to make additional profits by fully utilizing the existing assets. But such profiteering practices very soon inflicted the problem of unannounced arbitrary fees (*luan shoufei*.) Local cadres were found to charge arbitrary fees for drinking water on long-distance passenger trains, for standard ticketing services, and even providing space in the waiting room at the train station. Freight transport involved enormous categories of fees, such as security, inspection, cleaning, construction, maintenance, and insurance. These charges were incurred at different en-route railway stations, and from the place of origin to the destination could add up to over 100 types of arbitrary charges.[11]

The MOR tried to rectify the problem of *luan shoufei*. In July 1993, Han Shubin, the railway minister, led a team of railway leaders to offer drinking water to passengers waiting on the platform of the Beijing railway station and commanded that the railway sector should not charge passengers for such basic services.[12] Local cadres gradually realized that these kinds of profiteering activities were killing the goose that laid the golden egg:

We were not sure if the central policy of the dual-track system would last long. You know it takes quite a long time to start up new businesses, although we do have the resources and necessary connections. Obviously, it was short-sighted and not sustainable practice, but everybody wanted to make quick money and did not want to miss out on any opportunities.[13]

From arbitrary charges to sideline businesses

In 1994, when China's railway recorded an annual net loss of about RMB 3 billion, the MOR convened the first working meeting on diversified business in the railway sector to emphasize the policy's strategic importance. The ministry explicitly encouraged regional railway entities to diversify into the following businesses: freight forwarding, warehousing, trading, container transport, touring, advertising, catering, property, industrial engineering, planting and rearing, mining and construction material, and foreign transport and foreign trade.

In view of the railroad's declining market share, local cadres realized that imposing various fees was not a sustainable way to increase monetary income. Some capable cadres used their ties with regional governments and local enterprises to develop entrepreneurial sideline businesses:

> We were asked by our supervisors to think hard about golden opportunities (*jin dianzi*). Some people were paying lip service to the slogans of cost saving, others started to operate different sideline businesses with high return rates. In our words, the later projects were having a high percentage of golden value (*han jin liang gao*).[14]

Under the planned regime, the MOR leadership was simply unable to plan for the use of all the state assets. With limited information and bounded rationality, the reformer urged local cadres to explore possible "golden opportunities" and discouraged businesses using arbitrary charges. With the separate lines of income and expenditure and profit-sharing system still in place, local cadres were lured to negotiate with their supervisor on the fiscal arrangements of various initiatives on business diversifications. The combinations of a series of problem-solving policies unexpectedly opened up enormous streams of financial income as local cadres began to discover idle production resources amid the undemarcated property rights boundaries. The coordination of such idle assets was different from the deployment of typical physical assets in a capitalist economy, largely because these assets had been idle for a long time, and the property rights associated with them were intangible, individually based, "floating" in nature, and informal.

The 1990s has seen a boom in a wide range of transport-related and non-transport-related businesses growing out of these idle assets. Local railway cadres took part in various diversified businesses because they were given the opportunity to enjoy better-remunerated jobs. In many cases, they transferred some idle assets in the railway sector to the companies that they would later be running on their own. Table 6.2 shows a sample of a local unit's budgetary plan.

> We were supposed to report to the MOR the planned budgetary and extra-budgetary revenue and profits for the core and diversified businesses, but how could they possibly know for sure all the detailed arrangements down to earth. As long as we provided the required core services, the MOR would not challenge what we have reported for the diversified businesses. We were therefore able to retain more profits.[15]

During the 8th Five-Year Plan (1991–1995), business diversification within the transport sub-sector alone generated operating revenue of RMB 95 billion, about 35 percent of the total railway revenue, and an accumulated profit of RMB 12.2

Table 6.2 A sample form of a regional unit's budgetary plan, 2003

Annual targets				
Budgetary revenue targets under the responsibility contract (10,000 yuan)	Total assets (10,000 yuan)	Extra-budgetary revenue targets (10,000 yuan)	Profits (10,000 yuan)	Rate of remittance (%)

Machineries and gacilities		*Quality of product/service*		*Safety*	
Availability rate (%)	Efficiency rate (%)	Pass rate (%)	Distinction rate (%)	Casualty rate (%)	Death rate (%)

Source: interview, CHFBJ, 2003.

billion, 158 percent of the total railway profit. By 1995, there were approximately 354,000 railway cadres working in the railway sideline sector, which was about 10 percent of the total workforce in the MOR (Table 6.1 and Figure 6.2).

From scattered sidelines to large-scale corporations

Before 1995, most diversified businesses in the railway sector did not involve extensive coordination with other business partners and/or government entities. In 1995, the MOR formed four regional preparation groups, namely the Pudong,

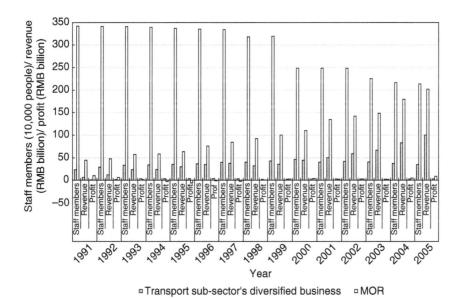

Figure 6.2 Number of staff members, revenue, and profit in diversified businesses of the MOR's transport sub-sector vs the MOR, 1991–2005 (source: based on Table 6.1).

Xiamen, Hainan, and Huatie Railway Corporations to initiate the establishment of railway corporations (*tielu jituan*). For example, the Huatie Jituan in Shenzhen would coordinate the efforts of more than 60 existing railway enterprises to develop intermodal service for international container transport.[16]

The establishment of the four railway corporations signified the MOR's support to develop and consolidate the diversified businesses. Given the green light for business diversification, local railway cadres were, in their own words, eager to go beyond "1435" and developed sideline businesses of a larger scale:

> 1435 cm is the distance between two rail tracks. We would like very much to try to go beyond 1435 which meant that we wanted to go beyond the core transport businesses and explore the opportunities of running sideline businesses.[17]

Gradually, local cadres started to develop sideline businesses which required more coordination and were of a larger scale. In 1997, Liuzhou railway cadres negotiated with local government to establish and develop a large-scale logistic center. Liuzhou Railway Administration, located at one of the southern nodes of the railway network, was a natural point of origin or destination. With the comparative advantage of its geographical location, local cadres used their existing connections with shippers and forwarders, and diversified into the fast-growing logistic service.

In the same year, Lanzhou and Hohhot Railway Administrations started local mining industries. Situated in regions endowed with mineral, coal, and petroleum resources, these two railway administrations had long been working with local governments to transport natural resources from the mines. The longstanding working relations thus helped in collaborating with new businesses beyond transportation.[18]

Between 1993 and 2001, Beijing Railway Administration established four subsidiary property development companies in Shijiazhuang, Beijing, Tianjin, and Taiyuan. These property development companies redeveloped the railway staff quarters into commercial residential blocks such as the "*Jingtie Jiayuan*" (Beijing Railway Homeland) in Yuejialou district of Beijing, and "*Shidai Mingju*" (Time's Famous Court) in Wangchuanchan district of Tianjin.[19] In 1999, Nanchang Railway Administration redeveloped a piece of wasteland of 8,000 hectares at Huangtugang district next to the Zhejiang–Jiangxi Railway, and turned it into farmland, an animal farm, a fish pond, and a food processing factory.[20]

Local railway cadres also expanded into R&D businesses. In May 1999, Nanjing Railway Sub-Administration established the Nanjing Technology and Railway Electronic Company Ltd. (Nanjing Ketie Dianzi Company Ltd), to work on R&D projects for the railway. In 2001, they successfully produced various high-tech systems, which were tailor-made for train cars in the mainland to ensure a steady supply of electricity. Three years later, in December 2002, the Nanjing Technology and Railway Electronic Company Ltd. formed a joint venture, *Nanjing Guotie Dianqi* Company Ltd., with the Guodian Nanjing Zhihua Company Ltd. to develop R&D products on electrification and automation.[21]

By identifying idle assets and reallocating excessive personnel, local railway cadres developed various sideline businesses with the existing establishment, and formed various joint ventures with railway and non-railway entities. Some of these joint venture partners were state-owned enterprises, some were the sideline companies of other state-owned sectors, or other railway subsidiaries, and a small fraction of shares went to private entities or individuals.

For example, in November 2000, the Urumqi Railway Administration formed a joint venture, Xinjiang Xibei Jiangshu Ronglian Company Limited (Xinjiang Northwest Furnace Company Limited) with the Urumqi Kexi'e Trading Company, the Zhejiang Province's People Electronic Factory, and an individual businessman, Liu Xinnian. The major business of the joint venture was to import recycled aluminum from neighboring countries and turn it into aluminum alloy ingots for both the international and domestic markets.[22]

In 1999, at a working meeting for Chinese railway's business diversification, then railway minister Fu Zhihuan admitted that diversified businesses in the railway sector were generally "small, dispersed, and weak" ("*xiao, san, ruo*").[23] Fu further identified five major areas of business diversification: freight forwarding, logistics, tourism, advertising, and property development. The top-down directive once again served as a guideline to re-organize the idle railway assets.[24] By 1999, the MOR established a number of special task forces, such as the China Railway Foreign Service Corporation (*Zhongguo tielu duiwai fuwu gongsi)*, the China Railway Import & Export Corporation (*Zhongtie jinchukou gongsi*), and the China Railway Travel Service Group (*Huayun luyou jituan*) at the Beijing headquarters to coordinate the diverse and dispersed business initiatives.

Consequently, the number of diversified enterprises (*duoyuan quje*) increased from 3,438 in 1990 to 9,345 in 1999, and then decreased to 4,941 in 2005. During the same period, the number of staff members increased from 237,000 in 1991 to 462,035 in 2000, but decreased to 347,267 in 2005. While business consolidation led to a decrease in the number of enterprises and staff members, it enhanced the revenue-generating ability for the diversified businesses. The revenue recorded more than 16-fold increase from RMB 6.03 billion in 1991 to RMB 100 billion in 2005. Yet the reported profit increased slowly from RMB 0.91 billion in 1990 to a maximum of RMB 3.43 billion in 1996, and then dropped to RMB 2.78 billion in 2005. What was more interesting was the ratio between revenue and profit. For example, in 2005, revenue for the whole railway sector was RMB 201.91 billion, which translated into a net profit of RMB 8.58 billion; and the revenue from the diversified business was RMB 100 billion, which produced a profit of RMB 2.78 billion. In both cases, the profit margin was only 2–4 percent (see Table 6.1).

How do we explain this anomaly? One of my informants told me that the policy of business diversification was not aimed at extracting more money from the sector; rather, the leadership wanted to identify and rejuvenate the idle assets:

> There were so many idle assets (*xianzhi zichan*) within the railway sector. During the planned regime, local cadres were all competing for funding, projects, and resources (*zheng touzi, zheng xiangmu, zheng zichan*). Much of the excessive amount of resources became idle assets. I don't think the MOR leadership know the exact boundary of such idle assets. Even local cadres who were used to having excessive resources may not have been fully aware of the potential production capacities of such idle assets.[25]

To a certain extent, the MOR turned a blind eye to the transfer of state assets from the core transport sector to the diversified sector, as long as local cadres squeezed resources from the existing provisions to operate these diversified businesses. If these sidelines could be operated without jeopardizing the transport services, they could later be separated from the core transport sector. But if these sidelines were competing with or involving the core business, the MOR would re-centralize it and put it under state control. In other words, under the policy of business diversification, local cadres carved up the railway assets which the MOR would later trim off from the railway sector, or retain and re-centralize under state ownership.

Property rights re-arrangements: spinning off, separation, and re-centralization

In July 1997, Premier Zhu Rongji called for an overall reduction in state employees.[26] In the same year, the MOR put forward the "*Tielu yunshu qiye jianyuan zhengxiao shishi yijian*" ("Opinion on Implementation of the Policy of Reducing the Establishment and Improving the Efficiency in the Transport Sub-sector of the MOR").[27] Accordingly, all transport sub-sectors could no longer recruit staff members from outside, and were requested to allocate idle staff members (*fuyu renyuan*) to diversified businesses.

Following the central directives, the MOR was separating the excessive assets from the railway sector. The following section will discuss the first phase of institutional reform, which detached the infrastructure services sector and the ancillary sector from the core sector of transport services. The next section focuses on the second phase, which re-arranged and separated the sideline sector from the core sector.

Spinning off the infrastructure services and ancillary sub-sectors

In 1998, the MOR removed four railway sub-administrations and 207 small railway stations, and reduced the total personnel level of its headquarters from 809 to 400. In November 2000, the MOR detached five large-scale entities in the infrastructure services sub-sector and their 800,000 staff members, including the China

Railway Engineering Corporation (CREC), the China Railway Construction Corporation (CRCC), the China Railway Signal & Communication Corporation (CRSCC), the China Railway Locomotive & Rolling Stock Industry Corporation (CRLRC), and the China Civil Engineering Construction Corporation (CCECC).

CRLRC soon split into two companies—the China Southern Locomotive and Rolling Stock Industry (Group) Corporation (CSR) and the China Northern Locomotive and Rolling Stock Industry (Group) Corporation (CNR). The six spin-off corporations were then put under the jurisdiction of the State-Owned Assets Supervision and Administration Commission (SASAC) of the State Council. Such large-scale corporations were still considered strategically important and therefore were only spun off from the railway sector, but not from the state sector.

In the same year, 2000, the MOR detached ten colleges and universities and put them under the jurisdiction of the Central Government Enterprise Affairs Commission, the Ministry of Education and local governments.[28] Consequently, the MOR reduced the number of its staff members from 3.34 million in 1997 to 2.49 million by the end of 2000.

Later, in the second half of 2003, the MOR spun off the China Rail Material & Supplies Corporation and China Railway Communication Company, and put them under the umbrella of the SASAC. The ministry also spun off four design institutes under the headquarters and 38 design enterprises under regional railway administrations, which were then merged into the China Railway Engineering Corporation and China Railway Construction Corporation of the SASAC. In addition, 319 railway primary and secondary schools, 50 railway kindergartens, and 52 railway hospitals were given back to the regional governments.[29] By 2004, the MOR further reduced its workforce from 2.49 million in 2000 to 2.14 million in 2005 (Table 6.1 and Figure 6.3).

Separating the non-transport related sideline businesses

On 26 March 2001, at the Working Meeting of the Railway's Business Diversification in Kunming, Wang Zhaocheng, the vice railway minister, announced the phase two reform policy of "*San fenkai*" ("Three Separations"):

> We have to separate the non-transport related and diversified businesses from the core business of transport services in terms of their institutional, financial and personnel arrangements, in the hope of regulating the relation between the holding companies and their subsidiaries; we have to establish an internal cost-center management system, in the hope of copying the market-like operation (*moni shichan yunzuo*); we also have to establish an internal labor market within the railway system, in the hope of providing a buffer against surplus labor.[30]

It was reported that such a policy had separated more than 10,000 enterprises and 600,000 people from the core transport sub-sector. During the process of

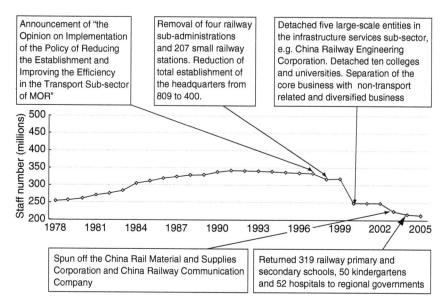

Figure 6.3 Total workforces in the MOR, 1978–2005 (source: data from *China Railways: 1949–2001* (Beijing: China Railway Publisher, 2003), pp. 226–271; *China Transport Yearbook*, 1993–2006).

separation, the MOR allocated some of the state assets, which had once been included in the railway sector had been left idle, to those local cadres who were able to put them to productive use. The diversified businesses were thus separated from the core businesses and the *duojing* enterprises were like satellite units, independent from the core businesses, decentralized from the MOR headquarters, but still under the railway regime.

However, not all newly identified businesses were decentralized. In December 2003, the MOR re-centralized and consolidated the diversified businesses which involved transport services and established three large-scale corporations. The China Railway Special Cargo Services Company Limited (CRSCS, Zhongtie tehuo yunshu Company Limited), China Railway Container Transport Company Limited (CRCTC, Zhongtie jizhuangxiang Company Limited), and China Railway Parcel Express Company Limited (CRPEC Zhongtie xinbao kuaidi Company Limited);[31] all were set up by local cadres.

The following section on the case study of CRPEC will show that while those non-transport-related diversified businesses were separated from the core transport sub-sector, the transport-related businesses, in particular those related to the logistics industry, would be consolidated and re-centralized. The previous decentralization policies helped the leadership to "pick the right assets," not "pick the right owner." (See Figures 6.4a and 6.4b for the schematic outline of the MOR restructuring.)

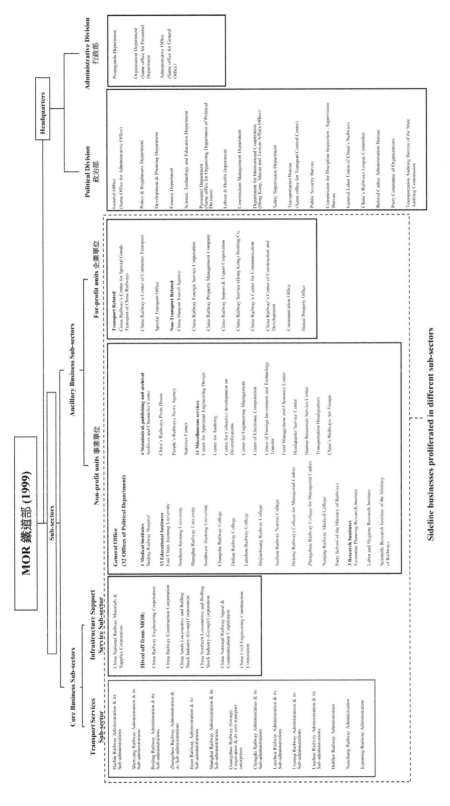

Figure 6.4a MOR's organizational chart, 1999.

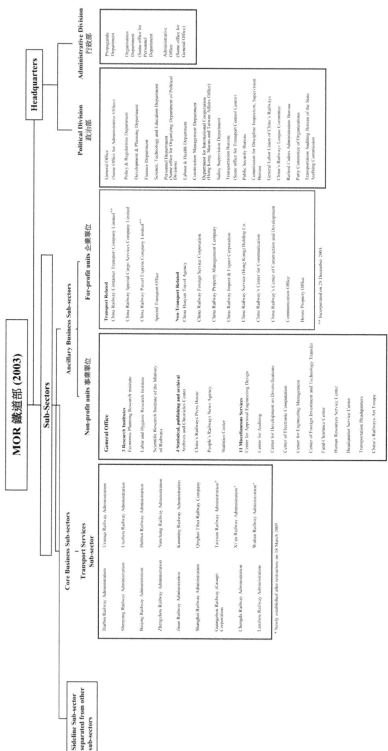

Figure 6.4b MOR's organizational chart, 2003 (source: CRCC website, www.chinarailway.com.hk/en/finance.htm (accessed 24 July 2007)).

Re-centralizing the transport-related sideline businesses

THE EMERGENCE OF RAILWAY EXPRESS SERVICES

As secondary and tertiary industries accounted for a large part of the stunning growth of China's GDP between 1991 and 2005, more and more shippers wanted to transport value-added goods rather than bulky raw materials. This kind of freight forwarding required safe, timely, and door-to-door service,[32] and such an emerging market was seen as a promising opportunity for the railway sector.

First, the Chinese railway network was very suitable for domestic express delivery. The railway network provided a nation-wide network. Recent technological enhancement of the speed of railway transport meant that it could provide transport service at reasonable speed and comparatively low cost. Also, the flexibility of adding luggage cars on passenger trains facilitated delivery of small parcels along the en-route stations.

Second, the dual-track system implemented in 1985 provided local railway cadres with the necessary policy accreditation to make use of their bureaucratic ties. Consequently, a few railway cadres, including some in the China Railway Foreign Service Corporation (CRFSC), an entity directly under the MOR, various regional railway administrations and sub-administrations, and some members of the railway research and educational units, took advantage of their political ties, technocratic knowledge and business network to stake a claim on the idle assets of the railway's luggage car. They started to negotiate with the MOR leadership to grant them rights to use the idle space to provide a full-fledged and complete express delivery service, and to assume part of the extra-budgetary income as other diversified businesses.

The railway's luggage cars were originally used for passengers to check-in their bulky luggage other than hand-carry luggage. But the luggage check-in service had long been underused in China's railway sector, and the unoccupied space of the luggage cars was therefore wasted.[33] In September 1993, CRFSC obtained the MOR's approval to operate a railway express parcel business in seven selected cities: Beijing, Shanghai, Tianjin, Guangzhou, Shenzhen, Shenyang, and Zhengzhou. To enlist support from these regional railway administrations, CRFSC signed cooperative agreements with them and agreed to offer 70 percent of the total profit.[34]

Regional railway administrators accepted the offer for two reasons. First, the cost of moving empty luggage cars was minimal as these regional railway administrators have to move the whole train anyway under the national train schedule. Under the system of separate lines of income and expenditure, as discussed in Chapter 3, local cadres could easily transfer the additional operating cost of moving parcels to the general operating cost, which would eventually be shared by the whole railway system. Second, by accepting the cooperative agreement, regional railway administrators enjoyed the additional profit as extra-budgetary income.

Although CRFSC and the regional railway administrators were taking advantage of state assets, their self-interested negotiations based on political ties and entrepreneurial considerations expanded the railway business and at the same time delineated the best possible property rights arrangements for the idle luggage cars. It was through such manipulations between political capitalism and technocratic managerialism that local cadres coordinated and discovered idle state assets. The railway express service was later considered as a transport-related sideline business and re-centralized under ministerial control.

In March 1994, CRFSC established a legal entity, the Beijing China Railway Foreign Service Express Company (Beijing Express Co.; Beijing zhongtie waifu kuaiyun gongsi), to look after the railway express business in Beijing. In the same year, it expanded the express business to cover Qingdao, Jinan, Harbin, Dalian, Nanjing, Xi'an, Lanzhou, and Chengdu. By 1997, the railway express service covered 61 cities. That same year, CRFSC and its wholly owned subsidiary, the Beijing Express Co., jointly registered the China Railway Express Company Ltd. (CRE), with the State Administration for Industry and Commerce.[35]

The cooperative agreement between CRFSC and the regional railway administrations on the 30:70 split of profit was maintained to ensure a seamless railway parcel service among different regional railway administrations, of which the local railway cadres had long been providing state-planned passenger and freight transport services. The cooperative agreement took advantage of the existing working ties, which had changed from purely command-driven to market-driven activities. As argued in Chapter 4, under the command-driven system, local cadres endeavored to lower production targets and increase operating costs because they want to maximize the above-target bonus and state-allocated resources, respectively. However, when dealing with the market-driven parcel express service, the same cadres negotiated with CRE to buy more shares of the company.

By 1997, 41 legal entities were established as regional subsidiaries of CRE. In each regional subsidiary, the related regional railway administration and sub-administration together bought 70 percent of the shares and thus maintained the original 70 percent profit share.[36] When some regional cadres were asked how they could possibly purchase shares of the CRE subsidiary, they said they contributed in cash or in kind: "We can provide support in terms of personnel, equipment or facilities."[37] In fact, such joint subsidiaries were run by the same group of people who were also in charge of the existing passenger and freight transport services. They were simply "one working team under two company names" ("*yige bangzi liangge paizi*").

These regional cadres were important gatekeepers for access to the resources which were vital to the provision of a seamless railway express service. In fact, all the interlocking procedures, such as loading and unloading, customs clearance, luggage car allocation, transit arrangement, and parcel tracking, took place within local cadres' jurisdiction. CRE was willing to give away 70 percent of the profits because the cadre in charge understood that the seamless service depended greatly on the cooperation of the en-route stations which were administered and controlled by regional railway administrations and sub-administrations.

Later, CRE realized that the company needed to focus on a strategic but unified development. From 2000 onwards, CRE started to re-organize the property rights arrangements of its 37 joint venture subsidiaries by increasing the parent company's investment share to 51 percent. Although CRE increased its investment in the subsidiaries, the profit share ratio remained unchanged, i.e., the subsidiaries could still obtain 70 percent of the profit. In return, CRE enforced and instilled a different set of corporate governance rules to the 37 subsidiary companies: each subsidiary had to form a board of directors of five members, three nominated by the holding company and two by the subsidiary.

In the second half of 2001, CRE negotiated again with its subsidiaries for a further change of the property rights arrangements. Consequently, all subsidiaries were switched from an independent legal entity to a regional branch of the China Railway Express Ltd. As a branch office, these regional joint ventures were restructured as regional cost centers. The share of profit between the branches and the holding company changed to 49:51, instead of the original 70:30.[38] The branch offices were expected to minimize the local operating costs so as to maximize the profits of both the mother company and the local branch. This property rights arrangement was different from the fiscal arrangement of the traditional passenger and freight transport services, which had separated lines for revenue and expenditures. Although the holding company took more of the profits, the regional subsidiaries agreed to do so because, gradually, they were becoming aware of the importance of integrated management in coordinating an express transport service:

> After a few years' operation, we were all aware of the importance of an overriding concern to ensure a seamless railway express business. It was just reasonable for the holding company to retain the majority shares of the business.[39]

Not only did the local cadres learn that express services require centralized coordination, the MOR leadership also shared the same view, especially when it took into consideration the strategic importance of the logistics industry. In 2003, the MOR began to re-centralize all transport-related sideline businesses.

LOGISTICS THREATS

By 2003 the Chinese government was under significant pressure regarding the country's inefficient distribution system, which was a result of various causes. First, China has become the manufacturing hub for the world. Between 1993 and 2003, the country's exports increased from RMB 528.5 billion to RMB 3,628.8 billion. Between 2003 and 2005, the figure almost doubled and reached RMB 6,264.8 billion. By 2003, China accounted for 5.8 percent of global exports, and was ranked fourth in the world in terms of export volume

(Tables 6.3 and 6.4). In order to benefit domestic companies, the Chinese government offered preferential tax rates to encourage export-oriented firms to produce goods from local raw materials and/or semi-manufactured products. The consequence of such a preferential policy was the need to provide the up-stream firms with a well-designed supply chain and distribution system within China so they can move the whole production process to China.[40]

Second, China has developed a huge retail market for consumer goods. Seeing that the country's population surpassed 1.3 billion, and its people were enjoying improving living standards, many world-famous retail companies, such as McDonalds, IKEA, Walmart, and Coca-Cola tried to expand their businesses in China; to do so, they needed to sort out how to distribute their goods across China. Some outsourced the distribution of goods to local or foreign partners. Other firms, such as Walmart, established their own distribution systems in China.[41]

Both the foreign trade and domestic retail markets created a huge demand for logistics services in China. However, the logistics industry was still in its infancy. When China entered the WTO in 2001, one of many other agreements was to phase out most restrictions on foreign companies' participation in the distribution sector by 2005 (Table 6.5). Since foreign companies would be allowed to own 100 percent of Chinese freight forwarding in 2005, third-party logistics, and customs brokerage firms, many major global, third-party logistics firms, such as DHL, Kuehne & Nagel, UPS, FedEx, TNT, APL Logistics, Maersk

Table 6.3 China's exports and imports volume, 1978–2005

Year	Exports volume (RMB billion)	Imports volume (RMB billion)
1978	16.8	18.7
1980	27.1	29.9
1985	80.9	125.8
1989	195.6	220.0
1990	298.6	257.4
1991	382.7	339.9
1992	467.6	444.3
1993	528.5	598.6
1994	1,042.2	996.0
1995	1,245.2	1,104.8
1996	1,257.6	1,155.7
1997	1,516.1	1,180.7
1998	1,522.4	1,162.6
1999	1,616.0	1,373.6
2000	2,063.4	1,863.9
2001	2,202.4	2,015.9
2002	2,694.8	2,443.0
2003	3,628.8	3,419.6
2004	4,910.3	4,643.6
2005	6,264.8	5,427.4

Source: China yearly statistical data; 2006, National Bureau of Statistics of China, www.stats.gov.cn/tjsj/ndsj/2006/html/R1803e.htm (accessed 28 June 2007).

Table 6.4 Share of world trade volume, 2003

Rank	Country	Value (billion US dollars)	Share
Exports			
1	Germany	748.3	10.0
2	United States	723.8	9.6
3	Japan	471.8	6.3
4	China	437.9	5.8
5	France	386.7	5.2
6	United Kingdom	304.6	4.1
7	Netherlands	294.1	3.9
8	Italy	292.1	3.9
9	Canada	272.2	3.6
10	Belgium	255.3	3.4
Imports			
1	United States	1303.1	16.8
2	Germany	601.7	7.7
3	China	413.1	5.3
4	United Kingdom	390.8	5.0
5	France	390.5	5.0
6	Japan	382.9	4.9
7	Italy	290.8	3.7
8	Netherlands	262.8	3.4
9	Canada	245.0	3.2
10	Belgium	235.4	3.0

Source: International Trade Statistics 2004, World Trade Organization, p. 19, www.wto.org/english/res_e/statis_e/its2004_e/its2004_e.pdf (accessed 3 May 2007).

Logistics, and Exel, were all eyeing China's huge market. Many had been working jointly with the government-owned transport giant Sinotrans and would continue to invest in the logistics sector in China.[42]

RE-CENTRALIZATION OF RAILWAY LOGISTICS BUSINESS

The MOR leadership was well aware of the fact that the logistics market would eventually be opened to foreign players. In view of the WTO timeline, the MOR began to re-centralize the transport-related sideline businesses in order to enhance the competitiveness of local logistics players. In August 2003, the MOR first put on its agenda the establishment of three freight transport companies. On 9–11 December 2003, at the Second High-level Conference on China's Logistics, Fu Xuanyi, Deputy Director of the Transport Bureau of the MOR, said that the ministry hoped that the specialized freight transport companies could upgrade the traditional station-to-station railway service to the level of door-to-door service, and provide modern logistic services, such as warehousing, allocation, and tracking services.[43]

On 28 December 2003, Sun Rongfu, the vice railway minister and vice party secretary, announced the re-centralization of CRE and turned it into the China

Table 6.5 WTO timetable for foreign participation in China's logistics sector

Sector	Minority-owned joint venture	Majority-owned joint venture	No restriction
Water International transport	2001: Establishment of registered companies for the purpose of operating a fleet under the national flag of the People's Republic of China. (No restriction for other forms of commercial presence.)	N.A.	N.A.
Maritime cargo-handling services, customs clearance services for maritime transport, container station and depot services	2001	2001	N.A.
Maritime agency services	2001	N.A.	N.A.
Road transport	2001	2002	2004
Rail transport	2001	2004	2007
International forwarding	2001: Licensing system applies; foreign companies should have at least three consecutive years' experience. The minimum registered capital of a joint venture shall be no less than US$1 million.	2002: The length of operation term shall not exceed 20 years; joint venture requires to have US$120,000 in additional registered capital per branch; foreign freight forwarder can set up another joint venture after its first joint venture has been in operation for five years.	2005
Storage and warehousing	2001	2002	2004
Packaging	2001	2002	2004
Courier service (except for those currently specifically reserved to Chinese postal authorities by law)	2001	2002	2005

Source: Report of the Working Party on the Accession of China, World Trade Organization, 1 October 2001, http://big5.mofcom.gov.cn/table/wto/03.doc (accessed 27 June 2007).

Railway Parcel Express Company Ltd. (CRPEC, Zhongtie xingbao kuaidi Co. Ltd.). Two other re-centralized transport-related sideline businesses were the China Railway Container Transport Company Ltd. (CRCTC, Zhongtie jizhuangxiang yunshu Co. Ltd.), and China Railway Special Cargo Company Ltd. (CRSCC, Zhongtie tehuo yunshu Co. Ltd.).

CRCTC was the biggest firm among the three the MOR companies, with RMB 2.2 billion registration capital. Its shareholders consisted of the MOR's China Railway Container Transport Center (*Zhongtie jizhuangxiang zhongxin*), which owned 51 percent of the company, and 14 local railway administrations, which together have a share of 49 percent. CRSCC's registration capital was RMB 1 billion. Its shareholders consisted of the MOR's China Railway Special Cargo Center (*Zhongtie tuhuo yunshu zhongxin*) and 14 regional railway administrations. CRPEC's registration capital is also RMB 1 billion. Its shareholders consist of China Railway Foreign Services Company (*Zhongguo tielu duiwei fuwu Company*) and 14 local railway administrations. The former holds 51 percent and the rest together holds 49 percent.[44]

Establishment of foreign joint ventures

The logistics industry is characterized by its special features—"systems, processes and perspectives, that is, the software of the business, is just as important as the physical assets, if not more so."[45] Therefore, China wanted to expedite the restructuring of the traditional logistics resources and promote the formation of Sino-foreign joint ventures in order to enhance the management know-how and competitiveness.[46] On the other hand, foreign players were eager to cooperate because they also required Chinese partners to minimize any operational difficulties and unnecessary hostility. Even foreign players realized the importance of nurturing good relationships with government if they wanted to streamline their supply and distribution chain. Jack Perkowski of ASIMCO, the successful car-parts manufacturer, believed that localization of their businesses in China would help to ensure a truly global supply chain because relationships with government at various levels are still vitally important and they need people who not only know the language, but also the socio-political structures that would otherwise take 50 years to learn.[47]

In response to the national policy, the MOR encouraged the incumbent cadres, who had been charged with managing the relevant physical assets during the planned era, to collaborate actively with foreign partners.[48] In 2002, the MOR's container transport sub-system, the China Railway International Freight Forwarding Co Ltd. (Zhongtie guoji huoyun daili Co. Ltd), a subsidiary of the China Railway Container Transport Center, and a group of Chinese companies established a joint venture logistics company, Lanzhou Pacific Logistics Corporation Limited (Jieshite Logistics Co. Ltd.), with Canada Pan Pacific Railway Company (Asian Company). The total investment of the joint venture was US$0.42 million, and was equally shared between the Canada Pan Pacific Railway Company and the Chinese team, which included the China Railway

International Freight Forwarding Co Ltd., the Container Transport Company of the Lanzhou Railway Administration, and three other branch companies of the Lanzhou Railway Administration.[49]

In 2003, after the centralization of the railway container transport businesses and the establishment of CRCTC, the Lanzhou Pacific Logistics Corporation Limited became jointly owned by Canadian Pacific Railway, China Railway International Freight Forwarding Company Limited, and CRCTC, with equity shares of 50 percent, 21 percent, and 29 percent, respectively. The Lanzhou Pacific Logistics Corporation Limited was one of many joint ventures with foreign logistics partners. After the establishment of such logistics joint ventures, the MOR soon re-centralized the transport-related sideline businesses:

> We need to learn from our foreign partner the management know-how and state-of-the-art technology in modern logistics industry, but we also need substantial foreign capital. The MOR first re-centralized the transport-related companies and then tried to enlist foreign investment by listing the companies in the public market.[50]

In June 2004, the media widely reported that the MOR had approved CRCTC to go public and both China International Capital Corporation Ltd (Zhongguo guoji jinrong Co. Ltd.) and KPMG were said to be involved in the feasibility study of the overseas listing project.[51] The fact that the Chinese government started listing large-scale state enterprises in domestic and overseas stock markets signified a second stage of reform, which we will discuss in more detail in the next chapter about the railway construction arm in Hong Kong and overseas markets.

In 2015, after the dissolution of the MOR and the establishment of CRC, CRE was broken up, with its luggage cars and cargo trains handed over to CRC and its 18 subordinate companies. CRE provides connecting services to and from the train stations with its vans and tractors, and the rail-borne express services has returned to CRC.[52]

Obviously, the establishment of CRE as a diversified business during the era of the dual-track system and decentralization was not intended to pick the right owner to receive and operate the productive assets. Ten years have passed and the government has started to recover and re-arrange the discovered assets.

Picking the right assets

The evolutionary approach in analyzing China's railway sector unveiled that the heritage of the planned economy endowed China's railway with excessive productive assets, but the separate financial arrangements of revenue and expenditure rendered many of these assets inefficient, idle, and invisible.

The efficiency model of railway reform advocates the concentration of railway assets into the hands of private owners. But how could reform leaders demarcate the boundary of property rights if they were not sure of the existence of the idle assets, and how do they deploy the assets in a productive way? The efficiency explanation failed to explain China's railway reform simply because it takes for granted the readiness and availability of a list of productive railway assets that can be re-allocated, if not privatized. Yet in China it took more than two decades for local railway cadres to adapt to the reform policy and productively deploy the embedded idle railway assets.

China's railway reform was a complicated process. Its property rights re-arrangements were a result of two consecutive processes. First, the planned economy failed to support the enormous state sector and thus adopted the dual-track system and encouraged local cadres to mobilize their working ties and make use of idle railway assets to engage in diversified businesses. When local railway cadres coordinated or allocated idle manpower and assets, they were actually moving resources which were outside the budgetary plan, and unknown to the railway leadership. But through business diversification, local cadres gradually demarcated the boundary between the budgetary and extra-budgetary property rights.

The unintended result of the first stage of the reform was that local cadres' survival strategies helped the railway leadership "pick the rights assets." Some of these assets were involved in non-transport-related diversified businesses, such as the operation of hotels, restaurants, touring services, etc. Such sideline businesses were later separated from the transport-related core sector to support the excessive personnel levels. Some other assets were involved in transport-related services, such as railway express services and railway container transport. These assets were considered as strategically important to the national economic development and were thus re-centralized under the MOR.

Seeing that transportation was one of the major bottlenecks for further economic development, and that the logistics industry was facing global competition after entry into the WTO, the MOR started to undertake the second stage of reform to carefully phase-in foreign involvement in the form of foreign joint ventures or public listings, so as to enhance the competitiveness of the domestic players and protect them from defeat by foreign partners.

The preparation for going public involves various procedural reforms in terms of the formation of the board of directors, the adoption of international accounting systems, and the implementation of transparent corporate governance. It is still unsure whether the property rights of these newly identified state assets will be re-arranged into a form predicted by economic theory. The following two chapters on the construction and signaling sub-sectors of the MOR deal with this research question as these two sub-sectors moved faster than the transport sub-sector in terms of corporatization and going public.

Notes

1 "The Core of the Reform Involves Property Rights and Property Rights Transaction Brings in a New Wave of Change," *Sina.net*, 11 August 2006, http://gov.finance.sina.com.cn/chanquan/2006-08-11/13769.html (accessed 21 April 2015).

2 Howell contends that "the snowball effect of the Open Policy has also served to extend the agenda of reform required for opening up from the foreign trade system to other state sectors." Jude Howell, *China Opens Its Door: The Politics of Economic Transition* (Boulder, CO: Lynne Rienner Publishers, 1993), p. 188.

3 Interview, LHCBJ, December 2003.

4 In 1984, the State Council put forward the principle of "*yiye weizhu, duozhong jingying*" ("Focusing on the core business and diversifying other businesses at the same time").

5 Hu Guoming, "*Zailun tielu yunshu qiye duoyuan jingyin de jingyin fanglue yu quxiang*" ("To Discuss again the Strategies and Directions of the Diversified Operations of the Transport Enterprises in the Railway Sector") in Wu Jianchong, *Xin duoyuan jingji lun* (Theory of Neo-economic Diversification; Bejing: Zhongguo tielu chubanshe, 2001), chapter 2, appendix, p. 89.

6 The Contemporary China Editing Department, ed., *Dangdai zhongguo de tiedao shiye* (The Contemporary Railway Business in China; Beijing: Chinese Social Science Publisher, 1990), p. 108.

7 Chinese Railway Publisher, ed., *Xin zongguo tielu wushinian* (Fifty-year Review of the New China's Railway; Beijing: China Railway Publisher, 1999), p. 320.

8 "*Guanyu jiaqiang fazhan tielu duozhong jingying de ruogan yujian*" ("Some Thoughts on Enhancing the Development of Business Diversifications in the Railway Sector"), www.law999.net/law/doc/c005/1994/06/07/00103097.html (accessed 3 June 2007).

9 Interview, CQBJ, October 2003.

10 Lida Ferguson Junghans, "Workers in Transit: Chinese Railway Workers and the Journey from Plan to Market" (PhD thesis, Harvard University, May 1999), p. 249.

11 Interview, WDHHK, September 2003.

12 "*Han Shubin tongzhi wai luke songshui*" ("Comrade Han Shubin offered Water to Passengers"), *People's Railway Daily*, 3 July 1993, as quoted in Junghans, "Workers in Transit."

13 Interview, CQBJ, December 2003.

14 Interview, CQBJ, December 2003.

15 Interview, HCBJ, December 2003.

16 "*Zhongguo tielu bumen nanxia kaizhan duoyuan jingying huatie nanfang jituan zhaishen choujian*" ("The Chinese Railway Bureau go South to Start the Diversified Business and Prepare the Establishment of Huatie Nanfang Corporation in Shenzhen"), *Shenzhen Special Zone Daily*, 7 August 1995, www.chinainfobank.com (accessed 5 March 2006).

17 Interview, CQBJ, December 2003.

18 Chinese Railway Publisher, *Xin zhongguo tielu wushinian*, p. 323.

19 "*Keituo jingqu de beijing tieluju duoyuan jingyin shiti*" ("The Proactive Beijing Railway Administrations and its Business Diversification"), *People's Railway Daily*, 18 February 2003.

20 "*Nanchang tieluju huangtogang bianqian xilie*" ("The Series on the Change of Huangtugang at the Nangchang Railway Administrations"), *People's Railway Daily*, 1 November 2000, p. 1.

21 "*Tielu duojing bahuayuan zhong de yiduo qiba*" ("One of the Many Railway Business Diversification"), *People's Railway Daily*, 29 December 2002.

22 "*'Xibei Ronglian' ronglian chule sheme?*" ("What had the 'Northwest Furnace' produced?), *People's Railway Daily*, 25 February 2003.

23 "*Zhongguo tielu duoyuan jinying shiwu nian chuangshou RMB 230 billion*" ("Chinese Railway's Business Diversification Gained RMB 230 Billion 15 Years"), *Jingji Rebao*, 22 November 1999.

24 "*Tielu goujian duoyuan jingyin geju*" ("The Railway Encourages Business Diversification"), *Jingji Renbao*, 30 November 1999.

25 Interview, SYMBJ, 2001.

26 Apo Leong and Stephen Frost, "From Security to Uncertainty: Labour and Welfare Reform in China," *Asian Labour Update*, vol. 35 (2000), www.amrc.org.hk/Arch/3502.htm (accessed 24 April 2007).

27 *"Tielu yunshu qiye jianyuan zhengxiao shishi yijian"* ("Opinion on Implementation of the Policy of Reducing the Establishment and Improving the Efficiency in the Transport Sub-sector of the MOR"), www.lawbook.com.cn/lawhtm/1997/64213.htm (accessed 6 June 2007).

28 *"Tielu xitong gaige saomiao"* ("Details of the Reform of the Railway System"), *People's Daily*, 17 January 2001, www.people.com.cn/BIG5/jinji/32/180/20010117/380412.html (accessed 2 April 2015).

29 *"Tielu gaige zhouchu chenmo jijiang chonglai"* ("Railway Reform Revives and Will be Back to the Stage Soon"), *Finance*, 2 August 2004, http://finance.sina.com.cn/b/20040802/1101918481.shtml (accessed 25 April 2007).

30 *"Tielu niannei quanmian shixian san fenkai"* ("The Policy of 'Three Separation' Roll Out in the Railway Sector this Year"), *People's Daily*, 26 March 2001, www.people.com.cn/GB/jinji/32/180/20010326/425801.html (accessed 25 April 2007).

31 *"Tupoxing jingzhan: tielu sanda huoyun gongsi jiepa"* ("Breakthrough Development: The Opening of the Three Big Railway Freight Transport Companies"), *21st Century*, 11 January 2004, http://channel.eastday.com/epublish/gb/paper94/20040111/class009400004/hwz1386376.htm (accessed 25 April 2007).

32 Helen Atkinson, "China's New Logistics Choices," *Traffic World*, 9 May 2005, p. 1.

33 Interview, RCHBJ, December 2003.

34 Rong Caohe, *"Zhongtie kuaiyun ji qi dui tielu yunshu tizhi gaige de qisi"* ("China Railway Express Transport and its Implications to the Institutional Reform of Railway Transport"), *Guangli Shijie* (*Management World*), vol. 11 (2003).

35 Li Bo, *"Chong zhongtie kuaiyun kan woguo tielu kuaiyun de zhidu zhuangxin"* ("To Understand the Institutional Innovation of China's Railway Express Businesses by the Case Study of the China Railway Express Company Ltd") (M. Phil thesis, North Jiaotong University, 2002), p. 39.

36 Li Bo, *"Chong zhongtie kuaiyun kan woguo tielu kuaiyun de zhidu zhuangxin,"* p. 39.

37 Interview, LLXGZ, October 2003.

38 Rong Caohe, *"Zhongtie kuaiyun ji qi dui tielu yunshu tizhi gaige de qisi."*

39 Interview, LLXGZ, October 2003.

40 Bin Jiang and Edmund Prater, "Distribution and Logistics Development in China: The Revolution has Begun," *International Journal of Physical Distribution and Logistics Management*, vol. 32, no. 9 (2002): 791.

41 Staffan Hertzell, "China's Evolving Logistics Landscape," McKinsey & Company, Greater China Office, 30 August 2001. See also Jiang and Prater, "Distribution and Logistics Development in China."

42 Atkinson, "China's New Logistics Choices"; and "WTO Entry Unleashes Greater Opportunity and Competition in Logistics Sector," *Hong Kong Trade Development Council*, vol. 8, 15 August 2002, www.tdctrade.com/alert/cba-e0208sp.htm (accessed 29 April 2007).

43 *"Tupoxing jingzhan: tielu sanda huoyun gongsi jiepai."*

44 *"Tupoxing jingzhan: tielu sanda huoyun gongsi jiepai."*

45 Luo Wenping and Christopher Findlay, "Logistics in China: Implications of Accession to the WTO," December 2002, http://siteresources.worldbank.org/INTRANET-TRADE/Resources/WenpingFindlay_logistics.pdf (accessed 21 April 2015).

46 "WTO Entry Unleashes Greater Opportunity and Competition in Logistics Sector."

47 See Michael Mackey, "China Integrates into Global Supply Chain," *Asia Times*, 28 April 2005, www.atimes.com/atimes/China/GD28Ad02.html (accessed 20 April 2015).

48 Hertzell, "China's Evolving Logistics Landscape."

49 "WTO Entry Unleashes Greater Opportunity and Competition in Logistics Sector"; *"Zhongjia qianyue chengli gangsusheng shoujia wuliu gongsi"* ("Chinese and

Canadian Companies Sign Contract to Establish the First Logistics Company in Gangsu"), http://unn.people.com.cn/BIG5/channel22/37/183/200111/30/132513.html (accessed 29 April 2007).
50 Interview WYBJ, December 2003.
51 "*Zhongtie jizhuangxiang huozun choubei shangsh*" ("China Railway Container Transport Company Ltd. was Approved to Prepare to go Public"), *Xingbao Caijing Xinwen*, 21 July 2004, p. 2; "*Tielu gaige zhouzhu shenmo jijiang zhonglai*," *Caijing*, 2 August 2004, http://finance.sina.com.cn/b/20040802/1101918481.shtml (accessed 21 April 2015).
52 Lu Bingyang, "Freight Transporter China Railway Express Co. is Broken Up," *Caixin Online*, 6 June 2013, http://english.caixin.com/2013-06-06/100538484.html (accessed 21 April 2015).

7 The railway's construction sub-sector

Emergence of a multi-layered, state-owned enterprise group

Overview

Chapter 6 argued that the profit-sharing and dual-track systems facilitated business diversification and paved the way for property rights re-arrangements for the transport sub-sectors within the Ministry of Railways (MOR). The hiving-off of the infrastructure support and ancillary sub-sectors, as well as the separation between the core and non-core businesses in terms of institutional, financial, and personnel arrangements, were possible only after local cadres had discovered and rejuvenated the idle assets. Later, the MOR re-centralized the transport-related sideline businesses in order to concentrate efforts to develop the logistics industry. This proves that the initial decentralization policies did not necessarily lead to privatization arrangements, but discovery of idle assets.

After "picking the right assets," the MOR's leadership re-arranged them according to their specific productive functions. As discussed in the previous chapter, the railway express and container transport businesses were re-centralized because both involved the use of the railway assets, and due to the network characteristics, market competition was not desirable. This was predicted by the hypothesis that the more likely market failure, and the more strategically important the newly identified assets, the more likely they will be re-centralized by the state.

The assets discovery and recovery mechanism applied not only within the MOR's transport sub-sector, but also the construction and signaling sub-sectors. The construction and signaling sub-sectors are chosen as they were part of the network services section which was different from the sideline business sector discussed in the last chapter. The construction and telecommunication sectors were strategically very important in China during the period of its economic take-off. The state-led policy in these sectors therefore was very significant and they serve as two case studies demonstrating the railway assets recovery mechanism.

Focusing on the railway's construction arm, this chapter shows that (H2) decentralization does not necessarily lead to privatization, and that (H3) decentralization identifies idle assets. More importantly, this chapter also demonstrates that (H4) the re-centralization of the railway construction assets involved strategic consolidation of specific, if not unique, productive resources and technology for large-scale infrastructure construction. Since market competition was not yet mature, the state consolidated and re-centralized construction assets in order to avoid fragmented development, enhance synergic effect, and nurture national champion corporations so they could compete with global competitors.

The first section of this chapter argues that although the break-up of the China Railway Construction Corporation (CRCC) followed the logic of vertical disintegration from the transport services sector in MOR, it should not be seen as a policy of decentralization, de-politicization, or anything close to partial privatization. Rather, it was part of the state policy to re-centralize the construction sector by taking over the construction sub-sectors from various ministries, including the MOR, and subsuming them back to the State Assets Management Commission (SAMC, which was later renamed State-owned Assets Supervision and Administration Commission, SASAC).

The second section briefly reviews the historical development of the MOR's construction sub-sector and illustrates that under the planned regime, the construction arm was included in the railway sector to ensure self-sufficiency. Such a comprehensive structure was typical for many other ministries and local governments. As a result, various sub-sectors performing the same construction function were scattered across different authorities all over the country. These construction sub-sectors were embedded with excessive and idle productive assets. They were strategically important to China's economic development, yet poorly coordinated and wastefully duplicated because they were administered under different supervisory units.

The third section goes on to discuss the property rights re-arrangements of the MOR's construction sub-sector. Similar to the transport sub-sector, the construction sub-sector adopted various profit-sharing and dual-track systems. After the initial rush to diversify into small-scale and non-construction related sideline businesses, local railway construction cadres gradually engaged in large-scale but non-railway-related construction projects. Later, the central leadership assembled the scattered construction assets, spun them off from the railway sector, and consolidated the resources under SAMC. In addition to the two construction sub-sectors originally under the MOR, the CRCC and the China Railway Engineering Corporation (CREC), the scattered construction components of other state sectors were also re-centralized and grouped as centralized enterprises (*yangqi*) under SAMC.

The last section discusses the property rights re-arrangements of the state assets upon the establishment of a number of construction group corporations. After re-grouping the existing and newly identified productive state assets according to their professional or industrial function, China's state sector is entering into its second phase of reform. With the pressing need for capital investment and technology know-how, the CRCC and CREC subsidiaries established different cooperative arrangements with foreign counterparts which resulted in the emergence of hybrid structures and diluted state ownership.

Discovery of excessive construction assets before spinning off from the MOR

In September 2000, the MOR spun-off CREC, the CRCC, and the China Loco-motive & Rolling Stock Industry (Group) Corporation (CLRSIC; Zhongguo jiche cheliang gongye zonggongsi). In 2003, it further spun-off the China Railway Resources Corporation (CRRC; *Zhongguo tielu wuzi zonggongsi*) and the China Railway Communication Co. Ltd. (CRCoC; *Tiedao tongxin xinxi yaoxian zheren gongsi*).

Such restructuring, however, did not involve decentralization of property rights bundles. The Chinese government did not give more autonomy to these large-scale infrastructure services sub-sectors after they had been spun-off from the railway sector, not to mention privatizing them. Rather, these sub-units were re-centralized and subsumed into another supervisory body: SAMC. As a result, the Chinese government agencies were involved in the shaping of the adminis-tration and operations of all the selected centralized enterprises (*yangqi*). The purpose of such restructuring was to solve the problems of fragmented distribu-tion of resources created by the ideology of self-sufficiency under which many state sectors had been so proud of being "large and self-sufficient (*da'er quan*)," with a wide range of ancillary sub-sectors supporting the core unit.

In view of the rising global competition, especially after China's entry into the WTO, the Chinese government selected a few strategic sectors and requested them to join forces and to achieve economies of scale. Instead of *da'er quan*, the state adopted the policy of "saving the large and letting the small go" (*zhuada fangxiao*). The main idea was, on the one hand, to redistribute the productive resources according to the sector's core function and to enhance its comparative advantage, and, on the other hand, to allow the small-scale sideline businesses to de-link from the core section and survive in the market.

The case study of the CRCC lays out a two-level argument. First, from the perspectives of the railway sector, the CRCC was spun-off to help the MOR focus on its core function. This was proved by the fact that all other infrastructure and ancillary sub-sectors, such as those involved in construction, signaling, manufacturing, engineering, education, medical, etc., were spun-off from the railway regime; and that the transport-related businesses, including the traditional passenger and freight transport and the newly developed special transport service, such as railway express services, were re-centralized within the MOR.

Second, from the perspective of the construction sector, the CRCC was sepa-rated from the railway sector as part of the re-centralization policy to tighten the state's iron grip on the coordination of the country's construction services. The following historical review of the CRCC, from its incorporation into the MOR in 1984 to its separation from the MOR in 2000, proves that the re-distribution of the construction resources were largely a factor of strategic consideration—when the construction industry was identified as an important component of the national development plan, either during wartime or on the edge of economic take-off, the Chinese leadership made sure that a critical mass of the sector's productive assets were put under close administrative scrutiny.

From the PLA to the MOR

During the Sino-Japanese War and the Civil War, the control of the railroad was very important militarily because most battles took place along the rail lines.[1] The Chinese Communist Party (CCP) had a special railway task force (*hulujun*) to repair and protect the railways and to ensure military transport using railways. On 5 July 1948, the CCP turned the railway task force into a formal unit of the Railway Troop (*tielu zongdui*) with 14,000 soldiers.

In January 1949, the Railway Bureau of the Chinese People's Revolutionary Army (*Zhongguo renmin geming junshi weiyuanhui tiedaobu*) was established to inherit and manage the fragmented railway system all over the country, and was later renamed as the Ministry of Railways of the Central People's Government (*Zhongyang renmin zhengfu tiedaobu*).[2] Stressing the importance of scale economy and self-sufficiency, the MOR integrated all functional components together, including the transport, manufacturing, engineering, construction, material supply, and signaling components.

The Railway Troop, established earlier in 1948 and under the administration of the Central Military Commission, was expanded to form the Chinese People's Liberation Army Corps of Railway Soldiers (*zhongguo renmin jiefangjun tielu bingtun*), and subsumed under the MOR. However, in June 1950, when the Korean War broke out, the Central Military Commission took back the power to command the railway soldiers, and sent the troop to North Korea to repair and build the railways there. In October 1953, the Railway Troop returned to China. In 1954, it was garrisoned in Beijing and became a technical task force under the People's Liberation Army.

The railway soldiers were retained within the army establishment, not returned to the MOR, because the Chinese leadership believed that such a special task force should be easily deployed to perform special missions whenever the country or its strategic partners required special military-technical support. Many railway cadres interviewed joined the Railway Troop when they were 15–18 years old: "The state centralized and retained us in the realm of its military capacities because we could be useful in foreign relationship building at a particular point of time."[3]

They quoted an old saying in Chinese, "*yangbing qianri, yongzhai yishi*" ("maintain the army for a thousand days to prepare for one particular moment"). Such a particular moment came again in 1964 when the Vietnam War broke out. As before, China sent its Railway Troops to repair the rail tracks under aerial attack. A railway manager, who was the head of a branch unit of the CRCC in 2003 at the time of interview, told me that he had been sent to Vietnam in 1969:

> It was part of the state's policy to help Vietnam to fight against the U.S. In 1969, I was about 15 years old when I was allocated to join the Railway

Troop as a railway soldier. Being paid RMB 6 yuan a month, we were sent to repair the signaling system along a rail track 20 km away from Hanoi in Vietnam. There were about 300,000 soldiers in the whole Railway Troop at that time, setting out from Guangxi and making shelters from palm-leaf and bamboo on our way to Hanoi.[4]

It was obviously very dangerous and costly to provide such technical aid to Vietnam, but the Chinese leadership believed that the entire mission to "save communist brothers" was a national strategy to forge an alliance against Western imperialism.

The Central Military Commission regarded the Railway Troop as the "triumph card" to enforce the legitimacy of the Communist Party, and thus kept the troops under close scrutiny, although the troops were functionally more related to the railway sector. It was only after 1978 that the CCP considered subsuming the Railway Troop back into the MOR.

In December 1982, the State Council and the Central Military Commission announced "The Decision about Subsuming the Railway Troop into the MOR" ("*guanyu tiedaobing pingru tiedaobu de jueding*"). On 1 January 1984, the Railway Troop, which comprised nearly 150,000 members, was officially merged into the MOR, and renamed the "Engineering Headquarters" (*gongcheng zhihuibu*).

From Engineering Headquarters to Construction Corporation

After what the railway army called the process of "*bing gai gong*" (migration from soldiers to workers), the newly established Engineering Headquarters started to take part in the construction of the national railway network. Like the transport sub-sector and many other sub-sectors, the Engineering Headquarters had to sign various responsibility contracts with the MOR. Following the same argument for the transport sub-sector in Chapter 3, local cadres negotiated with the MOR for a higher operating cost and lower construction targets.

The Railway Troop brought in 150,000 members to the MOR. The original army corporation (*shi*), division (*tuan*), brigade (*lian*), and company (*ying*) were renamed as engineering bureau (*gongcheng ju*), engineering division (*gongcheng chu*), engineering section (*gongcheng duan*), and engineering team (*gongcheng dui*). However, because of the existing construction team in the MOR, there were simply too many construction workers within the railway sector and insufficient budgetary funds to support the additional establishment. In 1985, after the MOR had adopted the dual-track system in all its sub-sectors to encourage local cadres to set up economic entities for self-financing purposes, the Engineering Headquarters started to look for business opportunities beyond its core function:

After the process of bing gai gong, railway soldiers brought with them huge number of dependents who need to work for their living. Also, many injured or sick members had to be settled with basic necessities ... as a result, local cadres began to develop diversified businesses.[5]

On 1 July 1989, the MOR turned the Engineering Headquarters into the China Railway Construction Corporation (CRCC, *zhongguo tielu jiangzhu zonggongsi*).

Between 1984 and 1995 there were 739 enterprises and 28,524 staff members in the CRCC working in diversified businesses, such as business catering, property development, and other processing industries.[6] By 1999, local cadres in the CRCC were involved in a wide range of sideline businesses in manufacturing, farming, livestock rearing, freight forwarding, touring, and catering, etc. The rush for diversification led to enormous duplications in businesses. As a result, supply exceeded demand, and the entire sideline sub-sector under the CRCC recorded an overall deficit of RMB 74.12 million yuan.[7]

In view of the unsatisfying result of the non-construction sideline businesses, the Engineering Headquarters re-arranged their idle production assets and their business networks to undertake various projects outside the railway sector, such as the construction of subways, bridges, buildings, highways, irrigation, and electrification systems:

> We simply did not have enough work to do at that time when we first joined the MOR. The MOR had another construction arm under their original establishment in 1949. Many of them are old comrades working in the railway sector for ages, and the MOR allocated more resources to them, so we had to look for construction projects outside the railway sector by ourselves.[8]

A cadre working in the CRCC subsidiary said they were trying very hard to look for businesses and their efforts paid off. They got a head-start over others because they accumulated business relations and mutual trust with the relevant working partners:

> We were all railway soldiers and used to travel around very often during wartime. Many of us therefore went out and searched for potential construction work all over the country. Since we had been under the PLA system, local governments gave us face, put their trust in us, and were willing to contract out various construction projects to us. Nearly 70 percent of our construction work came from outside the railway system.[9]

The major shift in terms of the share of construction work between railway and non-railway projects came in 1993 and 1994, when the share of construction investment for railway projects undertaken by the team of railway soldiers declined drastically from 71 percent to 23 percent. In 2000, the share recovered to 40 percent, and in 2002 it dropped again to 20 percent (Table 7.1).

Table 7.1 Total value of construction projects undertaken by the CRCC, 1992–2002 (RMB 100 million)

Year	Total	Railway (share of total %)	Road	Airport/pier	Water/electricity facility	Property	Others
1992	41.85	27.08 (64.72)	5.99	0.34	0.88	2.57	4.98
1993	129.16	91.65 (70.96)	11.59	1.66	3.31	9.88	11.07
1994	131.33	29.64 (22.57)	36.45	2.17	4.69	29.55	28.61
1995	N.A.	N.A.	N.A.	N.A.	N.A.	N.A.	N.A.
1996	152.00	21.00 (13.82)	55.50	2.88	6.57	36.70	29.20
1997	231.00	50.20 (21.73)	88.50	3.67	14.60	38.90	35.40
1998	320.00	118.00 (36.88)	122.00	2.41	16.30	35.40	25.80
1999	288.00	99.60 (34.58)	129.00	1.13	7.84	32.00	18.40
2000	372.00	151.00 (40.59)	133.00	1.90	11.10	34.90	40.10
2001	408.67	102.32 (25.04)	183.42	4.43	21.59	44.67	52.25
2002	533.99	107.44 (20.12)	262.85	n/a	24.53	53.97	52.58

Source: *China Railway Construction Corporation Annual Report*, 1993–2003.

From the MOR to Central Enterprise Industrial Committee

On 28 September 2000, the CRCC was spun off from the MOR and put under the administration of the Chinese Central Enterprise Industrial Committee (CCEIC, *zhongyang qiye gongwei*). Although the separation of the CRCC from the MOR was to transfer from one state agent to another, the consolidation of the once fragmented construction assets represented the state-led re-centralization effort to tighten control of selected industries.

The infrastructure construction industry, in particular railway construction, involves very specific technology and equipment. The high start-up cost thus rendered the market competition approach inappropriate when the government wanted to nurture national champions within a short period of time after entry into the WTO. The construction sector was going to be opened to foreign participation in a scheduled timeline after China's entry into the WTO. In view of the fierce competitive scenario, the Chinese government implemented horizontal economic integration, re-aligned production assets by their industrial function, and commanded the establishment of one or more domestic flagship companies in each industry.

Re-centralization of selected state-owned property rights

The origin of horizontal economic integration

Chapter 4 discussed the functionally, administratively, and socially integrated structure of the Chinese railway system. In order to ensure self-sufficiency, the MOR integrated everything—the transport and infrastructure services, the ministry, and the regional railway administrations, as well as the core profit-making and non-profit-making ancillary sectors. Without doubt, this was a highly centralized system.

The subsequent railway reform in terms of profit-sharing and responsibilities contracts did not bring about decentralization and privatization, yet they provided fuzzy property rights arrangements, which, together with the dual-track policy, helped identify idle production assets. After discovering the idle state assets by local cadres, the next stage of reform was for the central leaders to recover the newly discovered assets by re-grouping them according to their core businesses, and establishing flagship companies.

The rationale of such consolidation of strategically important assets to foster national economic development was not new in practice. As early as the mid-1980s, the Chinese government began to study the successful experience of Japanese *keiretsu* and Korean *chaebols*. These East Asian later-comer countries were able to catch up with the Western economies by nurturing conglomerate-type industrial organizations. In July 1980, the State Council put forward "The Provisional Regulation on Promoting Economic Association" ("*Guanyu tuidong jingjilianhe de zanxing guiding*") to initiate the policy of horizontal integration.[10]

In 1986 and 1987, the State Council put forward the "Regulations on the Problems of Further Promoting Horizontal Economic Association" ("*Guanyu jinyibu tuidong hengxiang jingji lianhe ruogan wenti de guiding*") and "Several Opinions on the Organization and Development of Enterprise Groups" ("*Guanyu zujian he fazhan qiye jituan de jidian yijian*"), respectively, and the Chinese government began to form selected enterprise groups by establishing multi-tiered organizational structures: the mother company at the first tier, closely related companies at the second tier, semi-closely related companies at the third tier, and loosely related companies at the outermost tier.

Under such horizontal associations, enterprise groups were formed among state enterprises which had close business relations. For example, they might be "in supplier and buyer relationships," or they wanted to "share brands, marketing channels, or production facilities, etc.," or "they might establish associations between civilian and military units, as well as associations between industry, university, and research units."[11] Such horizontal associations bound together those assets that could be useful for the core businesses. The purpose was to prevent duplicate investment and overproduction, and turn the newly aggregated productive assets into a flagship enterprise within the field of its core business.[12]

In May 1991, the State Economic Reform Commission (SERC, which was later renamed as the National Development and Reform Commission, NDRC) issued, and the State Council approved and announced, "The Major Points of the Economic and Institutional Reform in 1991" ("*Guanyu 1991 jingji tizhi gaige yaudian*"), which further encouraged horizontal integration (*hengxiang jingj lianhe*), and the establishment of large-scale, trans-departmental, and trans-regional enterprise groups (*qiye jituan*).[13]

By the end of 1993, there were more than 7,000 registered business groups (*qiye jituan*) in China. One type of these business groups was a small group of private firms voluntarily connected together with some kinds of family or social ties. Another type was formed by the state's administrative bureau, of which the chief selected a group of firms under the bureau's jurisdiction, and encouraged the establishment of various business relations among the firms. Typically, such business groups comprise a core parent company, which had investments in, or maintained some kind of control of, its member companies. The second type of the business groups were commonly found in a wide range of central industries in China, such as natural resources, transportation, raw materials, and high-tech industries.[14]

The successful experience of turning the medium- to large-scale state-owned enterprises into business groups paved the way for the horizontal integration of the last batch of super-sized centralized enterprises (*yangqi*). These centralized enterprises, involved in China's major industry and the policy of horizontal integration, were indeed a kind of "assets recovery mechanism" for the state to exhaust the best-quality assets and re-group them by their industrial functions. The recovered assets were then re-centralized under the newly established regulatory commission—the State-owned Assets Supervision and Administration Commission (SASAC).

The big boss: the SASAC

In 2003, the State Council combined CCEIC with the sub-units of different state agents, such as the former State Economic and Trade Commission, the former Work Committee of Enterprises of the Communist Party of China Central Committee, the special task force of the Ministry of Finance and the Ministry of Labor and Social Security, to form a super state agent: the SASAC. All these sub-units had been supervising various aspects of the reform of the state-owned enterprises.[15]

In 2003, Li Rongrong, the director of the SASAC, announced the Commission's missions at a press conference held by the Information Office of the State Council. He clearly stated that the Chinese government chose to re-centralize and re-regulate selected large enterprises (Table 7.2).

In order to regulate the centralized enterprises, the SASAC dispatched supervisory boards to the chosen large enterprises on behalf of the state and took charge of daily management of the supervisory board. However, working in one of the 196 central enterprises under the SASAC, a manager of the CRCC thought there was no difference between reporting to the MOR as "*popo*" and the SASAC as "*da laoban*":[16]

> When we were under the MOR, the state gave us administrative commands and supervised us through the vertical system of the ministry. Now that we are under the SASAC, the state still supervises us. The difference is that the state does not claim its legitimacy from its political authority as a party state, but from its economic identity as a major investor (*chuzizhe*). But the changes, so far, are nominal—it is true that we do not need to report to dozens of *popo*, but we still have to listen to our *da laoban*.[17]

Zhang Zuoyuan, the former director of the Economic Research Institute of the Chinese Academy of Social Science, explained that the SASAC was to exercise the rights of major shareholders:

> According to the Chinese Company Law, shareholders are entitled to three rights, namely the right to receive income generated from the invested property, the right to participate in the decision-making process for important issues, and the right to choose the management.[18]

Table 7.2 The SASAC's missions

1 Appoint, remove, and evaluate the executives of enterprises through legal procedures.
2 Reward and punish the executives according to their performance.
3 Draft laws, administrative regulations, and related rules on the management of the state-owned assets.
4 Direct and supervise the work of local state-owned assets management according to law.
5 Undertake other tasks assigned by the State Council.

Source: The "SASAC's Responsibilities & Targets," *People's Daily*, 22 May 2003, http://english. people.com.cn/200305/22/eng20030522_117060.shtm (accessed 23 April 2015).

The tightening policy: carving up the state assets and announcing the core businesses

When first established as the central enterprises' *da laoban*, the SASAC brought in nominal changes, and local cadres did not feel the difference between reporting to *popo* and reporting to *da laoban*. However, the Chinese government, through the SASAC, regrouped the state's productive assets according to their business function, and clarified the state's role as a major shareholder. Such reform was different from the planned regime in which the productive assets had been allocated according to administrative concerns, and the state assets were claimed to be owned by the people.

In view of the increasing interaction with the global economy, the SASAC soon merged and re-aligned the best combination of the state's productive assets and facilitated the establishment of a few national champions. In 2003, Zhang Zuoyuan, member of the Chinese People's Political Consultative Committee of the People's Republic of China and researcher of the Institute of Economics of the Chinese Academy of Social Sciences, expected that the share of state-owned assets would therefore decline from 35–36 percent to 20 percent:

> In the next few years, the state will re-arrange the state-owned sector by focusing more resources on industries which have strategic impact on China's economic development. The Chinese government will allocate state-owned capital to large-scale enterprises and decentralize small and medium enterprises. The absolute state-owned assets will increase, but the relative amount will decrease gradually.[19]

When the SASAC was established in 2003, director Li Rongrong asked all 198 central enterprises to compete for the top spot in their respective sector in three years' time; after these three years, he would subsume the losers into the top three enterprises.[20] At the end of 2004, the SASAC began to regulate in batches the core businesses of central enterprises so that the state-owned central enterprises could focus on the designated service. In October 2005, when the SASAC announced the core businesses of the third batch of central enterprises, Li Rongrong complained that most central enterprises were too diversified in their businesses scope:

> Some of them didn't even know what their core businesses were, and this led to inefficient resource allocation.... These designated industries were very important in enhancing our national security and economy development. We still need to control, influence and motivate the state-owned economy.[21]

It was under such a national policy of specialization of state assets that the China Railway Construction Corporation and China Railway Engineering Corporation were designated to focus on the construction and property development industries. All together the SASAC had recognized the core businesses of 96 central enterprises in three batches.[22] In the same year, 2005, at the Third Conference on Merging and Financing of Chinese Enterprises (*Zhongguo qiye pigou yongzhi gaofenghui*), Wang Zhongming, the director of the Policy Research Center of the SASAC, said that the SASAC would eventually merge the 198 central enterprises into 30–50 giant enterprises.[23]

Further discovery and recovery of construction assets under the SASAC

Through the SASAC, the Chinese government consolidated and tightened the control over the construction industry, and urged the CRCC to further expand its productive assets. As the CRCC was later ranked the 485th in the Fortune Global 500 companies in 2006,[24] the SASAC started to further re-arrange the assets with a view to arranging an IPO.

Global competition: the rise of the construction industry

The construction sector has been playing a very important role in China for many reasons. China's continual economic growth required enormous construction work on infrastructure, public utility systems, factories, warehouses, etc. Moreover, the increasing purchasing power of China's middle class meant that there would be enormous demand for housing projects.[25]

In fact, China's fixed asset investment surged enormously in the early 1990s. The annual rate of increase reached 23.8 percent, 42.6 percent, and 58.6 percent in 1991–1993, respectively. The Chinese government tried to curb the overheated investment and duplicated construction by enacting land-use regulations, suspending new development zones and restricting investment in raw materials. Consequently, the growth of the fixed asset investment fell from 58.6 percent in 1993 to 5.1 percent in 1999, and then picked up speed again and leapt from 5.1 percent in 1999 to 26 percent in 2005.

While China's construction market was expanding, it was considered a "labor intensive and less open industry."[26] As a result, foreign players had very limited access to the industry before China's entry into the WTO. Only in 2001 was the construction sector opened and foreign companies allowed to set up majority-owned, joint venture construction companies in China. From 2004 onwards, foreign companies could establish wholly foreign-owned enterprises and undertake certain types of construction projects.[27] By October 2006, there were 1,400 foreign companies from more than 30 countries/regions that set up construction and design enterprises in China, of which more than 700 were wholly foreign-owned or majority foreign-owned companies.[28] In view of the enormous list of infrastructure projects in China in its 11th Five-Year Plan, foreign construction counterparts, with their advanced construction technology and management know-how, would bring in fierce competition. The Chinese government therefore had to prepare local construction companies well to withstand this (see Table 7.3 for a list of China's key transport infrastructure projects for 2006–2010).[29]

Table 7.3 China's 11th Five-Year Plan for transport infrastructure

---

Construction of six inter-city passenger railways, including one between Beijing and Shanghai, which costs 140 billion yuan, and one between Beijing and Tianjin; and upgrading of five existing railways, including one between Datong and Qinhuangdao. The total investment in the construction of 19,800 km new railways is 1,200 billion yuan.

Construction of 14 expressways including one from Beijing to Hong Kong and Macao.

Construction of transit systems for the transportation of coal, imported oil, gas, and iron ore; construction of container transport systems at 12 seaports, such as Dalian, Tianjin and Shanghai; and construction of coal transit and storage bases in eastern and southern China.

Construction of channels at the Yangtze River, the Pearl River and the Beijing–Hangzhou Canal; and construction of ports along inland rivers.

Expansion of airports in Beijing, Shanghai, and Guangzhou; relocation of two airports in Kunming, Hefei, and other airports in central, western and northeastern China.

Source: "China's Key Transport Infrastructure Projects for 2006–2010," *People's Daily Online*, 6 March 2006, http://english.people.com.cn/200603/06/eng20060306_248313.html (accessed 23 April 2015).

In fact, foreign players had eyed the potential in the construction market well before China's entry into the WTO. Between 1994 and 1996, the number of minority foreign-owned construction joint ventures increased from 1,200 to more than 2,000.[30] Foreign companies also tried to get into the sector first by providing construction raw materials and machinery, such as timber, prefabricated homes, furniture, and other value-added wood commodities, to China. The US Department of Commerce estimated that the Chinese construction machinery market alone would reach US$16.7 billion with over US$3.6 billion in imports in 2004, and urged American construction equipment firms to move quickly into China.[31]

While joining the WTO posed enormous challenges for the Chinese construction enterprises, it also offered them golden opportunities to take part in the international construction market. The Chinese media reported that, between 1999 and 2003, the average growth rate of the global construction market was 5.2 percent.[32] Global Insight, Inc., a private information company, conducted "The Global Construction Study 2003," and forecasted a continued growth of 5 percent in construction investment through 2012, with India and China growing at considerably higher rates of 9.2 percent and 7.9 percent, respectively.[33] According to the Hong Kong Trade Development Council,

> Although Chinese construction enterprises have won some places in the top world 225 construction contractors, they are mostly placed behind in the ranking. The China Construction Corporation, a leader in the sector, only places at about twentieth. All the Chinese enterprises have less than 5% of the total market share the world over.

The fierce international competition thus pushed the Chinese government to establish a few flagship construction companies to avoid vicious competition and cut-throat price bidding for various projects at very low technical levels.[34]

Further consolidation of state-owned construction assets

In view of the global competition, the SASAC consolidated the large-scale and state-owned construction corporations and ensured an ordered competition. As a selected centralized enterprise in the construction sector, the CRCC had to grow big and become competitive in order to maintain its first-rank status:

> We were asked to be the national team, to be big and strong (*zuoda zuo-qiang*) and to get a place on the list of the Fortune Global 500. The SASAC gave us very specific targets. If we cannot become the top three in the construction sector in China, we will be subsumed under other construction enterprises in the near future. Of course we want to be able to report directly to the SASAC. This gives us more power to negotiate for more resources and preferential policies.[35]

Officials in the subsidiary of the CRCC worried that their status would be downgraded if the CRCC was no longer the first-tier centralized enterprise:

> We were all iron brothers (*tieger*) since the days when we were under the PLA. We want to be the "chicken head" (*jitou*), not the "phoenix tail" (*fengwei*). If we fail to be the leader in the industry, the SASAC will consider us as incompetent in making the best use of the state assets. As such, the SASAC could appoint another construction enterprise to take over our assets.[36]

Mergers were common practice among state-owned centralized enterprises. By March 2005, the SASAC reduced the number of central enterprises from 196 to 176 through state-led mergers. Li Rongrong told reporters that he had compiled a list of survivors and would further cut the number to 80–100 enterprises.[37] As a centralized enterprise under the SASAC, the CRCC was desperate to be on the list of survivors.

One way to grow big was to consolidate more productive assets. After the CRCC had been detached from the MOR, the SASAC recombined the fragmented and idle assets, which had been put under the MOR for administrative reasons, and integrated them with the CRCC according to their professional functions:

> When the CRCC joined the MOR in 1984, we were supposed to back up the railway sector and act as its construction arm. At that time, the state sectors were arranged in such a way that each administrative unit was self-sufficient. As such, many resources and production assets were duplicated and allocated at the convenience of various geographical locations of the regional administrations.[38]

Before the spin-off, each and every railway regional administration, as well as the railway headquarters, had their own survey, design, and construction teams for various railway construction projects. These research teams were fragmented and did not have any incentive to develop new technologies beyond the routine construction works. Wang Zhenhou, the general manager of the CRCC, admitted that the CRCC was large but not competitive (*daer buqiang*): "[W]e do not have a strong enough R&D capability and therefore cannot develop our own innovative technologies to catch up with other large-scale construction corporations in developed countries."[39]

Now that the MOR was focusing on its core transport businesses, the CRCC could have the small-scale and scattered survey and design institutes integrated, and so formed a stronger technical and research arm. In 2003 the SASAC merged 20 small-scale railway design institutes of various regional railway administrations into the design subsidiaries of the CRCC. Such a merger optimized the CRCC's production chains in the hope that it could become the flagship of the construction industry.[40] Later that year, the SASAC integrated the China Civil Engineering Construction Corporation (*zhongguo tumu gongcheng jituan gongsi*) into the CRCC. The China Civil Engineering Construction Corporation had been established by the MOR in 1979, and focused on overseas railway construction projects (see Figure 7.1 for the CRCC's re-organization in 2003).[41]

Local survival strategy: further discovery of idle assets

In addition to non-railway-related construction industry, CRCC officials began to discover idle assets which were embedded in the sector during the planning era and joined efforts to develop diversified businesses which were closely linked to its core business. For example, in 2006 the China Railway Material Corporation (CRMC) under the CRCC, took advantage of its previous role in sourcing and supplying construction raw materials to get involved in supply chain operation and logistics services.

Since they used to supply iron and steel to the MOR, the CRMC coordinated between the buyers and suppliers and established long-term and reliable business relations. Instead of material sourcing and delivery, the CRMC diversified the scope of its businesses and engaged in both the upper and lower streams of the supply chain services. For the upper stream operation, the CRMC estimated the demand for steel billets, iron ore, and pig iron, coordinated the production schedule, and cut down the cost for storage. For the lower stream operation, the CRMC supplied various construction materials, such as bulk cement, plywood, and haydite press bricks.[42]

The successful shift from engaging in non-construction-related sideline businesses to construction-related operations was a result of local cadres' willingness and abilities to discover the idle productive resources, which had been idle or were simply non-existent before. However, the initial rush to start various non-construction-related sideline businesses easily led to duplication of investment and wasteful allocation of state assets. There were many reported cases in which cadres were found siphoning off state resources. Such businesses were not sustainable and cadres with an entrepreneurial flair soon realized that, in order to

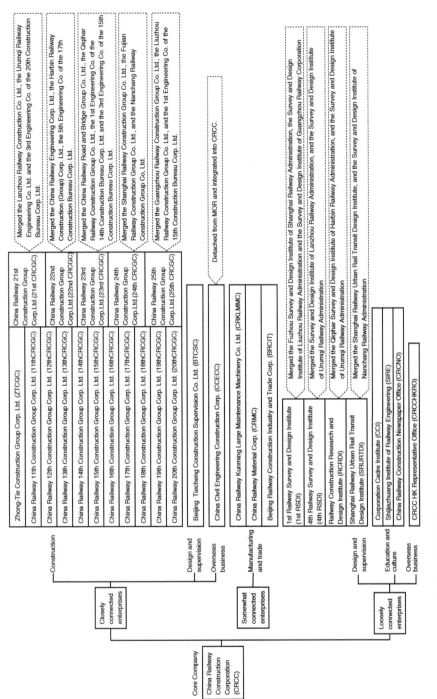

Figure 7.1 Re-organization of CRCC.

survive the global competition, they needed to be more competitive and diversify businesses along their comparative advantage.

Adopting the perspective of "picking the right owner," these CRCC cadres who had once been "bad managers" gradually turned out to be "good managers." This explains why it is more useful to analyze the transformation process with the framework of "picking the right assets."

The emergence of a construction business group: a property rights hybrid

After the centralization and consolidation of the construction-related assets, and the discovery of idle assets, the Chinese government became well aware of the available productive assets. Such an "assets picking strategy" paved the way for further property rights re-arrangements. The question was what further property rights arrangements were. Will the corporation converge to the efficiency model? Or will it emerge into a model of its own characteristics?

Similar to the case study of the transport sub-sector, the Chinese government did not follow the efficiency model and privatize the CRCC in any way close to what had happened in the Eastern European countries. There was no sign of mass privatization, voucher privatization, or management buy-out. Rather, a more pragmatic property rights adjustments took place and the resulting structure of a state-controlled, multi-layered ownership hybrid was in place to facilitate integration with the global system. Such a mimicry of the Western organizational structure was instrumental for getting into the overseas market, receiving FDI, or obtaining important technology and management know-how.

"Going out" strategy

As early as 2002, Zhen Silin, Deputy Party Secretary of the CCEIC, emphasized that China would develop a team of famous, independent, and competitive business groups in various strategic fields and hope that members of this national team would be on the Fortune Global 500 list.[43]

Before entering into the CCEIC, the CRCC had been involved in many overseas construction projects. During the 9th Five-Year Plan, the CRCC gained various overseas construction contracts with a total aggregated value of US$480 million, and achieved an operating revenue of US$390 million. Since 1995, the CRCC has been ranked in the top 225 international contractors by *Engineering News-Record* (ENR), an authoritative US engineering magazine.[44]

In 1999 and 2002, the CRCC, in a joint venture with other domestic and overseas companies, bid successfully for the construction contracts of the West Rail of the Kowloon Canton Railway Corporation, and the Disneyland Line of the Mass Transit Railway Corporation in Hong Kong.[45] According to the CRCC's web page, the corporation has successfully undertaken quite a number of overseas contracts to provide labor sources and construction service in projects such as the Upper Swat Water Diversion Project in Pakistan, the Supreme Court Building in Macau, the Wanhuabo in Osaka, Japan, the Waste Water Plant in Singapore, and the Mojiabo Flyover in Kuwait City.[46] In 2005, one of the CRCC's subsidiaries, the 18th Construction Bureau Corporation Ltd. participated in more than 30 construction projects in developing countries such as Pakistan, Nigeria, Saudi Arabia, Oman, Mauritania, Dubai, Thailand, Sudan, and Madagascar.[47]

In order to undertake overseas construction projects, the CRCC had to cooperate with foreign counterparts to establish conglomerates in compliance with the WTO tendering procedures. The corporation therefore adjusted the organizational structure to facilitate interaction with the global system, and yet maintain majority state ownership and control.

Emergence of a state-controlled, multi-layered hybrid

Following the policy of horizontal economic integration, the Chinese government further advocated the directive of "Saving the Large and Letting the Small Go," (*zhuada fangxiao*) and encouraged state-owned enterprises to rationalize their ownership by acquisition, management buyouts, and bankruptcy. As a result, from 1997 to 2004, the number of state enterprises decreased by 47 percent from 262,000 to 136,000, yet the total profits generated by the remaining state-owned enterprises increased ten times, from RMB 79 billion to RMB 737 billion (US$59.9 billion; Figure 7.2).

However, management buyouts (MBOs) have soon elicited public concern about asset stripping because of the legal loopholes and the resulting less-than-transparent privatization mechanism.[48] The MBOs thus required more supervision on managerial behavior. Otherwise, it would be very difficult for the government to protect the state's assets.[49] In April 2005, the SASAC put forward

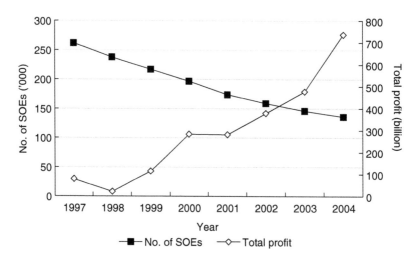

Figure 7.2 Number of and total profit generated by SOEs, 1997–2004 (source: China's Financial Yearbook, 2000 and 2005).

Document No. 78(2005) to regulate further MBOs in small- and medium-sized enterprises, and prohibit MBOs at large state-owned enterprises.[50]

As such, the SASAC sought to enhance central supervision over the property rights re-arrangements of the centralized enterprises. The Chinese government paid special attention to these centralized enterprises for a few reasons: First, the Chinese leaders did not want to see the unemployment rate soar and the complete demolition of communist ideology; second, it was simply impossible for the state to withdraw all at once.[51] Third, the leaders wanted to ensure that a critical mass of the strategic assets remained under state control so as to strategically "maintain the guiding role of the state-owned economy" ("*baochi guoyao jingji de zhudao diwei*").[52]

In view of the above-mentioned reasons, large-scale and key state-owned enterprises, such as the CRCC in the construction industry, and others in telecommunications, energy, and steel sectors, were all put under close scrutiny in 2005. A middle-ranking CRCC cadre explained that the multi-layered organizational structure of a business group was typical for many centralized enterprises, which needed central regulation, foreign capital, and technological input at the same time:

> The mother company is at the core (*hexing ceng*), surrounded by a second-tier of closely connected enterprises (*jinmi ceng*); and a third-tier of somewhat-closely connected (*ban jinmi ceng*) and loosely connected enterprises (*songsan cent*). While the core company remained state-owned, the closely connected enterprises became an insulating layer.... Nothing changed in terms of property rights arrangements within our mother company. But down to the second-tier level, we, according to the Company Law, turned 16 bureaus into limited liabilities group companies.[53]

Figure 7.3 shows the new organization of the CRCC.

Having worked in one of these limited liabilities companies for over 20 years, a CRCC middle-manager further explained that a limited liability company was established through joint investment by at least two and not more than 50 shareholders:

> Most of the CRCC's second-tier limited liabilities companies were established with two shareholders—the majority of 70–80 percent of the shares went to the mother companies, the CRCC, and the remaining 20–30 percent of the shares belong to a workers' shareholding committee (*zhigong chigu hui*).[54]

The fact that these second-tier closely connected enterprises were limited liability companies with multiple shareholders gave them a modern organizational structure. It became even easier for foreign companies to work with and to make sense of the management practice when the second-tier companies adopted the Western corporate governance model, which had boards of shareholders, boards of directors, boards of supervisors, and general managers.[55]

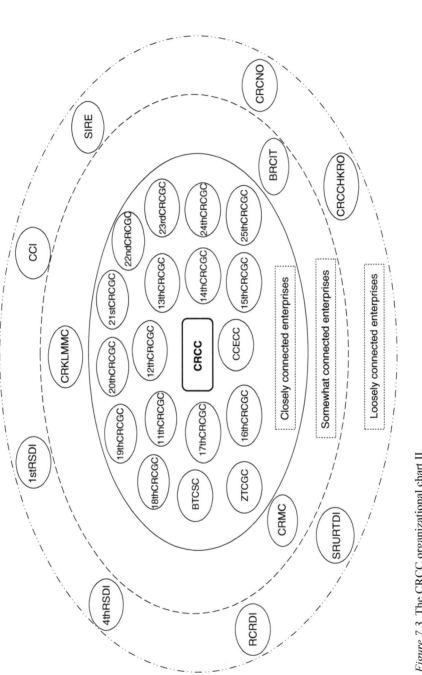

Figure 7.3 The CRCC organizational chart II.

Note

* See Figure 7.1 for full names of company initials.

Corporatization without privatization

According to the Company Law, shareholders should be liable to the extent of their capital contribution, and the company as a whole is liable for its debts to the extent of all of its assets. It appeared that the idea of corporatization of the second-tier closely connected enterprises, and the introduction of employees' shares, was at least to move toward de-politicization, if not partial privatization. But the trick here was two-fold. First, the state-owned mother company held the majority shares, and the leadership of the company remained more or less the same as before. Second, the workers' shares were owned collectively, in the name of a special fund which has been retained as reserve money—namely, *baihan jieyu* (saving from the extra-budgetary revenue).

Since 1985, *baihan jieyu* has been a typical arrangement in the state-owned construction sector, via which staff members could guarantee stable income. When the state planned for the annual construction work for a particular state-owned enterprise, it also set the ceiling for the total wage (*gongzi zong'e*) for that particular enterprise according to the fixed ratio called *baihan*, a short form for *baiyuan chanzhi gongzhi hanliang baogan zhidu* (Responsibility System of Total Wage per Every Production of One Hundred Renminbi), which stipulated the maximum amount of expenses in wages allowed to pay for every completed construction item worth RMB100. The companies were then free to allocate these funds among the staff, as long as the total amount did not exceed the wage ceiling. However, if the company undertook non-railway, extra-budgetary construction work and exceeded the planned output, the companies were allowed to retain a portion of the extra-budgetary revenue in a reserve fund called *baihan jieyu* (Saving for *baihan*). These funds were accumulative and would be used to top up staff salaries during the years when there were not enough construction projects. Local cadres called this practice "saving up during well-performing years for under-performing years" (*"yifeng buqian"*).

A second-tier company chief explained that although the state requested him to deposit the *baihan jieyu* into a special bank account, he chose to keep it as floating debt and used the funding as daily cash flow:

> During the process of corporatization, we formally set aside the reserve money as a kind of capital investment from the staff, and would allocate the shares according to the staff members' years of services and rank. In return, the staff members were entitled to a percentage of the bonus according to the size of the shares they received. However, they could not trade or transfer the shares when they left the company or retired from work.[56]

Since the staff members enjoyed only part of the income right and their control and transfer rights were attenuated, their so-called staff shares were considered as empty shares (*xugu*). As a result, the CRCC's first-tier subsidiaries were typical state-owned enterprises which become "modern enterprises" only nominally because they were still owned by the state de facto and lack independence from their parent state-owned enterprises.[57]

Dilution of state ownership taking shape

Dilution of state ownership usually occurred in two ways at the second-tier limited liabilities companies, which served as an insulating layer between the first-tier mother companies and the rest. First, local cadres might design a particular way to offer real shares (*shigu*) to their staff members. Compared to the incomplete shares mentioned in the last section, such substantial shares were transferable, although the transaction is limited to insiders at the time when the staff members quit or retired from their job.

Second, dilution of state ownership also took place when the CRCC and its subsidiaries set up joint ventures with private companies, either domestic or foreign, in order to join forces to bid for local or overseas construction tenders. For example, in 2004 the CRCC formed a joint venture with Beijing Metro Corporation and German-based Siemens to bid for the franchised operation of metro loop 4 in China.[58] In 2005 the China Railway Engineering Corporation co-invested RMB 3.75 billion with Baotou Iron and Steel Group and Inner Mongolia Qinghua Group in the Linhe–Ceke Railway. In 2006 the China Railway 20th Construction Bureau Company Limited formed a joint venture with Areeya Property Plc. to bid for the construction contracts for ten railway routes in Thailand, with an estimated value of Bt550 billion (US$17.3 million). Zhou Fu, China Railway 20th's vice president, said the group had been interested in partnering a Thailand firm to bid for the government's mega-projects since 2005.[59] Table 7.4 shows a selection of CRCC joint ventures.

The CRCC was therefore emerging into a property rights hybrid, with the state being the majority shareholder, and the staff members becoming minority shareholders, of which some were holding nominal and some substantial shares. There were also various domestic and foreign joint ventures growing out of the hybrid. The resulting structure, so far, was a state-controlled business group which was twisted to suit the form of the Western organizational structure. According to a construction manager of one of the CRCC subsidiaries, it was good to mimic the structure first:

> This is what we now call to follow the western framework and to retain the Chinese's essence (*xixue weiti zhongxue weiyong*). It will take some time for us to get used to the new system and when the operation is mature enough, the state could gradually retreat from the CRCC.[60]

However, whether the state will really give up its shares to private owners needs further empirical study on the development of the CRCC in the future.

Iron grip control

The Chinese government established the SASAC to realize the government's role as owner and investor. Instead of claiming that state assets were collectively owned by the people, the Chinese government for the first time acknowledged that a select group of centralized enterprises were owned by a "special organization

Table 7.4 Selected CRCC joint ventures

Projects	Cooperative or joint venture partners	Total investment (RMB)	Remarks
Xianyang Weihe No. 3 Bridge	The CRCC (55%) China Railway 20th Bureau Co. Ltd. (35%) Xianyang Urban Construction Bureau (10%)	120 million	Build–operate–transfer model
Jingcheng Highway phase II	The CRCC (80%) Beijing Capital Highway Development Company Ltd. (20%)	3.4 billion	Build–operate–transfer model
Yusui Highway (Chongqing Section)	The CRCC (80%) Chongqing Highway Development Co. (20%)	4.8 billion	Build–operate–transfer model
Naxu Railway	The CRCC (35%) Sichuan Railway Bureau (25%) Zhongtie Construction Center of the MOR (20%) Luzhou City Infrastructure Investment Co. & Sichuan Xinfu Group (20%)	1.45 billion	Build–own–operate model
Cross Yangtze River Tunnel in Nanjing	The CRCC (80%) Nanjing Transport Group (10%) Pukou Guozi Company (10%)	3 billion	Tunnel-boring machine (TBM) with diameter of nearly 15 meters would be adopted in the construction of the tunnel.

directly under the State Council (*guowuyuan teshe jigou.*)"[61] As a result, in view of various economic imperatives, the Chinese government did not really think of decentralization and privatization.

Various property rights re-arrangements took place within the CRCC as its cadres discovered and the SASAC recovered various productive assets, all of which were re-centralized under the SASAC. This "assets picking" process shaped the property rights boundaries of the CRCC, which paved the way for a corporatization arrangement that did not lead to privatization or reduction of state ownership. Rather, newly corporatized companies engaged in cooperative and joint venture construction projects, resulting in a state-owned multi-layered, property rights hybrid.

The property rights re-arrangements that took place within the construction sub-sector again illustrate that the Chinese government would not loosen its grip on strategically important industries. The next chapter will deal with another sub-sector of the railway regime, the telecommunication sub-sector, and will illustrate the formation of a more complicated property rights hybrid—with the introduction of more shareholders by exchange of shares among the telecommunication subsidiaries, which led to the emergence of a different type of state-owned, cross-ownership hybrid.

Notes

1 X. Xue, F. Schmid, and R. Smith, "An Introduction to China's Rail Transport Part 1: History, Preset and Future of China's Railways," *Proceedings of the Institution of Mechanical Engineers, Part F, Journal of Rail and Rapid Transit*, vol. 216, part 1, pp. 153–163.

2 Xue *et al.*, "An Introduction to China's Rail Transport," p. 157.

3 Interview, CHFBJ, December 2003.

4 Interview, CHFBJ, December 2003.

5 *Zhongguo tielu jianzhu zhonggongsi nianjian, 1945–1995* (China Railway Construction Corporation Perennial Report, 1945–1995; Beijing: China's Railway Publisher, 1999), p. 9.

6 *Zhongguo tielu jianzhu zhonggongsi nianjian, 1945–1995*, pp. 9–10.

7 Qin Yifang, "*Zhongguo tiedao jianzhu zhonggongsi duozhong jingying fazhan zhanlue yanjiu*" ("Research on the Development Strategies of Diversifying Businesses under the China Railway Construction Corporation") (MBA thesis, Beijing Jiaotong University, March 2001).

8 Interview, GKCBJ, 2003.

9 Interview, CHFBJ, December 2003.

10 Chen Jiagui and Huang Sujian, eds., *Shichang jingji yu qiye zuzhi jiegou de biange*, (Market Economy and Reform on Organizational Structure of Enterprise; Beijing: Jingji guanli chubanshe, 1995).

11 Lee Keun and Hahn Donghoon, "Market Competition, Plan Constraints, and Asset Diversion in the Enterprise Groups in China," (working paper, July 1999), p. 8.

12 Chen and Huang, *Shicang jingji yu qiye zhuzhi jiegou de biange*.

13 "*Guowuyuan pizhuan guojia tigaiwei 'guanyu 1991 jingji tizhi gaige yaudian' de tongzhi*" ("The State Council approved the State Reform Commission's Announcement on 'the Summary of the Economic and Institutional Reform in 1991'"), *People's Daily*, 20 May 1991, www.people.com.cn/BIG5/33831/33836/34146/34190/2543628.html (accessed 31 December 2005).

14 Lisa Keister, *Chinese Business Groups: The Structure and Impact of Interfirm Relations during Economic Development* (Oxford: Oxford University Press, 2000), pp. 68–71.

15 "China Set Targets for State-owned Assets Management," *China Daily*, 22 May 2003, www.chinadaily.com.cn/en/doc/2003-05/22/content_166023.htm (accessed 23 April 2015).

16 *Popo* (mothers-in-law) is the nickname for varying levels of government supervisory bodies, and represent a different authority. Chinese experts had long been arguing that too many mothers-in-law in China easily led to conflicting demands and inflicted the usual coping strategy—*guanxi*. See David Lampton, "The Implementation Problem in Post-Mao China," in David Lampton, ed., *Policy Implementation in Post-Mao China* (Berkeley, CA: University of California Press, 1987), pp. 3–24; and David Granick, *Chinese State Enterprises: A Regional Property Rights Analysis* (Chicago, IL: University of Chicago Press, 1990), ch. 8. *Da laoban* (big boss) refers to the SASAC, which has subsumed the supervising roles of *popo* at different levels.

17 Interview, ZJBJ, December 2003.

18 "*Sudu jigou gaige fangan, Zhang Zuoyuan: guoziwei zujian zhihou*" ("A Quick Look at the Institution Reform, Zhang Zuoyuan: After the establishment of the SASAC") *Chinese Industrial and Commercial Post*, 7 March 2003, http://big5.china.com.cn/chinese/zhuanti/288786.htm (accessed 23 April 2015).

19 "*Sudu jigou gaige fangan, Zhang Zuoyuan: guoziwei zujian zhihou*," 7 March 2003.

20 "*Yangqi chongzu buru 'jiaoshaqi*" ("The Restructuring of the Centralized Enterprises is Entering a Stage of "Competition and Demolition"), *Canquan shichang*, 29 November 2005, http://sme.sina.com.hk/cgi-bin/news/show_news.cgi?Type=build&date=2005-11-29&id=223076 (accessed 13 May 2007).

21 "*Disanpi yangqi zhuye gongbu*" ("Announcement of the Core Businesses of the Third Batch Centralized Enterprises"), *xinhuanet*, 13 October 2005, http://news.xinhuanet.com/house/2005-10/13/content_3611078.htm (accessed 13 May 2007).

22 "*Disanpi yangqi zhuye gongbu.*"

23 "*Yangqi chongzu buru 'jiaoshaqi.*'"

24 Fortune Global 500, http://money.cnn.com/magazines/fortune/global500/2006/full_list/401_500.html (accessed 25 January 2008)

25 Roseanne Freese, "China's Construction Market: A New Star in the East," *Ag Exporter*, January 2001, www.findarticles.com/p/articles/mi_m3723/is_1_13/ai_70395048#continue (accessed 18 December 2005).

26 Low Sui Pheng and Jiang Hongbin, "Internationalization of Chinese Construction Enterprises," *Journal of Construction Engineering and Management*, November/December (2003): 589–598.

27 Wholly foreign-owned enterprises can undertake the following four types of construction projects: (1) Construction projects wholly financed by foreign investment and/or grants; (2) construction projects financed by loans of international financial institutions and awarded through international tendering according to the terms of loans; (3) Chinese–foreign jointly constructed projects with foreign investment equal to or more than 50 per cent, and Chinese–foreign jointly constructed projects with foreign investment less than 50 per cent but technically difficult to be implemented by Chinese construction enterprises alone; and (4) Chinese-invested construction projects which are difficult to be implemented by Chinese construction enterprises alone can be jointly undertaken by Chinese and foreign construction enterprises with the approval of provincial government. See "Schedule of Specific Commitments on Services," in Annex 9 of the Legal Instruments on China's Accession to the World Trade Organization.

28 "*Zhongguo jianzhuye de duiwai kaifang zhiyi*," ("Open up China's Construction Industry, Part I"), *Zhongguo Jianshe bao*, 8 January 2007, China Infobank, http://210.177.11.50/gate/big5/www.chinainfobank.com/ifbase643-l0lyaxncaw4~/-VGV4 dC5kbGw~?-ZGI9Qkcmbm89MjI5Njc3JmNzPTI2MzQ0Njcmc3RyPc3i18q9qNb+# (accessed 29 September 2007).

29 Shi Liu, "Construction and WTO," tdctrade.com, 9 October 2000, www.tdctrade.com/report/indprof/indprof_001003.htm (accessed 18 December 2005).
30 *Zhongguo jianzhu nianjian 1997 and 1998* (China Construction Annual Report 1997 and 1998; Beijing: China Construction Industry Publisher, Ministry of Construction, 1998, 1999), pp. 230–231, 157–158.
31 "China Construction Machinery Market," US Commercial Service, United States of America Department of Commerce, www.buyusainfo.net/docs/x_7782452.pdf (accessed 30 June 2007).
32 *"Jianzhu qiye hawai kuozhang zhengdangshi"* ("Right Timing for Construction Enterprises to Expand Overseas Businesses"), *Dalian Construction Engineering Cost Information Net*, 9 September 2005, www.dlzj.com.cn/sitefunction/Reader.asp?URL=/manager/cmt/file/file2199.htm&Table=cmt&Class=1 (accessed 17 May 2007).
33 "New Study Forecasts Improving Outlook for Global Construction Industry," Global Insight, Inc., 10 June 2003, http://prninternational.com/cgi/news/release?Id=103640 (accessed 4 January 2006).
34 Liu, "Construction and WTO."
35 Interview, ZYLBJ, January 2004.
36 Interview, ZYLBJ, December 2003.
37 Barry Naughton, "SASAC Rising," *China Leadership Monitor*, vol. 14 (2005): 7.
38 Interview, WBTJ, January 2004.
39 *"'Zhongtie hangmu' yao yuanhang: Zhongguo tiedao jianzhu zonggongsi zongjingli Wang Zhenhou tan rushi"* ("'Chinese Railway's Flagship' are Sailing: Wang Zhenghou, the General Manager of CRCC Talks About the Entry into the WTO"), *Zhongguo jiaotong bao*, 22 January 2002.
40 *"Zhonggongsi, zhonggongsi dangwei fachu tongzhi gongbu zhenghe zhongzu huazuan zhonggongsi guanli de yuantielu sigong sheji danwei"* ("The CRCC and the Party Secretary of the CRCC Announce the Restructuring of the Construction and Design Units under the MOR"), *Zhongguo tiedao jianzhu bao* (China Railway Construction Post), 12 February 2004.
41 *"Zhongyang qiye zhongzu diyao"* ("Speeding up the Restructuring of Central Enterprises"), *Shanghai Securities News*, 17 December 2004, p. 1.
42 *"Zhongtie jianshe jituan wuzi gongsi kaizhan duoyuan jingying jiesheguo"* ("Successful Results of the Development of Diversified Businesses of the China Railway Construction Material Supply Corporation"), *Zhongguo jianshe bao*, 7 February 2007, China Infobank, http://210.177.11.50/gate/big5/www.chinainfobank.com/ifbase643-l0lyaxncaw4~/-VGV4dC5kbGw~?-ZGI9SEsmbm89MjY5MDQ1MCZjcz0zMjYzNz UxJnN0cj3W0Mz6vajJ6LyvzcXO79fKuavLvg~~ (accessed 1 July 2007).
43 *"Guojia jiang caiqu cuoshi peiyang yipi guoji jingzhengli qiang de daxing kuaguo gongsi da qiye"* ("The State Will Implement Policies to Nurture a Team of International Competitive and Large-scale Transnational Enterprises"), *Economic Times*, 31 January 2002, www.wisers.com.ezproxy.ust.hk (accessed 3 May 2006).
44 The ENR's Top 225 International Contractors is a comprehensive index based on the calculation of the non-home country revenue of international contractors. See *"Jianding xingxin tuanjie fenjin wai jianshe guonei yiliu juyou guoji jingzhenli de xiandai qiye jituan e fendou"* ("Be Confident and United in Endeavoring to Become the First-Grade, Domestically and Internationally Competitive Modern Enterprise Group"), *Zhongguo tiedao jianzhu bao* (China Railway Construction Post), 5 May 2001, www.wisers.com.ezproxy.ust.hk (accessed 3 May 2006).
45 *"Jiutie zhai pizun siyi xitie heyue"* ("KCRC Awarded Again the 0.4 Billion West Rail Contract"), *Tai Kung Po*, 28 July 1999, www.wisers.com.ezproxy.ust.hk (accessed 3 May 2006); *"Zonggongsi chuangru xianggang ditie jianshe shichang"* ("CRCC Enters into the Market of the Construction of the Mass Transit Railway in Hong Kong"), *Zhongguo tiedao jianzhu bao* (China Railway Construction Post), 16 September 2002,

www.wisers.com.ezproxy.ust.hk (accessed 3 May 2006); see also the CRCC webpage, www.chinarailway.com.hk/en/west_rail.htm (accessed 19 May 2007).

46 CRCC webpage, www.chinarailway.com.hk/en/p_overseas.htm (accessed 19 May 2007).

47 *Qiye de mingtian zainali?*" ("Where is the Future of the Enterprise?"), *Zhongguo tiedao jianzhu bao* (China Railway Construction Post), 3 December 2005, www.wisers.com.ezproxy.ust.hk (accessed 3 May 2006).

48 The debate about MBOs in China was stirred up by Larry Lang, a professor in the Business Administration Department of the Chinese University of Hong Kong, who gave a lecture on 9 August 2004 at the Fudan University in Shanghai. During the lecture, Lang charged that many state-owned enterprises, including high-profile firms such as Greencool, Kelon, and Haier, had engaged in MBOs as a way to strip state assets, benefit the new ownership, and cheat the public. See "Experts Debate MBO, Draining of State Assets," *China Daily*, 6 September 2004.

49 Andrew G. Walder, "Privatization and Elite Mobility: Rural China, 1979–1996," Working paper, Asia/Pacific Research Center, July 2002, http://aparc.stanford.edu/publications/20205 (accessed 19 May 2007).

50 See the document "*Qiye guoyou chanquan xiang guanliceng zhuanrang zangshi jueding*" ("Temporary Regulations on the Transfer of Assets of State Enterprises to Management") on the SASAC website, www.sasac.gov.cn/gzjg/cqgl/200504150122.htm (accessed 19 May 2007). For a more detailed discussion on MBOs in China, see Naughton, "SASAC Rising."

51 See Naughton, "SASAC Rising," p. 1.

52 Wang Shengke and Mo Fei, "*Guozi 'guanwang' gushi gaige*" ("The SASAC 'Wait and See' on Equity Market Reforms"), *21 shiji jingji baodao*, 16 May 2005, http://finance.sina.com.cn/stock/y/20050514/10581587629.shtml (accessed 23 April 2015).

53 Interview, ZYLBJ, December 2003.

54 Interview, ZYLBJ, December 2003.

55 "*Zhonggongsi, zhonggongsi dangwei fachu tongzhi gongbu zhenghe zhongzu huazuan zhonggongsi guanli de yuantielu sigong sheji danwei*" ("CRCC and the Party Secretary of CRCC Announce the Restructure of CRCC and Railway Construction and Design Units"), *Zhongguo tiedao jianzhu bao*, 12 February 2004; "*Tieyiyuan shili honghou gongji zuoyue*" ("The First Survey & Design Institute of the MOR is Well Established with Excellent Business record"), *Lanzhou Morning Post*, 22 November 2005.

56 Interview, GKCBJ, December 2003.

57 Simon S.M. Ho, "Corporate Governance in China: Key Problems and Prospects," Centre for Accounting Disclosure and Corporate Governance School of Accountancy Working Paper no. 1, Chinese University of Hong Kong, 2003, p. 5.

58 "Beijing to Seek Investors for new Metro Lines," *People's Daily*, 19 December 2004, http://english.people.com.cn/200412/19/eng20041219_167881.html (accessed 23 April 2015).

59 "Chinese Firm joins Railway Bidding Fray," *The Nation*, 21 January 2006, www.nationmultimedia.com/search/page.arcview.php?Clid=6&id=126505&usrsess= (accessed 20 May 2007).

60 Interview, HCBJ, December 2003.

61 Barry Naughton, "The State Asset Commission: A Powerful New Government Body," *China Leadership Monitor*, vol. 8 (2003): 1–10.

8   The railway's telecommunications sub-sector

Overview

Chapter 7 focused on the assets discovery and recovery of the Ministry of Railways' (MOR's) construction sub-sector, and argued that the restructuring did not lead to privatization. Rather, the reform led to fuzzy and negotiable fiscal arrangements and resulted in an unexpected process of "picking the right assets" before "picking the right owners." The study of the MOR's construction sub-sector also illustrates that when the state recovered the newly discovered assets, it re-arranged the property rights through the State-owned Assets Supervision and Administration Commission (SASAC), and created a state-owned, multi-layered business group. This chapter continues to strengthen the assets discovery and recovery argument by studying the restructuring of another railway sub-sector, the signaling sub-sector, and further illustrates the development of the resulting state-owned enterprise hybrid.

This last chapter on the railway's property rights re-arrangements studies the telecommunications sub-sector. As early as the late 1990s, China started to reform its telecommunication industry. Thus the reform of the MOR's telecommunications sub-sector has entered into the later stage of reform, which allows more historical data to illustrate and verify the assets discovery and recovery hypotheses. Moreover, the rapid technological development of the telecommunications industry perpetuated a wide range of new production capacities which did not rely on fixed line connections. Such production capacities had either become idle during the planned era or were simply non-existent because local cadres did not have the right incentives to innovate. During the reform era, the impending threat of fierce market competition and the desire to negotiate for the unidentified and unclaimed productive assets drove local cadres or managers to change to engage in diversified businesses. Such an "asset picking" strategy allowed the central leadership to recover the productive assets and paved the way for the emergence of a multi-layered, cross-ownership hybrid.

The organization of this chapter is as follows: The first section illustrates the strategic importance of the telecom industry in China. The second section documents the recent telecommunications restructuring, which involved a mixed policy of decentralization and re-centralization. The result was the creation of an orderly and yet competitive environment for the domestic telecommunication operators to gradually shape the best possible allocation of production assets.

The third section discusses the assets discovery process which took place in the signaling sub-sector of the MOR, and the emergence of the railway telecommunications company. Similar to what happened to the construction sub-sector, the signaling sub-sector first diversified into non-signaling businesses during the dual-track system, before it was spun-off from the MOR. It gradually turned to focus on commercialization of its telecommunications services and strove to become an independent and competitive telecommunications operator.

The last section focuses on the process of asset recovery. While local cadres tried to innovate and survive the orderly competitive environment, they got hold of unclassified production capacities quickly. They also developed the business as far as possible and formalized and retained the property rights before the state began to revert the policy. Soon the railway telecommunications assets were consolidated under the SASAC. On the one hand, local cadres further initiated various joint venture or cooperative projects to receive more foreign or domestic capital, management, and technology know-how. On the other hand, the Chinese government shaped the organizational structure of its state-owned companies to comply with the Western practice of transparent corporate governance, for example the state-owned companies were managed by boards of directors and general managers. The case of the telecommunications enterprises illustrates that while the Chinese government maintained its iron grip on the core enterprises, it allowed cross ownership or IPO arrangements in the second- or third-tier subsidiaries. The resulting property rights arrangements for reformed centralized enterprises were still state-owned, multi-layered enterprise groups, albeit with gradually diluted state ownership.

Telecommunications availability and economic development

A great deal of research argues that the availability of telecommunications and economic development are positively correlated. For example, the World Bank estimated that, by 2000, 70 percent of all employment in OECD countries would be information-related, and countries which could not provide adequate facilities to generate and transmit timely information would not be globally competitive and would suffer economic stagnation.[1] Ding and Haynes used a panel data of 29 regions in China between 1986 and 2002 and concluded that investment in telecommunications in China promoted regional economic growth and the effect was more significant in less developed regions.[2] The Chinese government was well aware of the importance of telecommunications for economic development. Both the Ministry of Aeronautics and Aerospace and the Ministry of Postal and Telecommunications had conducted quantitative research and concluded that investment in telecommunications was positively related to China's national income.[3]

However, China's investment in the telecommunications sector fell short of demand. Between 1953 and 1980, China increased its investment in the telecommunications and postal sectors from RMB 0.48 billion in the First Five-Year Plan (1953–1957) to RMB 1.8 billion in the Fifth Five-Year Plan (1976–1980).[4] But, in terms of the share of total fixed assets investment in China, it dropped from 0.8 percent to 0.6 percent. At that time, most resources were diverted into heavy industry.

The minimal initial investment in the first few Five-Year Plans set the pattern for proportionally low investment in the telecommunications sector in the following years. However, what was surprising was that, between 1989 and 1998, a decade after China had adopted the open policy and fueled a boom in economic development, China's telecommunications revenue expanded at an average annual rate of more than 30 percent, more than three times the growth of its GDP.[5]

In view of the positive relationship between telecommunications and economic development, the Chinese government needs to reform the sector and improve the telecommunications services. According to the efficiency model, the best way is to separate the operations of telecommunications from the regulatory authority, liberalize and commercialize telecommunications operations, introduce market competition, and attract enough financial resources to privatize the sector. For example, the World Bank's study on the performance indicator for the telecommunications sectors suggests that poor regulatory policy led to an imbalanced development pace between telecommunications infrastructure and economic activities in many developing countries.[6] In fact, the World Bank was very confident about transforming state telecommunications monopolies to private-led, competitive markets:

> When well done, this reform can be a positive-sum game in which all stakeholders gain—customers, existing and new operators, employees, domestic and foreign investors, and the government. Faster growth, better and new services, lower costs, and, eventually, lower prices follow.[7]

However, similar to the MOR's transport and construction sub-sectors, such an economic model of restructuring fails to explain the more complicated reform and restructuring in the telecommunications industry. In stark contrast to the orthodox advocates of decentralization and privatization,[8] the Chinese government centralized the dispersed and fragmented telecommunications assets into a few telecommunications operators, and administered an orderly competition among them in preparation for the foreign competition following the entry into the WTO.

State-led telecommunications reform in China

Spinning off the assets and hanging on to power

Telecommunications had long been a monopolistic sector in China. The national telecommunications network was largely put together for military use. After the

Chinese Communists took power in 1949, the new government established the Ministry of Posts and Telecommunications (MPT) in 1950 to oversee postal and telecommunications services in China. The MPT employed 1.2 million staff members and comprised 30 regional posts and telecommunications administrations (PTAs), each supervising numerous bureaus and enterprises at the municipal, prefecture, and county levels.

After its establishment, the MPT was organized in a semi-military fashion and telephone service was restricted to government use. In the 1960s, other ministerial and provincial bodies, such as the People's Liberation Army (PLA), the MOR, the Ministry of Electronics Industry (MEI), the Ministry of Electric Power (MEP), the Ministries of Transportation and Petroleum (MTP), the Ministry of Foreign Trade (MFT), the People's Bank of China, and other municipal governments were allowed to run their own dedicated telecommunications networks for internal use. While these telecommunications networks ensured that each dedicated user department was self-sufficient in terms of communications, they became fragmented, without much consistency and coordination.

In the early 1980s, China adopted the open door policy and rapid economic growth created enormous demand for telecommunications services. The vast opportunities for the expanding market provided enormous incentives for local cadres to gradually commercialize the fragmented, and sometimes idle, telecommunications assets.

In 1992, the MEI, the MOR, and the MEP submitted a joint proposal to the State Council to integrate the respective telecommunications networks and establish another national telecommunications operator. Such an initiative fitted well into China leadership's reform strategy at that time, which sought to introduce inter-firm competition but maintain state ownership and regulatory scrutiny.

In December 1993, the State Council approved the joint proposal and authorized the establishment of a new telecommunications operator called China United Communications Corporation (China Unicom, *Liantong*). Through China Unicom, the MEI, the MOR, and the MEP were allowed to combine the telecommunications assets to provide restricted local and long-distance services, and various other services such as radio communication, telecommunications engineering, and other value-added services.[9] These idle assets had been put under their jurisdiction for the purpose of self-sufficiency but were idle for a long time.

The establishment of China Unicom was the first move in China to re-arrange its fragmented and dispersed telecommunications assets and to introduce competition with the MPT in the telecommunications market. In the same year, the Chinese government spun-off China Telecom from the MPT, which will focus more on its regulatory role in the telecommunications market. In 1994 the MEI proposed to form another telecommunications company, the Ji Tong Communications Co. Ltd. (*Jitong*). Obviously, there were still some idle assets left in the MEI after the formation of China Unicom. As a result, after discovering the assets for development of ordinary telephone services, the MEI realized that there were remaining idle telecommunication assets which could best be used to provide specific e-government projects.

Jitong's three most famous projects were Golden Bridge, Golden Card, and Golden Customs. Golden Bridge was the principal backbone network for all other golden projects to operate on. Golden Card was a nationwide network linking all automatic teller machines of the People's Bank of China. Golden Customs was a network for customs offices to share trade- and customs-related information.[10] On 12 January 1994, *Jitong* was officially established, comprising 26 shareholders of which the MEI held a majority stake.[11]

Similar to the MOR's transport and construction sub-sectors, the first phase of the reform in the telecommunications sub-sector was actually a state-led strategy to re-partition the state assets. The separation of the telecommunications regulator and operator and the formation of three telecommunications companies were aimed at re-grouping different state assets by their economic or industrial functions, instead of the original attachment to specific administrative units. Such property rights re-arrangements, however, did not lead to outright privatization or even decentralization.

The "5 + 1" pattern: restructuring without decentralization

In 1996, after the formation of three telecommunications operators, the State Council formed the State Informatization Leading Small Group (SILSG) to look after the national strategy on telecommunications and informatization reform. The SILSG was chaired by Zou Jiahua, the vice prime minister, and comprised the senior officials of 24 commissions, ministries, and other government offices.[12]

In March 1998, the state centralized its regulatory power over the telecommunications industry by merging the MPT and the MEI and the Ministry of Radio, Film, and Television into a new authority, the Ministry of Information Industry (MII). The MII was supposed to play the role of a telecommunications regulator independent from the telecommunications operators.

In 1999, the MII further re-arranged China Telecom's production assets and formed two new telecommunications companies—China Mobile Corporation (China Mobile, *Zhongguo yidong tongxun jituan*), and China Satellite Communications Corporation (China Satellite, *Zhongguo weixing tongxun jituan*). China Mobile took up the mobile communications business from China Telecom, and China Satellite assumed part of the assets from China Telecom to operate satellite-related business and internet protocol telephone services. In addition, China Unicom was injected with China Telecom's paging networks, while China Telecom retained the fixed line telephone network. The five telecommunications carriers, China Telecom, China Unicom, Jitong, China Mobile, and China Satellite, were all closely linked with the MII.

In June 1999 the government established another state-owned telecommunications operator, China Network Communications Group Corporation (China Netcom, *Zhongguo wangluo tongxun jituan gongsi*). China Netcom was founded by the Chinese Academy of Sciences (CAS), the Information and Network Centre of the State Administration of Radio, Film and Television (INCSAR), China

Railways Telecommunications Centre (CRTC), and Shanghai Alliance Investment Limited (Shanghai Alliance). China Netcom focused on broadband networks.

In 2000, the MOR spun off its signaling assets and formed the China Railways Communications Corporation (China Railcom, *Zhongguo tielu tongxun jituan*), which provided domestic, fixed-line telecommunications, and internet-related businesses. Details of the emergence of China Railcom will be covered later.

So, in seven years' time, China created seven telecommunications companies, all state owned, and each providing one or two specific telecommunications services. These seven telecommunications operators more or less comprised all the existing operable telecommunications assets in the country, which had once been dispersed under different ministries. They were eventually re-arranged and put together under close scrutiny of the State Council, the MII and the SILSG.

On 12 December 2001, one day after China's entry into the WTO, the State Council announced the break-up of China Telecom into the northern and southern parts. The telecommunications assets in the northern part, including Beijing, Tianjin, Inner Mongolia, Hebei, Shanxi, Liaoning, Jilin, Heilongjiang, Henan, and Shandong, would merge with China Netcom and Jitong to form the China Netcom Group Corporation (China Netcom Group). The new China Netcom inherited about 30 percent of the network from the old China Telecom. The telecommunications assets in the southern part, covering 21 provinces, municipalities, and autonomous regions, would retain the original name and formed the China Telecommunications Corporation (China Telecom Corp). Renee Gamble, a telecom expert at International Data Corporation (IDC) Asia-Pacific, a renowned IT research firm, believed that splitting China Telecom was aimed at attracting foreign investors and listing the companies overseas.[13]

This second round of telecommunications restructuring re-demarcated the state-owned telecommunications assets into the "5+1" pattern: two mobile carriers—China Mobile and China Unicom—and three fixed-line operators—China Netcom, China Telecom, and China Railcom—and one satellite company—China Satcom.

China had committed to a schedule of market access six years after its accession into the WTO in 2001. Such an agreement stipulated a sliding scale for foreign investment in fixed-line, mobile, paging, and value-added services (Table 8.1). The Chinese government had to toughen up the domestic operators before foreign players could get into the market. Wu Jichuan, the minister of information industry explicitly expressed that he was happy to administer the necessary competition in the telecommunications sector,

> The move broke important ground in the war against monopolies. The two new fixed-line operators can gradually enter each other's business sovereignty to start competitive operation. And in the competition, more new services will be provided to convenience customers.... We finished a job which took European countries seven to eight years to complete in only three years. The telecoms market will then enter a relatively stable period which is good for the operators.[14]

Table 8.1 Maximum share of foreign investment in telecommunications joint venture after WTO accession

Sector	In 2001	By 2002	By 2003	By 2004	By 2005	By 2006	By 2007
Fixed-line services[a]	—	—	—	25% (geographical restriction: 3 cities)[b]	—	35% (geographical restriction: 17 cities)[c]	49% (no geographical restriction)[d]
Mobile services[e]	25% (geographical restriction: 3 cities)	35% (geographical restriction: 17 cities)	—	49% (geographical restriction: 17 cities)	—	49% (no geographical restriction)	—
Value-added telecommunication services[f] and Paging service	30% (geographical restriction: 3 cities)	49% (geographical restriction: 17 cities)	50% (no geographical restriction)	—	—	—	—

Source: Daniel Roseman, "The WTO and Telecommunications Services in China: Three Years on," *The Journal of Policy, Regulation and Strategy for Telecommunications*, vol. 7, no. 2 (2005): 30; and Addendum to the Report of the working party on the accession of China, WT/ACC/CHN/49/Add.2, 1 October 2001,(accessed 1 June 2007).

Notes

a Fixed-line services include domestic and international voice services, packet-switched and circuit-switched data transmission services, facsimile services, and private leased circuit services.

b Foreign suppliers can provide services in three cities: Shanghai, Guangzhou, and Beijing. There is no quantitative restriction.

c Foreign suppliers can provide services in 17 cities: Shanghai, Guangzhou, Beijing, Chengdu, Chongqing, Dalian, Fuzhou, Hangzhou, Nanjing, Ningbo, Qingdao, Shenyang, Shenzhen, Xiamen, Xi'an, Taiyuan, and Wuhan; foreign investment shall be no more than 49 per cent.

d Foreign suppliers can provide nationwide services.

e Mobile services include analogue, digital, and cellular services and personal communication services.

f Value-added services include electronic mail, voice mail, online information and database retrieval, electronic data interchange, enhanced/value-added facsimile services, code and protocol conversion, and online information and/or data processing.

Personnel reshuffle to curb over-heated competition

Similar to other strategic sectors discussed in the previous chapters, the telecommunications sector was put under the jurisdiction of the SASAC, which was established in March 2003. This comprehensive commission centralized the state's supervisory role over the centralized strategic enterprises. In addition to its primary mission of protecting and enhancing the value of the selected state assets, the SASAC also assumed part of the appointment power from the Organization Department (*zuzhi bu*), allowing it to dictate deployment of top-rank officials in the telecommunications sector.[15]

However, such personnel shuffling and discontinuity in management not only harmed individual firms' planning and development, but also jeopardized their international credibility. Francis Cheung, a telecom analyst at the CLSA, worried about the regulatory risks of the industry and concluded that "this isn't a good way to manage an industry."[16] Rohit Sobti, an analyst at Citigroup, agreed that the reshuffle represented a high risk for his clients: "We see this as a reminder to investors that managements at the Chinese telecoms are government employees who can be moved around without any notice, substantially and significantly undermining the independence of these telecoms."[17]

But the Chinese leadership still decided to play the game of musical chairs to maintain orderly competition. The Chinese Communist Party (CCP) has been controlling cadres' career paths since 1949, and it did not loosen its grip during the reform era. The idea was that the new boss would need time to re-adjust to the respective companies and therefore cool down the over-heated competition.[18] The first reshuffle of this kind in the telecommunications sector took place in 2003, two years after the split of the old China Telecom. According to a telecom insider, this reshuffle was aimed at further integrating the three constituent companies of the new China Netcom—the northern part of the old China Telecom, the old China Netcom, and Jitong:

> The three companies were all very different in their corporate cultures. The most difficult thing was to integrate the old China Netcom and the old China Telecom. The old China Netcom was found by Edward Tian, who employed a more transparent management style while the old China Telecom was more bureaucratic because of its deep-seated planned heritage. They were simply not willing to work together and in fact were competing in unhealthy ways with each other for subscription accounts.[19]

In April 2003, the MII sent Zhang Chunjiang, the Vice-Minister, to China Netcom and swapped his position with Xi Guohua, the general manager of China Netcom.[20] Zhang's mission was to ensure a smooth integration among the three companies. On 30 May 2003, he successfully halted Jitong's operation and integrated the assets into China Netcom. Obviously, the top-rank manager had been the leading and influential official of the companies before they were corporatized, and the central leadership hoped that such a "revolving door for personnel" could eliminate the deep-seated positional power and minimize any potential resistance to the state-planned competition among the telecom giants. Such personnel reshuffling suggested that the Chinese leadership has a set of nationwide reform imperatives which override corporate-specific interests, and sacrifice management continuity and autonomy when necessary. In fact, personnel reshuffles were abundant in other state sectors, such as the airline and banking sectors.[21]

The second wave of personnel reshuffling took place when the MII tried to curb the over-heated competition and asked all telecommunications operators to cease the price war. On 1 November 2004, Wang Xiaochu, the vice president of China Mobile, resigned from his existing position and joined China Telecom as the chairman. The next day, 2 November 2004, China Unicom announced that its chairman and president, Wang Jianzhou, had resigned and would become the chairman of China Mobile. On the same day, Chang Xiaobing, the vice president of China Telecom, became the Chairman of China Unicom, and Leng Rongquan, the vice president of China Netcom, became the vice president of China Telecom (Figure 8.1).[22]

Property rights re-arrangements for rail-borne telecommunications assets

The six telecommunications operators were detached and corporatized, yet they were still state-owned, with the same local cadres working in the same positions but under a different company name (Figures 8.2–8.7). Although each telecommunications company was well regulated by the state, local cadres who had controlled the telecommunications assets were more knowledgeable than the central regulatory agent about the potential production capacities of the telecommunications assets. During the reform era, local cadres combined their political, technocratic, and entrepreneurial skills to identify idle assets before they were known to the state leadership and put under central coordination.

Such local profiteering strategies were acceptable to the state as long as they discovered idle assets, demarcated the boundaries of the property rights of each company and gauged future restructuring. The following in-depth case study of the MOR's telecommunications sub-sector illustrates how local cadres discover embedded productive assets and how central leadership recovered the property rights.

The birth of China TieTong

The emergence of China Railcom (later renamed as China TieTong) was a result of the overall strategic state policy to re-centralize the once fragmented and uncoordinated telecommunications assets.

Decentralization, consolidations, and commercialization of rail-borne telecommunications assets

Railway transport requires reliable signaling and communications systems for the provision of safe and reliable services. When Wusong Railway, the first

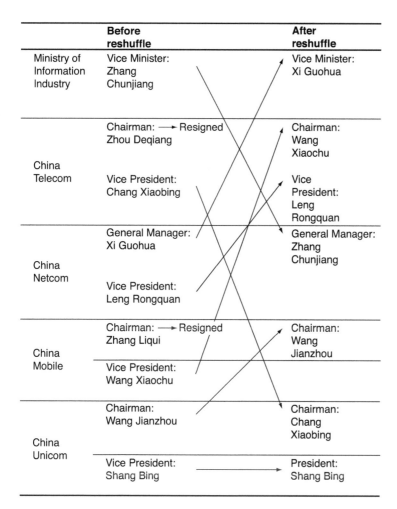

Figure 8.1 Personnel reshuffle in China's telecommunications sector in 2004 (source: "China Telecom Cos Reshuffle in prep for 3G?" China Comms Network, 3 November 2004, www.cn-c114.net/576/a285640.html (accessed 24 April 2015); Barry Naughton, "Market Economy, Hierarchy, and Single Party Rule: How Does the Transition Path in China Shape the Emerging Market Economy?" presented at the International Economic Association, Hong Kong, 14–15 January 2004).

railway in China, was constructed in 1879, the system was already equipped with a telecommunications facility. Later, the CCP government wanted to guarantee self-sufficiency, so the MOR decided to build the telecommunication network along the rail track when they undertook railway construction.

In order to centralize the control of the communications system, in 1950, the MOR standardized the institutional arrangement at all levels of the entire

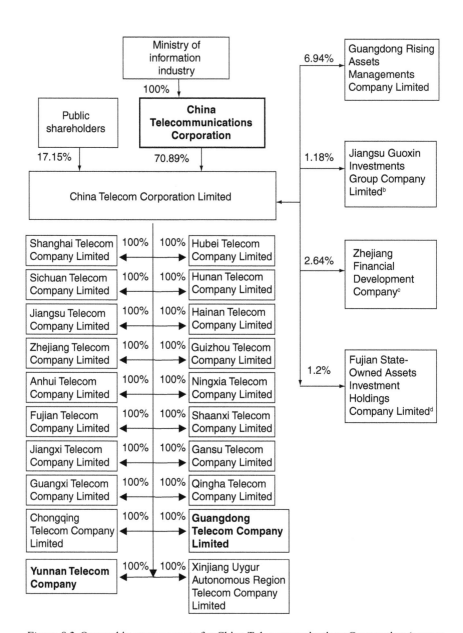

Figure 8.2 Ownership arrangements for China Telecommunications Corporation (source: China Telecom website www.chinatelecom-h.com/big5/corpinfo/structure.htm (accessed 1 November 2007)).

Note
* The four promoters are Unicom Xingye, Unicom Import & Export, Unicom Paging and Beijing Unicom Xingye. "China Unicom's Parent Company Unicom Group Announces a Share Offering," Press Release, China Unicom Limited, 17 September 2002, www.chinaunicom.com.hk/en/press/pressrelease/news.html?id=4346 (accessed 2 June 2007).

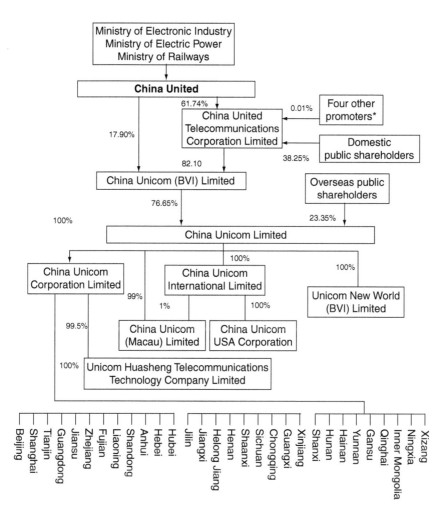

Figure 8.3 Ownership arrangements for China United Telecommunications Corporation (source: China Unicom webpage, www.chinaunicom.com.hk/en/aboutus/organization.html (accessed 1 November 2007)).

Note
* The four promoters are Unicom Xingye, Unicom Import & Export, Unicom Paging and Beijing Unicom Xingye. "China Unicom's Parent Company Unicom Group Announces A Share Offering," Press Release, China Unicom Limited, 17 September 2002, www.chinaunicom.com.hk/en/press/pressrelease/news.html?id=4346 (accessed 2 June 2007).

ministry to manage the railway's telecommunications and signaling systems across the country—the Telecommunications Bureau (*dianwu ju*) was the highest administrative body situated at the ministry headquarters in Beijing, which supervised the Telecommunications Divisions (*dianwu chu*) at regional railway administrations (*tielu ju*), the Telecommunications Sub-division (*dianwu*

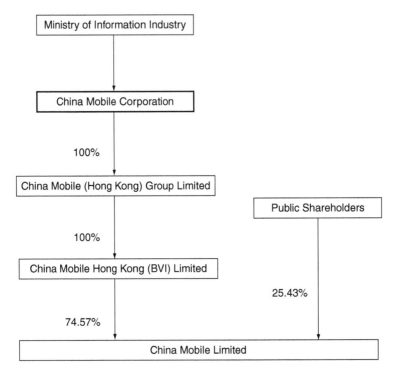

Figure 8.4 Ownership arrangements for China Mobile Corporation (source: China Mobile Limited website, www.chinamobileltd.com/about.php?lang=bg5 (accessed on 11 November 2006)).

fengchu) at railway sub-administrations (*tielu fengju*), and the Telecommunications Section (*dianwu ke*) at railway section level (*tielu duan*).

Although enormous bundles of communication cables were run between each railroad station, and along rail tracks, the massive level of telecommunications infrastructure was highly underused and had enormous spare capacity.[23] In 1985, when the MOR put forward the dual-track system, local cadres of the telecommunications system rushed to establish various non-telecommunications sidelines entities. A few of them still exist, such as the Xi'an TieTong Hotel, the Wuhan TieTong Holiday Travel Agent, and the Shanghai TieTong Theatre. However, the MOR soon realized that without guidance, business diversification could easily lead to excessive and duplicate allocation of resources in small-scale retail entities, which were easy to start-up and yet were not necessarily profitable.

In 1992, at a National Railway Telecommunications Working Meeting (*quanlu dianwu gongzhuo huiyi*), the head of the Telecommunications Bureau commanded that regional railway telecommunications cadres should make best use of their competitive edge in relation to the professional and technological knowledge

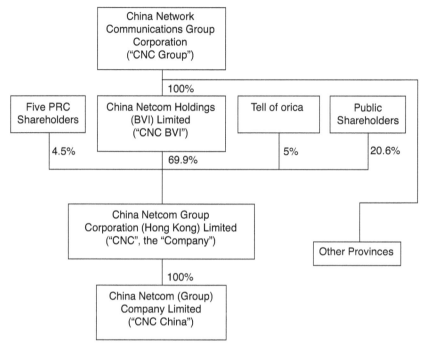

Figure 8.5 Ownership arrangements for China Network Communications Group Corporation (source: China Netcom website, www.china-netcom.com/english/inv/CorporateStructure.htm (accessed on 15 November 2007)).

on telecommunications, and diversify along the line of their core businesses to provided paid telecommunications services for the public at large.[24]

In 1994, in order to better coordinate the utilization of the underused cable infrastructure which was already in place, the MOR set up a preparation group to handle the telecommunications restructuring. In November 1995, the MOR established the China Railway Telecommunications Center (CRTC, *Zhongtie tongxun zhongxin*), which formally commenced commercial operation in February 1997. The CRTC was in charge of all the telecommunications operations within the MOR and became a legal entity through which the MOR injected parts of its telecommunications assets into China Unicom.

Separating and spinning off the railway telecommunications assets

In 1994, after the formation of China Telecom, China Unicom, and Jitong, other ministries which had dedicated telecommunications networks endeavored to discover, re-organize, and spin-off their own telecommunications assets. Local railway cadres who had previously worked in the telecommunications sub-sector

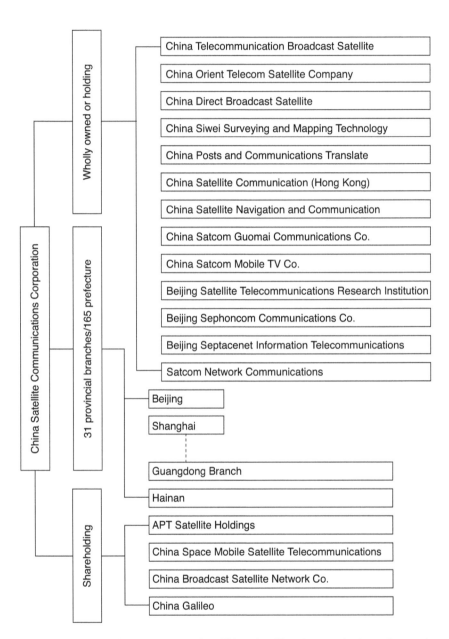

Figure 8.6 Ownership arrangement for China Satellite Communications Corporation (source: the website of China Satcom, www.chinasatcom.com/enterprise/showimg.asp?newsid=36 (accessed 15 November 2007)).

of the MOR also wanted to commercialize their professional services and share the huge market in China:

> We wanted to form our own telecommunications company. In 1992, the MOR lobbied together with the MEI and the MEP to integrate part of their abundant telecommunications assets and submitted a joint proposal to the State Council to form a new telecommunications operator. In 1993, the State Council approved the proposal and, in August 1994, established China Unicom. This was the first step for us to enter into the telecommunications industry.[25]

The CRTC soon started to offer phone services at cost to about one million people, mostly railway workers and their families residing along the rail tracks. Such service was known as *"ludian"* (railroad-borne telecommunications service), as compared to *"shidian"* (city-wide telecommunications service) provided by the MPT. The CRTC cadres believed that such service paved the way for full-scale commercialization of the MOR's telecommunications services in the future.[26]

In March 1999, in response to the State Council's request, the MOR agreed to separate its telecommunications arm, but insisted on maintaining the whole ownership of the railway telecommunications assets. In July 1999, the State Council decided to merge the entire railway telecommunication into China Unicom, which had been established in December 1993 with partial telecommunication assets from the MEI, the MOR, and the MEP. The MOR did not like the idea of the merger because that way the railway regime would lose control of the telecommunications system that the ministry had developed for decades. On the other hand, Unicom did not want to receive the MOR's telecommunications assets because by doing so, Unicom had to receive all 65,000 staff members from the CRCT. Having only 3,000 employees, Unicom was afraid that merging with the CRCT would render the company inefficient and unprofitable.

Between 1999 and 2000, the MOR and the CRCT leaders negotiated with Wu Jichuan, the minister of the MII, to gain his support on establishing an independent telecommunications entity. In June 2000, Wu filed a report to Zhu Rongji, the Premier, and Wu Bangguo, the Vice Premier, explaining that injecting CRCT into Unicom may affect Unicom's attractiveness to overseas investors when the company arranged IPOs. Wu suggested granting CRCT the right to operate telecommunications services independently for three years before reconsidering the plan of merger. On 15 July, Zhu approved Wu's proposal.[27]

On 26 December 2000, the MOR turned the CRTC into the China Railway Communications Company Ltd. (China Railcom, *Tietao tongxun xunxi yongxian gongsi*). At the same time, the MII granted China Railcom the sixth telecommunications operator license. In February 2001, China Railcom formally received the telecommunications network from the MOR, which was worth about RMB 13.6 million (US$1.64 billion), and sprawled along 65,000 km of the national railway network. Railcom's telecommunications network was the second largest telecommunication network, after China Telecom.[28] In return, the MOR held a 51 percent dominant stake in China Railcom, and the 13 regional

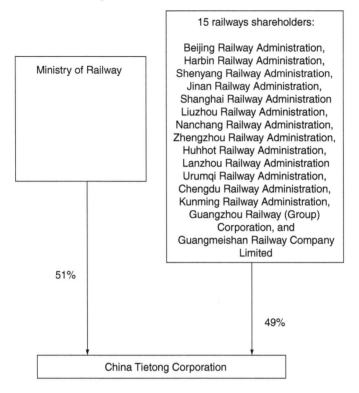

Figure 8.7 Ownership arrangement of China TieTong Corporation (source: China TieTong website, www.crcgd.com.cn/BIG/gs/tietong.htm (accessed 15 November 2007)).

railway administrations, the Guangzhou Railway (Group) Corporation, and the Guangmeishan Railway Co. Ltd. together held the remaining 49 percent of shares in the company (see Figure 8.7).[29]

A mixed policy of centralization and decentralization

During the transition, when the state was re-arranging and consolidating the fragmented telecommunications assets to form a few telecommunications companies, different telecommunications operators were, at the same time, discovering the idle or under-developed telecommunications capacities. The discovery process continued as the newly incorporated telecommunications operators were spun off from their original ministries and put under the SASAC. Since many of these idle assets were unclaimed or non-existent during the planned regime, the leaders of different telecommunications companies tried every means to compete for the ownership of various productive assets. While the technocratic competence and entrepreneurial leadership played a major role in the process of assets discovery, political power was as important in competing and formalizing these business initiatives. The state-controlled, phased competition allowed telecommunications cadres to showcase their various abilities in discovering the right assets.[30]

Such a discovery mechanism was especially important for the newly corporatized telecommunications companies to push their productive capacity to the limit and pick whatever assets might have potential to develop further, but were left unclaimed amid the entire telecommunications network. At this stage, the Chinese government was aware of the importance of the discovery mechanism and thus administered a pseudo-competition which drove different telecommunications companies to come up with lists of the best innovations. The Chinese government could later re-group the companies and the respective telecommunications assets according to their respective areas of specialization.

STATE-LED STRUCTURED PRICE WAR

Before 1996, the Working Committee for Large State-owned Enterprises supervised all Chinese telecommunications operators. In 1996, the state formed the SILSG, which kept a close eye on every move in the telecommunications sector, and ensured the six telecommunications operators, including China Railcom, competed in an orderly fashion. The resulting pseudo-competition was reflected in the structured price war between China Railcom and China Telecom.

Endowed with the second largest fixed line network in China, China Railcom was expected to be a rival competitor to China Telecom. Many cadres working at China Railcom were proud to work in the newly corporatized company, and were excited about being able to commercialize their telecommunications services:

> When China Telecom was the only telecommunications operator in China, the MII received so many complaints about it. With no competition, China Telecom did not care about customers' requests. When we started our service, we believed we could be competitive and provide much better services.[31]

In 2000, the MII received 6,588 complaints and investigated 1,025 of them. According to Zhang Chunjiang, the vice minister of the MII, China Telecom ranked top in the complaint list, with 732 cases under investigation. Among all the investigated cases, 35 percent were about poor and inconvenient services and 40 percent were related to high pricing. For example, customers complained that they had to go to one—and only one—designated place to pay the bill within 20 days upon the issuance of the invoice. Also, they did not have access to detailed call information. In addition, the first-time installation fee was as high as RMB 1,235 and air-time charges were counted on a per-minute basis for local calls, and a six-second basis for domestic long-distance calls.[32]

The major reason for such high charges and inconvenient services was the monopolistic operation of the fixed-line telecom service. With the introduction of China Railcom, the competition between the two companies should gradually bring down the price to an optimal level and improve the services to meet the market standard. However, according to a Railcom manager, the competition was under state regulation and the optimal price level was administratively distorted:

> When China Railcom first went into service, we planned to offer a first-time installation fee of RMB 680, and local phone call services at a price which was 10–20 percent lower than that of China Telecom. We also planned to improve the billing system to accommodate customers' different requests.[33]

But in July 2001, just before China Railcom commenced service, the MII ordered China Telecom to eliminate the installation fee. Consequently, Shanghai Telecom, a local unit of China Telecom, received 9,000 installation applications on 3 July 2001, as compared with a daily average of 3,000 before the fee cancellation.[34] In addition, on 2 August 2001, the MII officially launched eight new rules for all telecommunications carriers to protect subscribers' rights. One such rule is that all fixed-line operators, including China Telecom, China Railcom, and China Unicom, should launch more convenient charging packages, such as fixed monthly charges or tariffs to provide more choice to customers.[35] Although the introduction of more telecommunications operators successfully drove down the service charges, the competition was obviously state-regulated. The newcomer, China Railcom, could not pose any threat to the incumbent, as the Chinese government administered ordered competition which prevented price competition.

RESIDUAL POWER STRUGGLE OVER NETWORK INTEGRATION

Since nearly all telecommunications operators were backed up by different political leaders who could significantly affect business decisions, the power relations inherited from the planned regime played a major role in gaining access to key resources for providing telecommunications services. For example, China Telecom was spun off from the MII and backed by Wu Jichuan, the minister of information industry. China Netcom was backed by Jiang Mianheng, the son of China's president, Jiang Zemin. The company was based in Shanghai and about to go bankrupt before the state decided to merge it with the northern part of China Telecom. China Unicom was also backed by two important political protégés—Li Xiaopeng, the son of Li Peng, who bought into China Unicom through Huaneng Power International Inc; and China International Trust and Investment Corporation (CITIC), which was linked to Rong Yiren, China's former vice president. As a result, the informal struggle among residual powers in regard to network expansion and integration rendered the newcomer less competitive in traditional landline phone services compared to the incumbent telecommunications operator. Obviously, China Telecom did not want to cooperate with China Railcom to facilitate network integration.

In 2001, China Railcom received the telecommunications backbone networks from the MOR, which comprised 120,000 km of telecommunications links, of which 70,000 km were optical fiber cables and 12,000 were digital microwave lines.[36] The telecommunications backbone links were originally built to support the telephone switching network dedicated to the MOR, its regional railway administrations and sub-administrations, and had a capacity of only 2.28 million lines.[37] Although China Railcom had the exclusive right to lay network along the railway lines, interconnection with other operators had become a big headache for the company:

> We originally scheduled the nationwide operation in July 2001 because we had already signed a framework agreement on network integration with China Telecom's headquarters, which guaranteed to connect our networks so our customers could phone each other. However, we later realized that we indeed had to further negotiate with China Telecom's 31 provincial and municipal branches separately for the right to connect to each one of them to commence operations; this inevitably delayed our launch of service.[38]

In mid-August 2001, the provincial subsidiaries of China Railcom began to negotiate an implementation agreement with China Telecom. By late September 2001, China Railcom completed negotiations at the provincial level, but they still had to sort out various technical issues on the physical interconnection:

> We were left to arrange our own physical interconnection down to the technical level. For example, we had to negotiate for the most optimum physical site at which interconnection should take place. My experience was that China Telecom's exchange site was at quite a distance from us and it took a long and painful process to compromise on a mutually acceptable connection method to establish some kind of fibre-optical connection linking the two systems.[39]

By the end of September 2001, China Railcom managed to connect to China Telecom in just 101 cities.[40] By 2003, China Railcom claimed to have successful integration with the telephone switching networks of all other telecom carriers, giving the company a switching capacity of over 18 million lines. However, local network integration among telecom carriers was not as good as reported. *China Daily* reported that, between 6 and 14 June 2002, China Netcom "intentionally" cut off the telephone network of China Railcom three times, breaking down communication for the Railcom system in Tangshan in northern Hebei Province for several days. Liu Rongfu, President of China Railcom's Tangshan Branch, was quoted as saying: "Many users could not use their telephones.... This rude action severely hurt China Railcom's reputation."[41]

On 17 August 2002, the *Washington Post* carried an even more dramatic story about An Jianye, a manager of a six-floor hotel in Tangshan, who had two telephones sitting on his desk:

Over the past few weeks, workers from one of China's state-owned tele-communications behemoths, China Netcom, have twice severed the phone lines of China Railcom, a plucky rival that is also state-owned, to keep it out of An's hotel. Government regulators, allegedly in cahoots with Netcom, clipped little Railcom's wires a third time.

Other government departments also pressured An to keep China Netcom over Railcom, threatening to cut off his water and electricity. The local press has not touched the story because China Netcom is a major advertiser, according to local sources. Railcom, for its part, offered to pay for mobile phones for hotel staffers for a month if they signed up.

So An settled on a compromise—two phones on his desk, one black, one red, and a line from each phone company leading into his hotel.[42]

In addition to Hubei, local branches of China Telecom, China Unicom, and China Railcom were all setting up "technical barriers" in Guangdong, Henan and Sichuan to damage each other's fixed telephone lines and prevent mutual con-nection among their networks.[43]

RAILCOM'S SURVIVAL STRATEGIES I: FROM COPPER WIRE TO FIBER-OPTIC

In view of the destructive activities administered by various competitors, Peng Peng, the former president of China Railcom, soon learned that the company could not easily compete for the right to use the access network which had been claimed by other state agents during the planned era. Rather, China Railcom started to explore alternatives to improve the carrying capacity of its backbone network so that it could provide services different from those of the traditional backbone network. The state's preferential policy toward China Telecom, and the power struggle over network integration, therefore pushed China Railcom to develop its fiber-optic network, which could provide better service at lower cost.

When China Railcom received the telecommunications assets from the MOR, the backbone networks comprised 120,000 kilometers of telecommunications links, of which 70,000 kilometers were optical fiber cables. Before, the CRCT needed only to provide telecommunications services to railway units and staff located and residing within 3 km of the rail lines. Much of the communications capacity, in par-ticular that of the fiber-optic backbone, was unused. Seeing the future trend of digital technology, China Railcom decided to stake claims on this new business initiative so it could not only catch up, but actually leapfrog over its rivals:

This is the cheapest way to build a network based on internet rather than switches. We do not need to build many exchange hubs along the network to house switches for each phone line. The government also encouraged such development and thus did not set rates for calls on Internet-based networks.[44]

In July 2001, Peng Peng signed an agreement for about US$48 million with Nortel Networks to construct the Beijing–Shanghai–Guangzhou optical backbone ring. Nortel was a global internet and communications company and such a partnership helped China Railcom address its networking for high-speed connection in as little as six months.[45] Later, Peng Peng continued to build a nationwide fiber-optic ring, which included the southwest, southeast, northwest and northeast ring links. China Railcom not only intended to extend the fiber-optic backbone beyond the railway lines, but also to let Huawai upgrade its fiber-optic to a maximum bandwidth of 400 Gbs to provide video and multimedia services:

> The five ring links ... are intended to extend our fibre optic backbone beyond the railway lines. With regard to access networks within a city, we will review our various options, which certainly include using China Telecom's access networks, on a case-by-case basis, with the main criteria being market demand and customer needs.[46]

In 2002, China Railcom partnered with Cisco System for the second phase of expansion of CRNet, the company's internet backbone network. China Railcom and Cisco had already developed a long-term strategic partnership since the first phase of the project.[47] In 2005, after China Railcom was subsumed under the SASAC and renamed China TieTong, the company expanded the CRNet backbone again by migrating to the Cisco IP Next-Generation Network (IP NGN). IP NGN was an all-internet protocol network which allowed advanced network service with bandwidth of 10 Gbs. China TieTong and Cisco had developed mutual trust in terms of brand name and technology, which paved the way for the future joint venture cooperation.[48]

In 2005, China TieTong tried to explore the possibility of applying a new communication technology by which voice signals could be sent by packages through the internet, instead of as individual data. The company eventually contracted out the service of voice over internet protocol (VoIP) to a domestic provider, Beijing CVC Communication Co., which then subcontracted to General Components Inc, a leading US company focusing on broadband networking projects, with subsidiaries in Beijing.[49]

RAILCOM'S SURVIVAL STRATEGIES II: FROM INDIVIDUAL TO
RESIDENTIAL DIGITAL COMMUNITY AND COMMERCIAL CALL CENTER

In 2001, China Railcom had set a target of enlisting 12 million subscribers. However, in view of the problems of integration, Peng Peng discovered a new niche market which has not yet been covered by China Telecom's traditional services:

> Our targets have been revised. As we have been focusing our efforts on interconnection with China Telecom, our marketing has not been in full swing. In the meantime, the current lack of interconnection has also hampered our efforts in signing up subscribers. Of course, the issues regarding interconnection will be resolved one way or another, so in the longer time horizon we are confident that we can achieve our subscriber targets.[50]

With its national fiber loops and digital technology, China Railcom re-targeted to provide three types of advanced telecommunications services: group users, integrated information services, and cooperative services.

Since China Railcom had to commit huge resources in connecting to the areas which had already been well covered by China Telecom, the company changed to targeting group users, which would probably have tens or even hundreds of thousands of individual users. The group arrangement would be more cost-effective than getting only a few individual users signing up. Peng Peng admitted that most of their existing group users were railway units:

> for obvious reasons China Railcom has had a good working relationship with the railway units for several decades. We are nevertheless attempting to diversify our customer base by leveraging our experiences gained from serving group users in the railway industry.[51]

For example, China Railcom continued to provide and improve the signaling technology for the safe operation of railway transport services. One new tele-communications service combined the digital mobile telecommunication system with the GPS satellite navigation technology to ensure an automatic train opera-tion control system for the Qinghai–Tibet railway.[52]

China Railcom also endeavored to provide integrated information services to new residential communities. Again, wiring up such brand-new real-estate pro-jects saved the company the complicated negotiation and construction work of digging up the ground and integrating with the existing network. Peng Peng, who had established long-term, professional, and trusting relations with various ministries and the central government, competently handled bureaucratic negoti-ations and could easily enter cooperative projects with government units.

In April 1999, when China Netcom was incorporated, Peng Peng, with his close leadership connections, recommended Edward Tian to the Central leader-ship to set up a new telecommunications company. Soon after Tian became the Chairman of China Netcom, China Railcom cooperated with China Netcom, in which the MOR had shares, to provide digital community services to a showcase project at the newly constructed Lianhua Residential Area in Beijing, which was developed by the Ministry of Construction.

In September 2003, China Railcom and Huaxia Construction Group formed a joint venture called China Rail-Sino Telecommunications Co., Ltd. (Rail-Sino, TieTong huasha dianxun Co. Ltd.). Such a joint project was aimed at offering contract-out services to handle large volume of telephone calls for different com-mercial purposes, such as product after-sales services, information inquiries hot-lines, or telemarketing services. Tang Xiuyan, the vice-president of Rail-Sino, estimated that to establish an in-house 50-seat call center would cost RMB 2 million. It would therefore greatly reduce the costs if enterprises or government department outsourced their call center services to professional operators.[53]

The call center project was targeted at commercial corporate users. By means of centralizing the call services at its own subsidiary, which could be located in the vicinity of the backbone network, China Railcom did not need to deal with the problem of network integration.[54]

Later, China Railcom developed two special telecommunications services dedicated to corporate customers, which were distinguishable from general civilian telecommunications services.

The first one was *"Quanshitong"* ("Total Vision Communication"), which provided a virtual platform for headquarters and branch offices to link together for inexpensive and efficient data transmission, long-distance telecommunications, and video conferences. The second, *"Yixuntong"* ("Instant Communication"), was to provide government agencies and public enterprises with safe and reliable multi-function mobile communications.[55]

Re-centralization of telecommunications assets

CONSOLIDATION OF TELECOMMUNICATIONS ASSETS UNDER THE SASAC

When Zhu Rongji approved the separation of the telecommunications assets from the MOR and formed China Railcom, the State Council gave the company three years to develop and operate telecommunications services independently before reconsidering the feasibility of a merger with other existing telecommunications operators. Seeing that China Railcom was able to discover alternative communication capacity and produce various digital telecommunications products, the state leadership decided to re-centralize and put China Railcom under the SASAC for further restructuring. The MOR tried to resist such re-centralization, but the effort was in vain.

In the beginning of 2003, Peng Peng proposed to the State Council to separate the company from the MOR. Rumors soon arose that the railway leadership wanted to keep what it regarded as one of the most valuable assets and thus disliked Peng and his proposal.[56] In September 2003, the MOR decided to dismiss Peng Peng from the post of general manager, but he retained his position as the company's vice chairman. China Railcom explained that the decision was based on the routine appraisal of Peng's performance and was a normal personnel reshuffle.

In 2004, the State Council removed China Railcom from the railway regime and put it under the SASAC and renamed it as China TieTong. Although the Chinese name remained unchanged, the *pinyin* name *"tietong"* was less related to the railway system than the previous English name "railcom." In 2005, the SASAC appointed four non-executive directors to the board of TieTong—three were former top executives of other large state-owned enterprises, and another one was a university professor. These "external" directors were to discourage the MOR's interference in China TieTong.[57] The MII and the SASAC believed that introducing directors who were independent of the executive team would improve the company's corporate governance and attract strategic investors in the near future.

Figure 8.8 shows the restructuring of the telecommunications assets in the MOR.

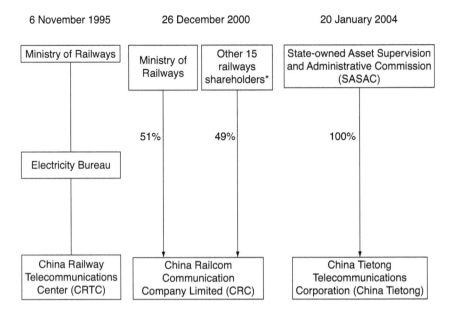

Figure 8.8 Restructuring of the telecommunications assets in the MOR, 1995, 2000, 2004 (source: *"Tietong Weilai Biansouduo,"* ("TieTong is Full of Uncertainties in the Future"), *People's Daily,* 30 January 2001, http://unn.people.com. cn/22220/61259/61261/4258731; and China TieTong, www.crcgd.com.cn/ BIG/gs/tietong.htm).

RATIFICATION OF MODERN AND MULTI-LAYERED ORGANIZATIONAL STRUCTURE

Before international telecommunication companies entered China's market, competition among different state-owned telecommunications operators was like a "civil war."[58] In about three years' time China Railcom successfully mapped out various business alternatives and explored the possible boundaries of the optical backbone and access networks. After "picking the right assets," the central leadership re-centralized the company, paving the way for the second phase of property rights re-arrangements. Whether the second phase of re-arrangements would lead to privatization was still unknown, but what was certain was that such reform resulted in a modern organizational structure, with a board of directors established to appear compliant with the international standard of transparent governance. On the other hand, large-scale centralized enterprises under the SASAC were turned into a multi-layer shareholding structure, so that when such group enterprises wanted foreign technology through a joint venture, or wanted to attract foreign capital by listing on the stock market, the holding company could remain state-owned and state-controlled, irrespective of its subsidiaries' property rights.

When China Railcom was still under the MOR, most of its funding came from state sources.[59] In 2004, when China Railcom was subsumed under the

SASAC and renamed China TieTong, the State Council asked the MOR to exempt the company from a total debt of RMB 2.38 billion yuan (US$286 million), and took care of the loans from the World Bank and Swiss Bank.[60] In June of the same year, the State Development and Reform Commission ratified the plan for China TieTong to set up a board of directors, and *People's Daily* reported that such a move was to "diversify its capital structure and reform itself into a stock company."[61]

In 2005, Zhao Jibin, China TieTong's new Chairman, contended that the company still relied heavily on bank loans to fund more than 70 percent of its total investment, but he said that the company would diversify its financing channels:

> The company will take advantage of preferential government policies to accelerate any reshuffling to consolidate its business as well as build up a positive image for investors.... We will take advantage of our experience in the railway network to co-operate with specific sectors, such as petroleum, coal, irrigation works and broadcasting and television in order to explore our network resources, as well as save on investment costs.

Next, Zhao encouraged property rights re-arrangements at the subsidiaries of the company:

> We are going to be involved in business integration and adjusting our subsidiaries in developed regions to attract strategic investors from home and abroad.... Those subsidiaries will be characterized by high-quality assets, complete network coverage and huge market potential.[62]

Eventually, Zhao expected to seek cooperation with foreign financial organizations and investment companies, and pursue public listings on both the domestic A-share market and overseas markets. In August 2005, with permission from the State Development and Reform Commission, China TieTong first entered the capital market by issuing one billion yuan (US$123 million) of corporate bonds.

Similar to other large-scale centralized enterprises, China TieTong was restructured to form a business group (*qiye jituan*) with a multi-layered organizational structure, which included 31 closely related provincial branch companies and 321 city branch companies, five somewhat closely related subsidiaries, and 18 loosely related railway service centers. The closely related branches were wholly owned regional companies which focused on the core profit-making telecommunications services, such as fixed-line and long-distance telephone services. The somewhat closely related companies were joint ventures between China TieTong and other domestic or foreign telecommunications counterparts. The loosely related institutes were regional service centers providing support services to the MOR at cost (Figure 8.9).

Although China TieTong has issued one billion yuan worth of corporate bonds, and planned to purse an IPO in 2008, the company was not restructured

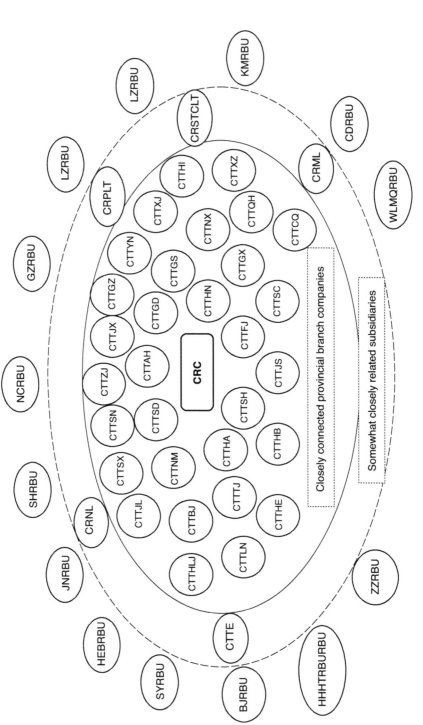

Figure 8.9 China Railcom's property rights hybrid.

as predicted by the economic model of convergence toward capitalism. On the contrary, a new model of economic coordination was emerging—one in which the parent company remained state-owned, and various joint venture projects took place at the subsidiaries of the parent company. When the companies go public in the future, they will probably follow other telecommunications companies by creating a holding company which will become an insulating layer between the parent company and the listing subsidiary. (See the case of China Unicom in Figure 8.3, of which the MOR owned 0.56 percent through the China Railway Telecommunication Center.)

In May 2008, the state further combined the six telecom operators into three, with a view to enhancing the development of 3G businesses and full telecom services. As a result, China Netcom was acquired by China Unicom, China Satcom was merged with China Telecom, and China Tietong was merged with China Mobile.

Robert Lewis, a partner at international lawyers Lovells, had anticipated that "the Chinese partner won't step aside and let you take control. The deck is stacked in favour of the Chinese partner."[63] Denis Fred Simon, then president of Monitor Group China, said: "there is more uncertainty to come as the rules and regulations aren't clear.... The Chinese version of the WTO hasn't been checked for consistencies. In China, the Chinese version's already got political and economic intent."[64] Francis Cheung, telecom-industry analyst at the CLSA-Asia Pacific in Hong Kong, opined that acquiring shares in these telecommunications companies "are buying a proxy to China." Although these "utility-like" companies seemed to generate sizable profits, investors should be aware of "potential shocks down the road as the government adjusts the industry's structure."[65]

Mixed policies of decentralization and re-centralization

The reform of the MOR's telecommunications sub-sector involved mixed policies of decentralization and re-centralization. First, the MOR allowed regional railway telecommunications cadres to diversify into various non-telecommunications-related sideline businesses, and soon asked local cadres to focus on commercialization of its telecommunications services. Second, the SASAC consolidated the country's fragmented telecommunication assets to form a few domestic operators, and allowed them to further toughen up under orderly competition. This applied to the MOR's telecommunication sub-sector as well.

The mixed polices further urged domestic telecommunications operators to discover idle productive assets, rejuvenate hidden communication capacity, and explore undeveloped niche markets. The case of China Railcom demonstrates that, suffering from unfavorable pricing policy and uneasy network integration, China Railcom shifted to expand the transmission capacity of its optical fiber backbone and provide digital services to group and corporate users.

The second stage of reform involved the state's effort to recombine the newly discovered assets according to each operator's areas of specialization. Since the telecommunications industry involved a large initial sunk investment to provide a nationwide communication network, the prohibitively high start-up cost favored incumbent operators and rendered pure market competition impossible. In addition, in view of the pressure of opening up the market after the entry into the WTO, the Chinese government chose to consolidate and restructure all the newly discovered telecommunications assets. The resulting property rights arrangements, so far, were the formation of a few multi-layered state hybrids, with cross-ownership and joint ventures at the subsidiary level. The multi-layered state hybrids were also characterized with Western-like organizational structure. Such Western mimicry was aimed at facilitating the second phase of reform by arranging an international public offering. In the case of China Tietong, it was merged with China Mobile as a wholly owned subsidiary. The development of China's telecommunication industry clearly demonstrates the Chinese government's determination to nurture a few national champions in such a strategically important industry.

Notes

1 "Performance Indicators for the Telecommunications Sector," Telecommunications and Informatics Division, Industry and Energy Department, May 1995, www.world-bank.org/html/opr/pmi/telecom/telecom0.html (accessed 29 May 2007).
2 Lei Ding and Kingsley E. Haynes, "The Role of Telecommunications Infrastructure in Regional Economic Growth of China," Paper presented at the Telecommunications Policy Research Conference, Washington, 1–3 October 2004. See also David Canning, "Infrastructure's Contribution to Aggregate Output," Policy Research Working Paper no. 2246 (1999), World Bank; and Leonard Waverman, Meloria Meschi, and Melvyn Fuss, "The Impact of Telecoms on Economic Growth in Developing Countries," The Vodafone Policy Paper Series no. 2 (March 2005): 10–23.
3 Y.Q. Chen, "Speed up the Development of Telecommunication," *Modernization*, p. 5. [Chinese and quoted in Jianguo Zhu "Telecommunications and Development in Shanghai: A Case Study," in Paul Lee, ed., *Telecommunications and Development in China* (Cresskill, NJ: Hampton Press, 1997), p. 137].
4 *Zhongguo guding zichan touzi tongji ziliao 1950–1985 (China Fixed Assets Investments Statistical Information 1950–1985)*, National Bureau of Statistics of China, p. 101.
5 *Zhongguo tongji nianjian 1983, 1992, 2002 and 2005 (Chinese Statistical Yearbook 1983, 1992, 2002, 2005)*; *Zhongguo tongxun tongji niandu baogao* (China Communications Statistics Annual Report; Renmin youdian chubanshe/People's Telecommunications Publisher, 2002), p. 273; Zen Jianqiu, *Dianxun canye fazhan gailun* (Development Theory of Telecommunications Industry; Beijing: Youdian xueyuan chubanshe, 2001), p. 126; *Xinzhongguo 55 nian tongji lubian 1949–2005 (New China 55 Year's Statistics 1949–2004*, China Infobank, http://210.177.11.50.ezproxy.ust.hk/gate/big5/www.chinainfobank.com/ifbase643-L0lyaXNCaW4~/-VGV4dC5kbGw~?ZGI9VE ombm89Mjk3MzQ2JmNzPTEyNDA0MDcyJnN0cj3Stc7x (accessed 4 October 2007).
6 "Performance Indicators for the Telecommunications Sector."
7 "Telecommunication Reform: How to succeed," *Public Policy Journal*, vol. 130 (1997), http://rru.worldbank.org/Documents/PublicPolicyJournal/130welle.pdf (accessed 1 October 2007).
8 "Best Practices for Telecommunications Reform," Global Internet Policy Initiative Papers (August 2002), www.internetpolicy.net/practices/telecomreform.pdf (accessed 1 October 2007).

9 Milton Mueller and Zixiang Tan, *China in the Information Age: Telecommunications and the Dilemmas of Reform* (Westport, CT: Praeger, 1997), p. 51.
10 "Joint Venturing in China Telecoms," Telecoms InfoTech Forum Briefing paper, 22 January 1997 http://trpc.biz/wp-content/uploads/1996-00_TIF_JointVenturingInCN-sTelcos_BackgroundBriefing1.pdf (accessed 25 April 2015).
11 "Creating an Independent Telecom Regulator," United States Information Technology Office, 30 September 2002, www.usito.org/USITO/uploads/112/independent_regulator.PDF (accessed 1 June 2007).
12 "Chronology of the Development of China's Internet, 1994–1996," China Internet Network Information Center (May 2003), www.cnnic.net.cn/html/Dir/2003/10/22/1003.htm (accessed 1 October 2007); see also Margaret Pearson, "The Business of Governing Business in China: Institutions and Norms of the Emerging Regulatory State," *World Politics*, vol. 57, no. 2 (2005): 306.
13 Liu Baijia, "Telecom Monopoly Set to Split," *China Daily* (North American edition), 12 December 2001, p. 5. www.china.org.cn/english/2001/Dec/23497.htm (accessed 25 April 2015).
14 "Minister Answers IT queries," *China Daily* (North American edition), 8 January 2002, p. 5.
15 Barry Naughton, "Market Economy, Hierarchy, and Single Party Rule: How Does the Transition Path in China Shape the Emerging Market Economy?" Paper presented at the International Economic Association, Hong Kong, 14–15 January 2004); Pearson, "The Business of Governing Business in China," p. 206. One of my informants also believed in such party influence. In fact, he later resigned from China Railcom partly because his boss left the company during the personnel reshuffle in the telecom sector. Although the exact mechanisms were not transparent, it was very likely that the SASAC served as an agent for the Party leadership.
16 "China Telecom Cos Reshuffle Seen as Backward Step," *China Comms Network*, 3 November 2004, www.cn-c114.net/576/a285642.html (accessed 25 April 2015).
17 "China Telecom Cos Reshuffle Seen as Backward Step."
18 Chen Yu, "Reshuffle a Prelude to Mergers," *China Daily* (North American edition), 10 November 2004, p. 11.
19 Interview, CQBJ, 2003.
20 Pearson, "The Business of Governing Business in China."
21 Naughton, "Market Economy, Hierarchy, and Single Party Rule," and Pearson, "The Business of Governing Business in China."
22 "China Telecom Cos Reshuffle in Prep for 3G?" *China Comms Network*, 3 November 2004, www.cn-c114.net/576/a285640.html (accessed 25 April 2015).
23 Other major telecommunications networks were owned by the People's Liberation Army, the Ministry of Electric Power, the Ministries of Transportation and Petroleum, the People's Bank of China, and the Ministry of Foreign Trade. See Mueller and Tan, *China in the Information Age*, p. 46; and Li Zhaoyan, "Private and Overlay Networks in the PRC," Paper presented at the conference on Telecommunications and the Integration of China, Hong Kong Center, as quoted in Mueller and Tan, *China in the Information Age*, p. 141.
24 Hu Yauhua and Zhu Junan, ed., *Zhongguo Tielu Tongxin Shiji Huigu* (Review of China's Railway Telecommunications in this Century; Beijing: China Railway Publisher, 2001), p. 70.
25 Interview, CQBJ, January 2004.
26 Interview, BJCQ, January 2004. Also see Hu Yauhua and Zhu Junan, ed., *Zhongguo Tielu Tongxin Shiji Huigu*, p. 73.
27 "*Tietong shiduo zhongguo dianxun ¼ guhua fen'e*" ("Railcom Swire to Take Away One-Fourth Market Share from China Telecom"), ChinaByte, 9 May 2001, http://news.chinabyte.com/124/1220124.shtml (accessed 25 April 2015).

28 *"Xiang dabo dianxun canye de longduan: tietong ping sheme jingzheng?"* ("Want to Break the Telecommunications Monopoly: How Could Tietong Compete?"), *Zhongguo jingying bao*, 16 January 2001, China.org, http://big5.china.com.cn/chinese/EC-c/17010.htm (accessed 25 April 2015).

29 China TieTong, www.crcgd.com.cn/BIG/gs/tietong.htm (accessed 10 June 2007).

30 For a more detailed discussion on China's "phased competition" approach toward telecommunications reform at large, see Qing Duan, "China's IT Leadership" (PhD Thesis, University of Maryland, 2005).

31 Interview, LAXBJ, January 2004.

32 "Competition in Telecom Sector will Cut Complaints," in *People's Daily*, 13 March 2001, http://english.people.com.cn/english/200103/13/eng20010313_64854.html (accessed 25 April 2015).

33 Interview, CQBJ, January 2004.

34 "China: Fee Cut Spurs Phone Demand," *Asiainfo Daily China News*, 11 July 2001.

35 Hou Mingjuan, "New Rules to Improve Services," *China Daily* (North American edition), 3 August 2001, p. 5.

36 "China Railcom to Focus on Fibre Access Networks," Telecommunications Development, Asia-Pacific, 25 June 2002, www.tdap.co.uk/uk/archive/interviews/inter (railcom_0203).html (accessed 11 June 2007).

37 China TieTong, www.chinatietong.com/english/index.him (accessed 11 June 2007).

38 Interview, BJCQ, 2001. See also "China Railcom launches Operation," *China Daily*, 13 August 2001, www.chinadaily.com.cn/en/doc/2001-08/13/content_76419.htm (accessed 25 April 2015). The same problems also happened for China Unicom; see Vineeta Shetty, "The China Syndrome," *Communications International*, April 2001, pp. 22–25.

39 Interview, BJWY, 2003.

40 "China Railcom to Focus on Fibre Access Networks."

41 China Unicom also experienced similar unfair treatment. In Sichuan Province, China Unicom's fixed-line telephone connection was cut off by China Telecom, which led to an eight-hour disconnection for Unicom users. On 12 April 2002, employees of China Telecom even intruded into Unicom's operation center and cut off the telephone trunk lines. See Hou Mingjuan, "Government May Throw Carriers a Line," *China Daily* (North American edition), 4 July 2002, p. 5, www.chinadaily.com.cn/en/doc/2002-07/04/content_126373.htm (accessed 12 June 2000).

42 John Pomfret, "Lines Crossed in China," *Washington Post*, 17 August 2002, p. A01.

43 Xiao Yang, "Order Essential in Telecom Market," *China Daily* (North American edition), 10 August 2002, p. 4.

44 Interview, LAXBJ, January 2004.

45 "China Railcom Opens National High-Speed Optical Ring Using Nortel Networks Solution," Nortel news release, 21 July 2001, www.nortel.com/corporate/news/news releases/2001c/07_12_0101477_china_railcom.html (accessed 19 June 2007).

46 "China Railcom to Focus on Fibre Access Networks."

47 "Cisco to Provide Backbone Technology for China Railcom Network Expansion," *People's Daily*, 28 April 2002, http://english.peopledaily.com.cn/200204/19/print20020419_94369.html (accessed 25 April 2015).

48 "China TieTong Again Selects Cisco for Expansion of its CRNET Backbone Network," Cisco news release, 22 June 2005, http://newsroom.cisco.com/dlls/global/asiapac/news/2005/pr_06-28.html (accessed 25 April 2015).

49 "General Components to Provide VoIP Enterprise Solution to China Railcom," *Business Wire*, 14 November 2005, www.thefreelibrary.com/General+Components+to+provide+VoIP+Enterprise+Solution+to+China...-a0138650511 (accessed 25 April 2015).

50 "China Railcom to Focus on Fibre Access Networks."

51 "China Railcom to Focus on Fibre Access Networks."

52 *"Zhongguo tietong: lizhu tielu zhuanwang, kaizhang teshe yewu"* ("China Railcom: Based on the Railway Network to Develop Businesses with Special Features"),

Tongxun Shijie, 30 November 2006, www.51telecom.com/Get/syyw/200611304922. htm (accessed 18 June 2007).

53 "China Railcom to Occupy China's Call Center Market," *SinoCast China Business Daily News London (UK)*, 23 September 2003, p. 1.

54 "Sino Call to Cover 300 Chinese Cities," *SinoCast China Business Daily News London (UK)*, 23 September 2003, p. 1. See also the home page of Rail-Sino, www. sinocall.com/about_us.asp (accessed 19 June 2007).

55 "*Zhongguo tietong: lizhu tielu zhuanwang, kaizhang teshe yewu.*"

56 Interview, BJCQ, 2003. See also "*Peng Peng rehuo chuju, tietong 'duli yundong' yanqi sigu*" ("Peng Peng was Out Amid China Railcom's Independent Movement"), *Jingji Guangcha Bao (The Economic Observer)*, 1 November 2003, http://it.sohu. com/17/75/article215057517.shtml (accessed 25 April 2015).

57 Li Weitao, "Regulators Alter Tietong's Board," *China Daily* (North American edition), 3 December 2005, p. 5.

58 "Intense Competition in Telecommunications Industry," 19 November 2001, www. tdctrade.com/report/indprof/indprof_011103.htm (accessed 20 June 2007).

59 For example, in 2001, China Development Bank signed a Finance Cooperation Agreement with China Railcom and provided the company a total loan of RMB 20 billion yuan to construct its backbone communications networks and facilitate technological innovation; see "Railcom Gets 10 Billion Yuan Loan to Construct Network," *Asiainfo Daily China News Dallas*, 28 June 2002, p. 1.

60 Chen Zhiming, "China Tietong to be Officially Launched in Early August," *China Daily* (North American edition), 23 July 2004, p. 10.

61 "China Railcom to Issue One Billion Yuan in Bonds," *People's Daily*, 11 April 2005, http://my.tdctrade.com/airnewse/index.asp?id=6205 (accessed 20 June 2007).

62 Chen Zhiming, "Tietong Seeks Co-operation, Listing," *China Daily* (North American edition) 18 January 2005, p. 10, http://english.sohu.com/20050118/n223990968.shtml (accessed 24 April 2015).

63 Nathalie Raffray, "Open and Closed," *Communications International London*, February 2002, pp. 9–10.

64 Raffray, "Open and Closed."

65 Evan Ramstad, "Heard in Asia: Telecom-Consolidation Rumor in China Fails to Stir Investors," *Asian Wall Street Journal Victoria, Hong Kong*, 12 July 2004, p. M.1.

9 Conclusion

Confusing property rights re-arrangement policies

China's railway reform confused many people, particularly in terms of its property rights arrangements and the conflicting policies of decentralization and re-centralization. To recap, between 1978 and 2003, the Ministry of Railways (MOR) administered a series of profit-sharing systems: responsibility contracts, the full-scale and integrated contracting responsibility system, and the responsibility system of assets management. At first glance, such profit-sharing contracts appeared to allow regional railway administrations to assume increasing rights to retain income, to control the productive assets, and to facilitate at least partial privatization of the railway assets.

However, since the Chinese railway was still wholly state-owned, such reform policies did not clarify the boundary of the three bundles of property rights, namely the right to retain income, the right to control the productive assets, and the right to transfer them. By giving a different percentage of the transport operating, railroad construction, and telecommunications network construction funds to the regional railway administrations directly, profit sharing arrangements merely simplified the internal fiscal system so that regional railway administrations did not need to first remit the revenue and later request the funds back from the MOR. Also, the control rights were granted with conditions and subjected to negotiations, and the bundles of property rights were thus not as clearly partitioned and decentralized as expected. In a nutshell, under the planned system, regional railway administrations did not really enjoy more income rights through the profit-sharing policies.

In 2001 the MOR rolled out the plan of vertical separation between the transport services sub-sectors and the network sub-sector. Again, such a reform strategy had been projected as theoretically sound and practically feasible for the sector to move further toward the best railway model. However, in 2003 Liu Zhijun, the new railway minister, called off the plan and put forward a Great-Leap approach to railway development.

In 2005, all railway sub-administrations were removed. Railway administrations started to manage the stations and sections directly and a few large railway administrations were split into smaller ones, and Minister Liu called for a

Great-Leap style of railway construction and development. The centralized and ambitious approach to developing the railway network has resulted in 17,000 kilometers of high-speed rail supporting high-speed trains running at an average speed of 200 km/h or more in 2012.[1]

However, the tragic accidents in Shandong, Hunan, and Wenzhou in 2008, 2009, and 2013, respectively, and the announcement of the death penalty of Minister Liu for taking bribes, led to further re-centralization of the railway sector by dissolution of the MOR. The China Railway Corporation was established to operate the national railway. The administrative functions of the railway sector were put under the control of the State Railway Administration under the Ministry of Transport.[2]

In March 2015, China announced the framework of its Belt and Road Initiative, running through the continents of Asia, Europe, and Africa to "enhance regional connectivity and embrace a brighter future together."[3] Such a centralized strategy of the construction of the Railroad Economic Belt (*yilu yidai*) exemplifies the government's iron grip on the railway sector.

What was confusing was that the cyclical reform strategies of decentralization and re-centralization were administered over years when there was continuous declining railway market share and shrinking profits. Thus, in the Chinese railway reform, economic imperatives do not necessarily lead to decentralization. Even if we consider the arrangement of responsibility contracts to be decentralizing policies, they did not lead to clarification of property rights, not to mention privatization.

Another puzzle was why the MOR would bother to design and put forward a series of complicated profit-sharing formulae, and yet was unable to achieve the "efficient" property rights arrangements in the end? If searching for the most efficient model was not the primary drive for railway reform, what was the hidden agenda aside from mere mimicry of the Western model?

Property rights re-arrangements as a discovery process

The problem of applying the efficiency model to understanding China's railway reform is that the efficiency model is aimed at prescribing the best property rights arrangement and explaining why some countries adopt the best model and some do not. Such positive reasoning falls into a blind spot in treating property rights arrangements as an outcome of the reform. In fact, property rights arrangements can be seen as a process through which idle state assets created by the inefficiencies of state ownership are discovered and re-covered.

Since the efficiency model sees property rights arrangements as an outcome of the reform, the focus of the discussion is on the pursuance of property rights specificity, or why some systems fail to achieve the desired assets specificity, which is to look for the right person or the good manager to receive the state assets and to concentrate the income, control, and transfer rights of the assets.

This book, on the contrary, treats property rights arrangement as a process of reform, and explains the significance, and to a certain extent the beauty, of the fuzzy property rights arrangements. Graber and Stark's study on the post-socialist economies provides an important insight in theorizing the "assets discovery mechanism." Their research focuses on the post-socialist economy, in which asset ambiguity was a result of the local recombination of the property rights from the ruins of the previous socialist system. Accordingly, such property rights ambiguity provides the necessary "friction" to slow down the transformation process so that managers could "acquire resources." They argued that "organizations that learn too quickly exploit at the expense of exploration thereby locking in to suboptimal routines and strategies."[4]

The post-socialist experience could be useful. Graber and Stark focus on the time after the big bang reform, when the post-reformed managers were exploring the optimal way to function and operate their companies in the post-socialist economy. This study, on the other hand, focuses on the reform era in China, when the socialist system was still in place, and local cadres discovered the idle resources within the existing socialist system. In my theoretical framework of assets discovery, the transformation needs to take time so that idle assets are discovered and bad or incompetent managers become good and competent ones. It was therefore logical to hypothesize that the cyclical, and sometimes mixed, policies of decentralization and re-centralization was the state's exploratory measures to get around the major issues. The unexpected result of the fuzzy property rights arrangements and "asset ambiguity" in turn facilitated the process of asset discovery and recovery.

The case of railway reform illustrates that the heritage of the planned economy endowed the state sector with enormous productive assets, and the separate financial arrangements of revenue and expenditure rendered many of these assets exceptionally inefficient, idle, and "invisible." As the profit-sharing and dual-track systems encouraged local cadres to mobilize their working ties and make use of idle state assets to engage in diversified businesses, local cadres learned to explore the resources outside the budgetary plan and eventually made them known to the state leadership.

Gradually, the central leadership realized that it was all the more important for the government to know what it possesses and how to elicit the true value of the state's assets before the leaders could decide on whether and how to put them under private or state ownership.

Recovery of state assets: consolidation and specialization of business groups

After identifying the idle productive assets, the central government began to recover them selectively. For productive assets relating to those industries in which market competition alone could not improve efficiency, the Chinese government would maintain the state's ownership in order to re-regulate and re-arrange the respective property rights. These industries usually possess certain market constraints, such as involving high start-up costs, provision of public goods, or are national pillar industry, which required state-led efforts to coordinate and regulate the sector strategically. As a result, the more likely the result of market failure and the more strategically important the newly identified assets, the more likely it is that they will be centralized by the state.

For those which were less strategically important, the government would decentralize and, perhaps, privatize them. But privatization was not the major purpose of such an assets recovery mechanism—it could just be "an occasional side-effect" of the corporatization of large-scale state enterprises.[5] The main purpose was still to retain state ownership and control over the strategic assets.

In the case study of the MOR's three sub-sectors, some of the newly discovered assets, which involved non-transport-, non-construction-, and non-telecommunications-related diversified businesses, such as the operation of hotels, restaurants, touring services, etc., were later separated from the transport-related core sector to support the excessive personnel levels. Some other newly discovered strategic assets which involved the core businesses were later consolidated and centralized under the MOR's headquarters or the Assets Supervision and Administration Commission (SASAC).

The Chinese government refers to the selected large-scale, centralized enterprises as the pillar industries or "lifeline industries" (*jingji mingmai*). Such centralization of the lifeline industries and consolidation of related productive resources facilitated assets specialization and professionalization, which is desirable for the accumulation and specialization of knowledge, and avoids duplication of resources allocation. The arrangement also streamlined the system for the central leadership to manipulate various incentives, administer an orderly domestic competition, and control the socialist hierarchy.[6]

The policy of consolidation of strategically important assets to foster national economic development can be traced back to the mid-1980s, when the Chinese government began to study the successful experience of Japanese *keiretsu* and Korean *chaebols*. In July 1980, the State Council put forward "The Provisional Regulation on Promoting Economic Association" (*Guanyu tuidong jingjilianhe de zanxing guiding*) to initiate the policy of horizontal integration.[7] In 1986 and 1987, the State Council put forward the "Regulations on the Problems of Further Promoting Horizontal Economic Association" (*Guanyu jinyibu tuidong hengxiang jingji lianhe ruogan wenti de guiding*), and "Several Opinions on the Organization and Development of Enterprise Groups" (*Guanyu zujian he fazhan qiye jituan de jidian yijian*), respectively. In May 1991, the State Economic Reform Commission (SERC, which was later renamed the National Development and Reform Commission, NDRC) issued, and the State Council approved and announced, "The Major Points of the Economic and Institutional Reform in 1991" (*Guanyu 1991 jingji tizhi gaige yaudian*), which further encouraged horizontal economic integration (*hengxiang jingj lianhe*), and the establishment of large-scale, trans-departmental, and trans-regional enterprise groups (*qiye jituan*).[8] By the end of 1993, there were more than 7,000 registered business groups (*qiye jituan*) in China.

The successful experience in turning the medium- to large-scale state-owned enterprises into business groups paved the way for the government to implement a similar policy of horizontal integration when the state started to reform its last batch of super-sized centralized enterprises (*yangqi*). The consolidation and centralization policies turned out to be the "assets recovery mechanism" for the state to exhaust the best-quality assets and re-group them by their industrial functions. The result was that the Chinese government maintained, via the SASAC, a crucial mass of state assets to form a bunch of national champions to "catch-up" with the developed countries.[9]

"Statization" versus "privatization"

In 2003, with a view to better regulating and nurturing the national champions, the Chinese government sought to establish a "special organization directly under the State Council" (*guowuyuan teshe jigou*)—the State Assets Commission—to formalize its ownership over a group of selected central enterprises, a process this book refers to as "statitization."[10] Despite various economic imperatives, the Chinese government did not really think of decentralization and privatization. Rather, by having a few state administrative ministries and commissions performing regulatory roles, the Chinese government separated the roles of owners and regulators of state assets within the State Council.[11]

In the case study of the railway regime, for example, China Railcom was detached from the MOR, put under the ownership of the SASAC and renamed as China TieTong. Together with other telecommunications companies, such as China Telecom, China Unicom, and China Netcom, China TieTong was regulated by the NDRC and the Ministry of Information (MII). However, since both the owner, the SASAC, and the regulators, NDRC and the MII, were all under the wing of the State Council, it was difficult to conclude that the Chinese government was moving toward an "independent regulatory model"—a Western model of governance under which the regulatory body is separated from the owner and independent from government intervention.

Emergence of a multi-tiered hybrid: dilution of state ownership

With a view to enhancing the competitiveness and enlisting domestic or foreign capital and technology, the SASAC urged the centralized enterprises to engage in joint ventures or cooperative projects to receive foreign capital, as well as management and technology know-how. At the same time, the SASAC forced the central enterprises to establish boards of directors and general managers, and to comply with the Western practice of transparent corporate governance. The SASAC also ensured an orderly competition among a few selected centralized enterprises and encouraged local managers to further explore any potential productive resources.

While the SASAC retained state ownership of the core company of the centralized enterprises, it allowed cross-ownership or IPO arrangements in the second- or third-tier subsidiaries. The resulting property rights arrangements for the reformed centralized enterprises were therefore a multi-layered shareholding corporation group, with insulating layers separating the public listing arrangements at the periphery from the state-owned enterprises at the core. Although the overall state ownership was diluted, a critical mass of strategic assets was still centrally controlled.

The reformed state enterprises under the arm of the SASAC, such as the MOR enterprises, were developing into state-owned multi-layered business groups. Although more and more state-owned group corporations started to arrange IPOs in Hong Kong and overseas stock markets, the governance of these "red chips" was largely influenced by the Chinese government and the Communist Party. Richard Huang, the associate principal of McKinsey's Beijing office, and Gordon Orr, the director of McKinsey's Shanghai office, thus advised Western strategic investors to be aware of the "invisible power" behind and locate the real decision makers:

> Strategic investors should thus strive to ensure that the directors they appoint join the strategy committees of the companies in which they invest. The best time to put this arrangement in place is during the negotiations over the initial strategic investment, when investors have maximum leverage.... Best practice is to obtain the state-owned enterprises' organization chart showing party committee members and senior executives. Then investors must ask themselves whether they have covered most of the real decision makers and whether their influence is broad enough to get the party committee's attention.[12]

As a result, the property rights arrangements of the "red chips" so far involved state ownership dilution but not privatization. There was no sign yet that this bunch of reformed state-owned enterprises would move along the direction of privatization. However, it is worthwhile to further research on whether the corporate governance of these reformed SOEs would have substantial changes after the IPOs arrangements if foreign strategic investors were allowed to become the companies' international board member and thus gain greater influence over the decision-making process.

Notes

1 "Important High-Speed Railway Lines in China," www.chinahighlights.com/travelguide/transportation/china-high-speed-rail.htm (accessed 17 April 2015).
2 David Briginshaw, "China Confirms Plans to Abolish Ministry of Railways," *International Railway Journal*, 11 March 2013, www.railjournal.com/index.php/policy/china-confirms-plans-to-abolish-ministry-of-railways.html?channel=542 (accessed 18 April 2015).
3 "Chronology of China's Belt and Road Initiative," Xinhua net, 28 March 2015, http://news.xinhuanet.com/english/2015-03/28/c_134105435.htm (accessed 21 April 2015).
4 Gernot Grabher and David Stark, eds., *Restructuring Networks in Post-Socialism: Legacies, Linkages, and Localities* (New York: Oxford University Press, 1997), pp. 1–22.

5 "Corporatisation Versus Privatisation," *China Economic Quarterly*, third quarter, 2003.

6 Dylan Sutherland, "Policies to Build National Champions: China's 'National Team' of Enterprise Groups," in Peter Nolan, ed., *China and the Global Business Revolution* (Basingstoke: Palgrave, 2001), pp. 67–139; and Barry Naughton, "Market Economy, Hierarchy, and Single Party Rule: How Does the Transition Path in China Shape the Emerging Market Economy?" International Economic Association, Hong Kong, 14–15 January 2004.

7 Chen Jiagui and Huang Sujian, eds., *Shichang jingji yu qiye zuzhi jiegou de biange* (Market Economy and Reform on Organizational Structure of Enterprise; Beijing: Jingji guanli chubanshe, 1995).

8 "*Guowuyuan pizhuan guojia tigaiwei 'guanyu 1991 jingji tizhi gaige yaudian' de tongzhi*" ("The State Council Approved the State Reform Commission's Announcement on 'the Summary of the Economic and Institutional Reform in 1991'"), *People's Daily*, 20 May 1991, www.people.com.cn/BIG5/33831/33836/34146/34190/254 3628.html (accessed 31 December 2005).

9 Peter Nolan, ed., *China and the Global Business Revolution* (New York: Palgrave, 2001), pp. 1–25; and Peter Nolan, *China and the Global Economy: National Champions, Industrial Policy and the Big Business Revolution* (New York: Palgrave, 2001), pp. 1–17.

10 Barry Naughton, "The State Asset Commission: A Powerful New Government Body," *China Leadership Monitor*, vol. 8 (2003).

11 James Kynge, "China Lays Out Plans for Reform of Business State-owned Companies," *Financial Times*, 23 May 2003, p. 13.

12 Richard Huang and Gordon Orr, "China's State-owned Enterprises: Board Governance and the Communist Party," *Mckinsey Quarterly*, vol. 1 (2007): 108–111.

Appendix

List of interviewees

Code	Sub-sectors	Position
1 CHFBJ	Construction	Division chief
2 GKCBJ	Construction	Manager
3 WHYWH	Construction	Director
4 ZJBJ	Construction	Manger
5 ZYLBJ	Construction	Manager
6 WBTJ	Signaling	Director
7 CQBJ	Signaling	Secretary
8 HZBJ	Signaling	Deputy manager
9 JWGTJ	Signaling	Division chief
10 YAXBJ	Signaling	Division chief
11 FRSH	Transport	Division chief
12 LBRBJ	Transport	Director
13 LHCBJ	Transport	Division chief
14 LLXGZ	Transport	Section chief
15 MGXGZ	Transport	Division chief
16 OGLBJ	Transport	Section chief
17 RCHBJ	Transport	Division chief
18 SYMBJ	Transport	Director
19 TZYBJ	Transport	Project manager
20 WYBJ	Transport	Division chief
21 YFFGZ	Transport	Section chief

Bibliography

"*2001 nian zhongguo 14 ge tieluju jiang zhujian keyun gongshi shixian wanyun fengli*" ("In 2001 China's 14 Railway Administrations will Establish Passenger Transport Companies and Separate the Railway Network from Transport Services"), *Zhongguo jingying bao*, 1 May 2001, China Infobank.

"*30 zai cunyun*" ("Thirty Years of Spring Transport"), *China News Digest*, 15 March 2005, http://my.cnd.org/modules/wfsection/article.php?articleid=9593.

Adamson, Mike, Wynne Jones and Robin Pratt, 1991, "Competition Issues in Privatization: Lessons for the Railways," in David Banister and Kenneth Butlon, eds., *Transport in a Free Market Economy*, Houndmills: Macmillan.

Aghion, Philippe and Olivier J. Blanchard, 1998, "On Privatization Methods in Eastern Europe and their Implication," *Economics of Transition*, vol. 6, no. 1: 87–99.

"Airfares to Float," *Shenzhen Daily*, 28 March 2001, http://pdf.sznews.com/szdaily/2001/0328/2.htm.

Alchian, Armen, 1997, "Some Economics of Property Rights," *Economic Forces at Work*, vol. 30: 142.

Alexandersson, G. and K. Rigas, 2013, "Rail Liberalisation in Sweden: Policy Development in a European context," *Research in Transportation Business & Management*, vol. 6, pp. 88–98.

Archives and Records Centre, Ministry of Railways, 1999, "The Brilliant 50 Years History of China's Railway Development," in *China Railway Monthly*, vol. 2, no. 13: 3–14.

Atkinson, Helen, 9 May 2005, "China's New Logistics Choices," *Traffic World*.

Baldinger, Pamelar, 1998, "Secrets of the Supply Chains," *The China Business Review*, September–October: 8–14.

Banister, David and Kenneth Button, 1991, eds., *Transport in a Free Market Economy*, Houndmills: Macmillan.

Barkey, Karen and Sunita Parikh, 1991, "Comparative Perspectives on the State," *Annual Review of Sociology*, vol. 17: 525–536.

Barzel, Yoram, 2003, "Property Rights in the Firm," in Terry Anderson and Fred McChesney, eds., *Property Rights: Cooperation Conflict and Law*, Princeton, NJ: Princeton University Press.

"Beijing to Seek Investors for New Metro Lines," *People's Daily*, 19 December 2004, http://english.people.com.cn/200412/19/eng20041219_167881.html.

"Best Practices for Telecommunications Reform," Global Internet Policy Initiative Papers, August 2002, www.internetpolicy.net/practices/telecomreform.pdf.

Bienkowski, Wojciech, 1992, "The Bermuda Triangle: Why Self-governed Firms Work for their Own Destruction," *Journal of Comparative Economics*, vol. 16, no. 4: 750–762.

Bo, Jingwei, 17 July 2001, *"Zhongguo tielu zhongzu: hengqie? haishishuqie?"* ("The Restructuring of China's Railway: Horizontal Separation? Or Vertical Separation?"), People.com.cn, www.people.com.cn/BIG5/jinji/36/20010719/515398.html.

Bornstein, Morris, 1997, "Non-standard Methods in the Privatization Strategies of the Czech Republic, Hungary and Poland," *Economics of Transition*, vol. 5, no. 2: 323–338.

Boycko, Maxim, Andrei Shleifer, and Robert Vishny, 1996, *Privatizing Russia*, Cambridge, MA: MIT Press.

Brenner, Robert, 1986, "The Social Basis of Economic Development," in John Roemer, ed., *Analytical Marxis*, New York: Cambridge University Press.

Briginshaw, David, 11 March 2013 "China Confirms Plans to Abolish Ministry of Railways," *International Railway Journal*, www.railjournal.com/index.php/policy/china-confirms-plans-to-abolish-ministry-of-railways.html?channel=542.

Button, Kenneth, 1991, "Regulatory Reform," in Kenneth Button and David Pitfield, eds., *Transport Deregulation: An International Movement*, New York: St. Martin's Press..

Button, Kenneth and David Pitfield, 1991, eds., *Transport Deregulation: An International Movement*, New York: St. Martin's Press.

"Call for China to Develop Multiple Energy Sources," *ABC News*, 18 April 2005, www.abc.net.au/news/newsitems/200504/s1347165.htm.

Campos, Javier and Pedro Cantos, 1999, "Rail Transport Regulation," World Bank Group Working Paper, www.worldbank.org/html/dec/Publications/Workpapers/wps2000 series/wps2064/wps2064.pdf.

Cavana, R.Y., 1995, "Restructuring the New Zealand Railway System: 1982–1993," *Transport Reviews*, , vol. 15, no. 2: 119–139.

Canning, David, "Infrastructure's Contribution to Aggregate Output," Policy Research Working Paper no. 2246, World Bank.

Cao, Desheng, 10 August 2005, "Transport to Focus on Moving Key Goods," *China Daily*, www.chinadaily.com.cn/english/doc/2005-08/10/content_467771.htm.

Caohe, Rong, 2003, *"Zhongtie kuaiyun ji qi dui tielu yunshu tizhi gaige de qisi"* ("China Railway Express Transport and its Implications for the Institutional Reform of Railway Transport"), *Guangli Shijie*, vol. 11.

Chandler, Alfred D., 1997, *The Visible Hand: The Managerial Revolution in American Business*, London: The Belknap Press of Harvard University Press.

Chen, Chih-Jou Jay, "Local Institutions and the Transformation of Property Rights in Southern Fujian," in Jean C. Oi and Andrew G. Walder, eds., *Property Rights and Economic Reform in China* (Stanford, CA: Stanford University Press, 1999).

Chen, Jiagui and Huang Sujian, 1995, ed., *Shichang jingji yu qiye zuzhi jiegou de biange* (Market Economy and Reform on Organizational Structure of Enterprise) Beijing: Jingji guanli chubanshe.

Chen, Yu, 10 November 2004, "Reshuffle a Prelude to Mergers," *China Daily*, North American edition.

Chen, Zhiming, 18 January 2005, "Tietong Seeks Co-operation, Listing," *China Daily*, North American edition., http://english.sohu.com/20050118/n223990968.shtml.

Chen, Zhiming, 23 July 2004, "China Tietong to be Officially Launched in Early August," *China Daily*, North American edition.

Cheung, Peter, 1998, ed., *Provincial Strategies of Economic Reform in Post-Mao China: Leadership, Politics, and Implementation*, Armonk, NY: M.E. Sharpe.

"China Construction Machinery Market," US Department of Commerce, www.buyu-sainfo.net/docs/x_7782452.pdf.

"China Looks to Coal to Oil the Wheels of Industry," *Asia Times*, 27 May 2005, www.atimes.com/atimes/China/GE27Ad03.html.

"China Railcom Launches Operation," *China Daily*, 13 August 2001, www.chinadaily.com.cn/en/doc/2001-08/13/content_76419.htm.

"China Railcom Opens National High-Speed Optical Ring Using Nortel Networks Solution," Nortel news release, 21 July 2001, www.nortel.com/corporate/news/newsreleases/2001c/07_12_0101477_china_railcom.html.

"China Railcom to Focus on Fibre Access Networks," *Telecommunications Development, Asia-Pacific*, 25 June 2002, www.tdap.co.uk/uk/archive/interviews/inter(railcom_0203).html.

"China Railcom to Issue One Billion Yuan in Bonds," *People's Daily*, 11 April 2005, http://my.tdctrade.com/airnewse/index.asp?id=6205.

"China Railcom to Occupy China's Call Center Market," *SinoCast China Business Daily News London (UK)*, 23 September 2003.

"China Set Targets for State-owned Assets Management," *China Daily*, 22 May 2003, www.chinadaily.com.cn/en/doc/2003-05/22/content_166023.htm.

"China Telecom Cos Reshuffle in Prep for 3G?" *China Comms Network*, 3 November 2004, www.cn-c114.net/newscarrier_html/20041139365-1.Html.

"China Telecom Cos Reshuffle Seen as Backward Step," *China Comms Network*, 3 November 2004, www.c114.net/cn-c11404/newscarrier_html/200411394957-1.Html.

"China TieTong Again Selects Cisco for Expansion of its CRNET Backbone Network," Cisco news release, 22 June 2005, http://newsroom.cisco.com/dlls/global/asiapac/news/2005/pr_06-28.html.

"China: Fee Cut Spurs Phone Demand," *Asiainfo Daily China News*, 11 July 2001.

"China-Seventh Railway Project," Staff Appraisal Report, World Bank, 14 April 1995, www-wds.worldbank.org/servlet/WDS_IBank_Servlet?pcont=details&eid=000009265_3961019100557.

"Chinese Firm Joins Railway Bidding Fray," *The Nation*, 21 January 2006, www.nation-multimedia.com/search/page.arcview.php?clid=6&id=126505&usrsess=.

"Chinese Institutions in Detail: GRC," Intercity Services Department, Kowloon-Canton Railway Corporation, September 2001.

"Chinese Railway has New Image," *People's Daily*, 12 December 2001, http://english.peopledaily.com.cn/other/archive.html.

Chinese Railway Publisher, 1999, ed., *Xin zongguo tielu wushinian* (Fifty-year Review of the New China's Railway), Beijing: China Railway Publisher.

"Chronology of the Development of China's Internet, 1994–1996," China Internet Network Information Center, www.cnnic.net.cn/html/Dir/2003/10/22/1003.htm.

Chung, Jae Ho, 2003, "The Political Economy of Industrial Restructuring in China: The Case of Civil Aviation," *The China Journal*, vol. 50: 61–82.

"Cisco to Provide Backbone Technology for China Railcom Network Expansion," *People's Daily*, 28 April 2002, http://english.peopledaily.com.cn/200204/19/print20020419_94369.html.

Coase, Ronald H., 1959, "The Federal Communications Commission," *Journal of Law and Economics*, 2: 1–41.

"Competition in Telecom Sector Will Cut Complaints," *People's Daily*, 13 March 2001, http://english.people.com.cn/english/200103/13/eng20010313_64854.html.

Comtois, Claude, 1999, "The Integration of China's Port System into Global Container Shipping," *GeoJournal*, vol. 48, no. 1: 35–42.

Contemporary China Editing Department, 1990, ed., *Dangdai zhongguo de tiedao shiye* (The Contemporary Railway Business in China), Beijing: Chinese Social Science Publisher.

"Corporatisation Versus Privatisation," *China Economic Quarterly*, third quarter, 2003.

"Country Risk? Chinese Historical GDP Growth Rates Revised," Economic Intelligence Unit, 12 January 2006, www.riskcenter.com/story.php?id=12085.

"Creating an Independent Telecom Regulator," United States Information Technology Office, 30 September 2002, www.usito.org/USITO/uploads/112/independent_regulator.pdf.

Dai, Yan, 19 May 2005, "Logistics Industry Moving Forward," *China Daily*, www.chinadaily.com.cn/english/doc/2005-05/19/content_443922.htm#.

Dang dai zhongguo congshu bianjibu, 1990, ed., *Dangdai zhongguo de tiedao shiye* (The Contemporary Railway Business in China), Beijing: *Zhongguo shehui kexue chubanshe*.

Demsetz, Harold, 1967, "Towards a Theory of Property Rights," *American Economic Review*, vol. 57, no. 2: 355

Demsetz, Harold, 1988, *Ownership Control and the Firm*, Oxford: Basil Blackwell.

Ding, Xueliang, 2000, "The Illicit Asset Stripping of Chinese State Firms," *The China Journal*, 43: 1–28.

"Disanpi yangqi zhuye gongbu" ("Announcement of the Core Businesses of the Third Batch of Centralized Enterprises"), Xinhua Net, 13 October 2005, http://news.xinhuanet.com/house/2005-10/13/content_3611078.htm.

Duan, Qing, 2005, "China's IT Leadership," PhD Thesis, University of Maryland.

Duckett, Jane, 1998, *The Entrepreneurial State in China*, New York: Routledge.

Earle, John S. and Almos Telegdy, 1998, "The Results of 'Mass Privatization' in Romania: A First Empirical Study," *Economics of Transition*, vol. 6, no. 2: 313–332.

Energy Information Administration, 2006, *Annual Energy Outlook 2006*, Report # DOE/EIA-0484, www.eia.doe.gov/oiaf/ieo/pdf/ieoreftab_4.pdf.

"Experts Debate MBO, Draining of State Assets," *China Daily*, 6 September 2004.

Eyal, Gil, Ivan Szelenyi, and Eleanor Townsley, 1998, *Making Capitalism without Capitalists: Class Formation and Elite Struggles in Post-Communist Central Europe*, London: Verso.

Fethi, Meryem Duygun, "Measuring the Efficiency of European Airlines: An Application of DEA and Tobit Analysis," Discussion paper in Management and Organization Studies, University of Leicester, School of Management, No. 01/20.

Fingar, Thomas, 1987, "Implementing Energy Policy: The Rise and Demise of the State Energy Commission" in D. Lampton, ed., *Policy Implementation in Post-Mao China*, Berkeley, CA: University of California Press.

Fong, Shiaw-Chian, 1999, "The Shareholding System in a Shandong Township: Practice and Impact," *Issues & Studies*, vol. 35, no. 4: 33–54.

Freese, Roseanne, 2001, "China's Construction Market: A New Star in the East," Ag Exporter, www.findarticles.com/p/articles/mi_m3723/is_1_13/ai_70395048#continue.

Frydman, Roman and Andrzej Rapaczynski, 1994, *Privatization in Eastern Europe: Is the State Withering Away*, Budapest: CEU.

Gates, Robert, 2001, "Beyond Sinotrans: China's Distribution Infrastructure," *The China Business Review*, July–August: 14–17.

"General Components to Provide VoIP Enterprise Solution to China Railcom," *Business*

Wire, 14 November 2005, www.findarticles.com/p/articles/mi_m0EIN/is_2005_Nov_14/ai_n15793986.

Gibson, Ken, 27 September 2001, "Analysing the Trends: Predicting the Future of Logistics in Asia," Presentation to the conference on "Toward the Final Frontier: Logistics and the Efficient Supply Chain."

Government Work Report delivered by Premier Zhu Rongji at the 5th Meeting of the 9th National People's Congress, 16 March 2002, http://focus.hustonline.net/html/2005-12-7/25454_4.shtml.

Grabher, Gernot and David Stark, 1997, eds., *Restructuring Networks in Post-Socialism: Legacies, Linkages, and Localities*, New York: Oxford University Press.

Granick, David, 1990, *Chinese State Enterprises: A Regional Property Rights Analysis*, Chicago, IL: University of Chicago Press.

Groombridge, Mark Allen, 1998, "The Politics of Industrial Bargaining: The Restructuring of State-owned Enterprises in the People's Republic of China, 1978–1995," PhD dissertation, Columbia University.

Gu, Chaolin, Shen Jianfa, Wong Kwan-yiu, and Zhen Feng, 2001, "Regional Polarization under the Socialist-market System since 1978: A Case Study of Guangdong Province in South China," *Environment and Planning*, vol. 33, no. 1: 97–119.

"*Guanyu jiaqiang fazhan tielu duozhong jingying de ruogan yijian*" ("Some Thoughts on Enhancing the Development of Business Diversifications in the Railway Sector"), www.law999.net/law/doc/c005/1994/06/07/00103097.html.

"*Guojia jiang caiqu cuoshi peiyang yipi guoji jingzhengli qiang de daxing kuaguo gongsi da qiye*" ("The State Will Implement Policies to Nurture a Team of International Competitive and Large-scale Transnational Enterprises"), *Economic Times*, 31 January 2002, www.wisers.com.ezproxy.ust.hk.

"*Guowuyuan pizhuan guojia tigaiwei 'guanyu 1991 jingji tizhi gaige yaudian' de tongzhi*" ("The State Council Approved the State Reform Commission's Announcement on 'the Summary of the Economic and Institutional Reform in 1991'"), *People's Daily*, 20 May 1991, www.people.com.cn/BIG5/33831/33836/34146/34190/2543628.html.

Guthrie, Douglas, 1997, "Between Markets and Politics: Organizational Responses to Reform in China," *American Journal of Sociology*, vol. 102: 1258–1304.

Guthrie, Douglas, 1999, *Dragon in a Three-Piece Suit: The Emergence of Capitalism in China*, Princeton, NJ: Princeton University Press.

"*Han Shubin tongzhi wei luke songshui*" ("Comrade Han Shubin offered Water to Passengers"), *Renmin tiedao bao*, 3 July 1993.

He, Qinglian, 1998, *Xiandaihua de xianjing: dangdai zhongguo de jingji shehui wenti* (The Trap of Modernization: The Economic and Social Problems of Contemporary China), Beijing: Jingre zhongguo.

Hertzell, Staffan, 2001, "China's Evolving Logistics Landscape," McKinsey & Company, Greater China Office.

Ho, Simon S.M., 2003, "Corporate Governance in China: Key Problems and Prospects," Centre for Accounting Disclosure and Corporate Governance School of Accountancy, Chinese University of Hong Kong.

Hong Kong Trade Development Council, 2002, "China's WTO Accession: Enhancing Supply Chain Efficiency—Transportation and Logistics," www.tdctrade.com/econforum/tdc/tdc020501.htm#.

Hou, Mingjuan, 3 August 2001, "New Rules to Improve Services," *China Daily* (North American edition).

Hou, Mingjuan, 4 July 2002, "Government May Throw Carriers a Line," *China Daily* (North American edition), www.chinadaily.com.cn/en/doc/2002-07/04/content_126373. htm.

Howell, Jude, 1993, *China Opens Its Door: The Politics of Economic Transition*, Boulder, CO: Lynner Rienner Publishers.

Hu, Guoming, 2001, "*Zailun tielu yunshu qiye duoyuan jingyin de jingyin fanglue yu quxiang*" ("To Discuss Again the Strategies and Directions of the Diversified Operations of the Transport Enterprises in the Railway Sector") in Wu Jianchong, *Xin duoyuan jingji lun* (Theory of Neo-economic Diversification), Bejing: zhongguo tielu chubanshe.

Hu, Xiaobo, 8 December 2003, "Choices and Path-Dependency of China's Property Rights Transformation: The Institutional Origins," Working paper presented at the Social Science Seminar, Hong Kong University of Science and Technology.

Hu, Yauhua and Zhu Junan, 2001, eds., *Zhongguo tielu tongxin shiji huigu* (Review of China's Railway Telecommunications in this Century), Beijing: China Railway Publisher.

"Intense Competition in Telecommunications Industry," 19 November 2001, tcdtrade. com, www.tdctrade.com/report/indprof/indprof_011103.htm.

"Introduction of China's Medium- to Long-term Railway Network Construction Plan," Central People's Government of the People Republic of China, www.gov.cn/ztzl/2005-09/16/content_64413.htm.

Jefferson, Gary H. and Thomas G. Rawski, 1994, "Enterprise Reform in Chinese Industry," *Journal of Economic Perspectives*, vol. 8, no. 2: 47–70.

"Ji Tong Communications Co Ltd," Telecommunications Research Project Paper, University of Hong Kong, December 1996, www.trp.hku.hk/papers/1996/JITONG.DOC.

"*Jianding xingxin tuanjie fenjin wei jianshe guonei yiliu juyou guoji jingzhenli de xiandai qiye jituan e fendou*" ("Be Confident and United in Endeavoring to Become the First-Grade, Domestically and Internationally Competitive Modern Enterprise Group"), *Zhongguo tiedao jianzu bao*, 5 May 2001, www.wisers.com.ezproxy.ust.hk.

Jiang, Bin and Edmund Prater, 2002, "Distribution and Logistics Development in China: The Revolution has Begun," *International Journal of Physical Distribution and Logistics Management*, vol. 32, no. 9: 783–798.

Jiang, Shijie, 2001, "*Yu wushengchu ting jingle: tielu xitong gaige shaomiao*" ("A Quiet Surprise: To Scan Through the Railway Reform"), People.com.cn, www.people.com. cn/BIG5/jinji/32/180/20010117/380412.html.

Jiang, Wenran, 2005, "Fueling the Dragon: China's Quest for Energy Security and Canada's Opportunities," *Asia Pacific Foundation of Canada*, www.asiapacific.ca/analysis/ pubs/pdfs/can_in_asia/cia_fueling_dragon.pdf.

Jianguo, Zhu, 1997, "Telecommunications and Development in Shanghai: A Case Study," in Paul Lee, ed., *Telecommunications and Development in China*, Cresskill, NJ: Hampton Press.

"*Jianzhu qiye hawai kuozhang zhengdangshi*" ("Right Timing for Construction Enterprises to Expand Overseas Businesses"), *Dalian Construction Engineering Cost Information Net*, 9 September 2005, www.dlzj.com.cn/sitefunction/Reader.asp?URL=/ manager/cmt/file/file2199.htm&Table=cmt&Class=1.

"*Jiutie zhai pizun siyi xitie heyue*" ("KCRC Awarded Again the 0.4 billion West Rail Contract"), *Tai Kung Po*, 28 July 1999, www.wisers.com.ezproxy.ust.hk.

Junghans, Lida Ferguson, 1999, "Workers in Transit: Chinese Railway Workers and the Journey from Plan to Market," PhD thesis, Harvard University.

Kasarda, D.J., 1996, "Transportation Infrastructure for Competitive Success," *Transportation Quarterly*, vol. 50, no. 1: 35–50.

Kay, John and David Thompson, 1991, "Regulatory Reform in Transport in the United Kingdom: Principles and Application," in D. Banister and K. Button, eds., *Transport in a Free Market Economy*, Houndmills: Macmillan.

Keister, Lisa, 2000, *Chinese Business Groups: The Structure and Impact of Interfirm Relations during Economic Development*, Oxford: Oxford University Press.

"*Keituo jingqu de beijing tieluju duoyuan jingyin shiti*" ("The Proactive Beijing Railway Administrations and its Business Diversification"), *Renmin tiedao bao*, 18 February 2003.

Kerr, John, 2005, "10 Key Challenges for the Chinese Logistics Industry," *Logistics Management 2002*, vol. 44, no. 2: S64–68.

King, Lawrence P., 2001, *The Basic Features of Postcommunist Capitalism in Eastern Europe*, Westport, CT: Praeger.

Kopicki, Ron and Louis S. Thompson, 1995, "Best Methods of Railway Restructuring and Privatization," World Bank CFS Discussion Paper Series.

Kornai, Janos, 1990, *Vision and Reality, Market and State: Contradictions and Dilemmas Revisited*, New York: Routledge.

Kung, James Kai-sing, 1999, "The Evolution of Property Rights in Village Enterprises: The Case of Wuxi County," in Jean C. Oi and Andrew G. Walder, eds., *Property Rights and Economic Reform in China*, Stanford, CA: Stanford University Press.

Kung, James Kai-sing and Lin Yi-min, "Markets, the Local State, and Ownership Transformation: The Rise and Decline of Local Public Enterprises in China's Economic Transition," forthcoming.

Kynge, James, 2003, "China Lays out Plans for Reform of Business State-owned Companies," *Financial Times*.

Lampton, David M, 1987, "The Implementation Problem in Post-Mao China," in D. Lampton, ed., *Policy Implementation in Post-Mao China*, Berkeley, CA: University of California Press.

Lampton, David M., "Water: Challenge to a Fragmented Political System," in D. Lampton, ed., *Policy Implementation in Post-Mao China*, Berkeley, CA: University of California Press.

Lee, Keun and Hahn Donghoon, 1999, "Market Competition, Plan Constraints, and Asset Diversion in the Enterprise Groups in China," Institute of Economic Research Working Paper.

Lee, Keun, 1991, *Chinese Firms and the State in Transition: Property Rights and Agency Problems in the Reform Era*, London: M.E. Sharpe.

Lei, Ding and Kingsley E. Haynes, 1–3 October 2004, "The Role of Telecommunications Infrastructure in Regional Economic Growth of China," Paper presented at the Telecommunications Policy Research Conference, Washington.

Leong, Apo and Stephen Frost, 2000, "From Security to Uncertainty-Labour and Welfare Reform in China," *Asian Labour Update*, vol. 35, www.amrc.org.hk/Arch/3502.htm.

Li, Bo, 2002, "*Chong zhongtie kuaiyun kan woguo tielu kuaiyun de zhidu zhuangxin*" ("To Understand the Institutional Innovation of China's Railway Express Businesses by the Case Study of the China Railway Express Company Ltd"), MPhil Thesis, North Jiaotong University.

Li, Hongbin and Scott Rozelle, 2003, "Privatizing Rural China: Insider Privatization, Innovative Contracts and the Performance of Township Enterprises, *The China Quarterly*, vol. 176: 981–1005.

Li, Hongbin and Scott Rozelle, 2004, "Insider Privatization with a Tail: The Screening Contract and Performance of Privatized Firms in Rural China," *Journal of Development Economics*, 75: 1–26.

Li, Shi, 7 February 2005, "Time to Stoke up Railway Reform," *China Daily* (North American edition), Wisenews, http://libwisenews.wisers.net.

Li, Wai-ching, 2001, "The Reform Programme of the Ministry of Railways and Its Impact on Rail Development in China," MA Dissertation, University of Hong Kong.

Li, Weitao, 3 December 2005, "Regulators Alter Tietong's Board," *China Daily* (North American edition).

Li, Xuechong, 1999, *Boyilun yu jingji zhuanxin: jianlun zhongguo yielu gaige* (Game Theory and Economic Transformation: Including a Discussion on China's Railway Reform), Beijing: Shehui kexue wenxin chubanshe.

Li, Zhaoyan, "Private and Overlay Networks in the PRC," Paper presented at the conference on Telecommunications and the Integration of China, Hong Kong Center.

Lieberthal, Kenneth and Michel Oksenberg, 1988, *Policy Making in China: Leaders, Structures, and Processes*, Princeton, NJ: Princeton University Press.

Limao, Nuno and Anthony Venables, 1999, "Infrastructure, Geographical Disadvantage, and Transport Costs," World Bank Policy Research Working Paper, no. 2257, http://ssrn.com/abstract=629195.

Lin, Yi-min, 2001, "Economic Institutional Change in Post-Mao China: Reflections on the Triggering, Orienting, and Sustaining Mechanisms," *Asian Perspective*, vol. 25, no. 4: 33–66.

Lin, Yi-min and Zhang Zhanxin, 1999, "Backyard Profit Centers: The Private Assets of Public Agencies," in Jean Oi and Andrew Walder, eds., *Property Rights and Economic Reform in China*, Stanford: Stanford University Press.

Lin, Yi-min and Zhu Tian, 2001, "Ownership Restructuring in Chinese State Industry: An Analysis of Evidence on Initial Organizational Changes," *The China Quarterly*, 166: 305–341.

Liu, Baijia, 12 December 2001, "Telecom Monopoly Set to Split," *China Daily*, North American edition.

Liu, Qinglin, 2001, ed., *Teilu qiye banzhu guanli jichu zhishi* (Basic Knowledge of Work Group Management of Railway Enterprises), Beijing: Zhongguo tielu chubanshe.

Liu, Yia-Ling, 1992, "Reform from Below: The Private Economy and Local Politics in the Rural Industrialization of Wenzhou," *The China Quarterly*, 130: 293–316.

"*Liu Zhijun shiqi: chefenju, yong fazhen huan gaige*" ("The Era of Liu Zhijun: Removing Railway Sub-administration and Slowing Down the Reform in Exchange for Railway Development"), 25 January 2015, *Caijing.com.cn.*

Low, Sui Pheng and Jiang Hongbin, 2003, "Internationalization of Chinese Construction Enterprises," *Journal of Construction Engineering and Management*, November–December: 589–598.

Lu Bingyang, "Freight Transporter China Railway Express Co. is Broken Up," *Caixin Online*, 6 June 2013, http://english.caixin.com/2013-06-06/100538484.html.

Lu, Haoding, 8 August 2005, "Railway Financing Plan Chugging Along," *China Daily*, www.chinadaily.com.cn/english/doc/2004-08/08/content_363168.htm.

Luo, Wenping and Christopher Findlay, 2002, "Logistics in China: Implications of Accession to the WTO," http://siteresources.worldbank.org/INTRANETTRADE/Resources/WenpingFindlay_logistics.pdf.

"*Luotuo tiaowu*" ("Camel Dances"), *Zhongguo gaige bao*, 26 February 2001.

Ma, Ngok, 1998, "The Political Economy of Privatization in Eastern Europe: Trans-formative Politics and Competing Imperatives of Privatization in Hungary, Poland and the Czech Republic," PhD Dissertation, University of California, Los Angeles.

Mackey, Michael, 17 June 2005, "China's Working on the Railroad," *Asia Times*, http://atimes01.atimes.com/atimes/China/GF17Ad02.html.

Mackey, Michael, 18 June 2005, "Privatizing the 'Iron Rooster,'" *Asia Times*, www.atimes.com/atimes/China/GF18Ad03.html.

Mackey, Michael, 28 April 2005, "China Integrates into Global Supply Chain," *Asia Times*, www.atimes.com/atimes/China/GD28Ad02.html.

Mann, Ainsley, 2001, "Dry Packaged Goods: Overcoming Logistical Hurdles," *The Chinese Business Review*, July–August: 24–29.

Marx, Karl and Friedrich Engels, 1967, *The Communist Manifest*, Harmondsworth: Penguin.

McMillan, John, 1988, "Market in Transition," Symposium address at the Seventh World Congress of the Econometric Society, Tokyo.

Milor, Vedat, 1994, "Changing Political Economies: An Introduction," in Vedat Milor, ed., *Changing Political Economies: Privatization in Post-Communist and Reforming Communist States*, Boulder, CO and London: Lynne Rienner Publishers, pp. 1–23.

"Minister Answers IT Queries," *China Daily* (North American edition), 8 January 2002.

"Ministry Control on Railways Questioned," *China Daily*, 5 December 2004, www.chinadaily.com.cn/english/doc/2004-12/05/content_397425.htm.

Mizutani, Fumitoshi, 1999, "An Assessment of the Japan Railway Companies Since Pri-vatization: Performance, Local Rail Service and Debts," *Transport Review*, vol. 19, no. 2: 117–139.

Milgrom, Paul and John Roberts "Moral Hazard and Performance Incentives," in Paul Milgrom and John Roberts, *Economics, Organization and Management* (Englewood Cliffs, NJ: Prentice-Hall, 1992), ch. 6.

Mueller, Milton and Zixiang Tan, 1997, *China in the Information Age: Telecommuni-cations and the Dilemmas of Reform*, Westport, CT: Praeger.

Murrell, Peter, 1992, "Conservative Political Philosophy and Strategy of Economic Transition," *East European Politics and Societies*, vol. 6, no. 1: 3–16.

Nan, Lin, 1995, "Local Market Socialism: Local Corporatism in Action in Rural China," *Theory and Society*, 24: 301–354.

"*Nanchang tieluju huangtogang bianqian xilie*" ("Series Report on the Changes of Huangtugang at Nangchang Railway Administrations"), *Renmin tiedao bao*, 1 Novem-ber 2000.

Nash, C.A. and J. Preston, 1993, "United Kingdom: Privatization of Railways," Report of the Ninetieth Round Table on Transport Economics, European Conference of Ministers of Transport.

Naughton, Barry, 1987, "The Decline of Central Control over Investment in Post-Mao China," in David Lampton, ed., *Policy Implementation in Post-Mao China*, Berkeley, CA: University of California Press.

Naughton, Barry, 1995, *Growing Out of the Plan: Chinese Economic Reform, 1978–1993*, Cambridge: Cambridge University Press.

Naughton, Barry, 2003, "The State Asset Commission: A Powerful New Government Body," *China Leadership Monitor*, vol. 8.

Naughton, Barry, 2004, "Market Economy, Hierarchy, and Single Party Rule: How Does the Transition Path in China Shape the Emerging Market Economy," Paper presented at the International Economic Association, Hong Kong.

Naughton, Barry, 2005, "SASAC Rising," *China Leadership Monitor*, vol. 14, www.chinaleadershipmonitor.org/20052/bn.html.

"New Study Forecasts Improving Outlook for Global Construction Industry," Global Insight, Inc, 10 June 2003, http://prninternational.com/cgi/news/release?id=103640.

Nolan, Peter, 2001, *China and the Global Economy: National Champions, Industrial Policy and the Big Business Revolution*, New York: Palgrave.

Nolan, Peter, 2001, ed., *China and the Global Business Revolution*, New York: Palgrave, pp. 1–25.

OECD, 28–29 January 2002, "Railway Reform in China: Promoting Competition," Summary and Recommendations of an OECD/DRC Seminar on Rail Reform, Beijing.

Oi, Jean, "Fiscal Reform and the Economic Foundations of Local State Corporatism in China," Nan Lin, "Local Market Socialism: Local Corporatism in Action in Rural China," in Jean Oi and Andrew Walder, eds., *Property Rights and Economic Reform in China*, Stanford: Stanford University Press.

Oi, Jean, 1999, *Rural China Takes Off: Institutional Foundations of Economic Reform*, Berkeley, CA: University of California Press.

"Opinion: Public Rail Price Hearing a Good Start," *China Daily*, 15 January 2002.

Organization for Economic Co-operation and Development, 28–29 January 2002, "Railway Reform in China Promoting Competition," Proceedings of an OECD/DRC Seminar on Rail Reform in Beijing.

Orr, Gordon and Richard Huang, 2007, "China's State-owned Enterprises: Board Governance and the Communist Party," *Mckinsey Quarterly*, vol. 1: 108–111.

Osnos, Evan, 2012 "Boss Rail: Letter from China," *The New Yorker*, vol. 88, no. 33: 44.

Pearson, Margaret, 2005, "The Business of Governing Business in China: Institutions and Norms of the Emerging Regulatory State," *World Politics*, vol. 57: 206, 314.

"*Peng Peng rehuo chuju, tietong 'duli yundong' yanqi sigu*" ("Peng Peng was Out Amid China Railcom's Independent Movement"), *Jingji guangcha bao*, 1 November 2003, http://it.sohu.com/17/75/article215057517.shtml.

"Performance Indicators for the Telecommunications Sector," Telecommunications and Informatics Division, Industry and Energy Department, May 1995, www.worldbank.org/html/opr/pmi/telecom/telecom0.html.

Pfeffer, Jeffrey and Gerald R. Salancik, 1978, *The External Control of Organizations: A Resource Dependence Perspective*, New York: Harper & Row.

Pickel, Andreas, 1992, "Jump-Starting a Market Economy: A Critique of the Radical Strategy for Economic Reform in Light of the East German Experience," *Studies in Comparative Communism*, vol. 25, no. 2: 177–191.

Pittman, Russel, 2004, "Chinese Railway Reform and Competition: Lessons from the Experience in Other Countries," *Journal of Transport Economics and Policy*, vol. 38, no. 2: 309–332.

Pomfret, John, 17 August 2002, "Lines Crossed in China," *Washington Post*.

Popov, Vladimir, 2000, "Shock Therapy Versus Gradualism: The End of the Debate (Explaining the Magnitude of Transformational Recession)," *Comparative Economic Studies*, vol. 42, no. 1: 1–57.

Porta, Rafael La and Florencio López-de-Silanes, 1999, "The Benefits of Privatization: Evidence from Mexico," *The Quarterly Journal of Economics*, vol. 114, no. 4: 1193–1242.

Powers, Patrick, 2001, "Distribution in China: The End of the Beginning," *The China Business Review*, July–August: 9–12, www.chinabusinessreview.com/public/0107/powers.html.

"Premier Wen Heads New Energy Group," *China Daily*, 27 May 2005, www.chinadaily. com.cn/english/doc/2005-05/27/content_446253.htm.

"Private Cash to Help Build Railway Line," *China Daily*, 23 February 2005.

"Po chulai de chexiaolin: yichang 'caosui' de tielu gaige," ("A Forced Order of Removal: an Arbitrary Railway Reform." *Shangwu zhoukan* (Commercial Weekly), 14 April 2005.

Prybyla, Jan, 1991, "The Road from Socialism: Why, Where, What and How," *Problems of Communism*, vol. 40: 1–17.

Pryor, Frederic, 1973, *Property and Industrial Organization in Communist and Capitalist Nations*, Indiana, IN: Indiana University Press.

"Public Services Due for Private Business," *China Daily* (North American edition), 26 July 2000. http://proquest.umi.com.

Qiu, Xin, 3 June 2005, "China Overhauls Energy Bureaucracy," *Asia Times*, www.atimes. com/atimes/China/GF03Ad01.html.

"*Qiye de mingtian zainali*" ("Where is the Future of the Enterprise?"), *Zhongguo tiedao jianzu bao*, 3 December 2005, www.wisers.com.ezproxy.ust.hk.

"*Qiye guoyou chanquan xiang guanliceng zhuanrang zangshi jueding*" ("Temporary Regulations on the Transfer of Assets of State Enterprises to Management"), SASAC, www.sasac.gov.cn/gzjg/cqgl/200504150122.htm.

Raffray, Nathalie, February 2000, "Open and Closed," *Communications International London*.

"Rail Ministry to Carry on its Reforms," *China Daily*, 19 October 2002, www.chinadaily. com.cn/en/doc/2002-10/19/content_140249.htm.

"Railcom Gets 10 Billion Yuan Loan to Construct Network," *Asiainfo Daily China News Dallas*, 28 June 2002.

Ramstad, Evan, 12 July 2004, "Heard in Asia: Telecom-Consolidation Ministry of Railways in China Fails to Stir Investors," *Asian Wall Street Journal Victoria*.

Rawski, Thomas G., 1995, "Implications of China's Reform Experience," *The China Quarterly*, vol. 144: 1156.

Rong, Chaohe, "*Cong yunshu changpin kang tielu chongzhu de fangxiang*" ("To Study the Direction of Railway Reform in the Light of the Characteristics of Transport Product"), www.china.org.cn/chinese/OP-c/434301.htm.

Rosen, Stanley, "Restoring Key Secondary Schools in Post-Mao China: The Politics of Competition and Educational Quality," in D. Lampton, ed., *Policy Implementation in Post-Mao China*, Berkeley, CA: University of California Press.

Ross, Lester, "Obligatory Tree Planting: The Role of Campaigns in Policy Implementation in Post-Mao China, in D. Lampton, ed., *Policy Implementation in Post-Mao China*, Berkeley, CA: University of California Press.

Rothsman, Andy, 2005, "China Eats the World: Sustainability of Chinese Commodities," Credit Lyonnais Securities Agency, Asia-Pacific Markets, www.cctr.ust.hk/articles/pdf/China%20Eats%20the%20World%20Spring%202005.pdf.

Ruf, Gregory A., 1999, Collective Enterprise and Property Rights in a Sichuan Village: The Rise and Decline of Managerial Corporatism," in Jean C. Oi and Andrew G. Walder, eds., *Property Rights and Economic Reform in China*, Stanford, CA: Stanford University Press.

"Schedule of Specific Commitments on Services," Annex 9 of the Legal Instruments on China's Accession to the World Trade Organization.

Shaw, Jon, 2000, *Competition, Regulation and the Privatization of British Rail*, Aldershot: Ashgate.

Sheng, Guangzu, 1999, "*Guanyu tielu de gaige yu fazhan wenti*" ("Problems in Railway Reform and Development"), *Zhongguo tielu*, vol. 7, no. 2, serial no. 13: 1–3.

Shetty, Vineeta, April 2001, "The China Syndrome," *Communications International, London.*

Shi, Liu, 2000, "Construction and WTO," www.tdctrade.com/report/indprof/indprof_001003.htm.

Simon, Denis Fred, "Implementing China's S & T Modernization Program," in D. Lampton, ed., *Policy Implementation in post-Mao China*, Berkeley, CA: University of California Press.

"Sino Call to Cover 300 Chinese Cities," *SinoCast China Business Daily News London (UK)*, 23 September 2003.

Smith, Adam, 1796, *An Inquiry into the Nature and Causes of the Wealth of Nations*, London: Printed for A. Strahan, T. Cadell and W. Davies.

So, Alvin Y., ed., 2003, *China's Development Miracle: Origins, Transformation, and Challenges*, London: M.E. Sharpe.

Solinger, Dorothy, 1996, "Despite Decentralization," *China Quarterly*, vol. 145: 1–34.

Song, Lina and Du He, 1990, "The Role of Township Governments in Rural Industrialization," in William A. Byrd and Lin Qingsong, eds., *China's Rural Industry: Structure, Development, and Reform*, New York: Oxford University Press.

Staniszkis, Jadwiga, 1991, " 'Political Capitalism' in Poland," *East European Politics and Societies*, vol. 5, no. 1: 127–141.

Stark, David, 1992, "Path Dependence and Privatization Strategies in Eastern Europe," *East European Politics and Societies*, vol. 6, no. 1: 17–54.

Stark, David, 1996, "Networks of Assets, Chains of Debt: Recombinant Property in Hungary" in Roman Frydman, Cheryl Gray, and Andrzej Rapaczynski, eds., *Corporate Governance in Central Europe & Russia*, vol. 2, Budapest: Central European University Press.

Stark, David, 1997, "Recombinant Property in East European Capitalism," in Gernot Grabher and David Stark, eds., *Restructuring Networks in Post-Socialism: Legacies, Linkages, and Localities*, Oxford: Oxford University Press.

Steinfeld, Edward, 1998, *Forging Reform in China: The Fate of State-owned Industry*, Cambridge: Cambridge University Press.

"*Sudu jigou gaige fangan, Zhang Zuoyuan: guoziwei zujian zhihou*" ("A Quick Look at the Institution Reform, Zhang Zuoyuan: After the Establishment of the SASAC") *Chinese Industrial and Commercial Post*, 7 March 2003, http://big5.china.com.cn/chinese/zhuanti/288786.htm.

Sutherland, Dylan, 2001, "Policies to Build National Champions: China's 'National Team' of Enterprise Groups," in Peter Nolan, ed., *China and the Global Business Revolution*, Basingstoke: Palgrave.

Szalai, Erzsebet, 1994, "Political and Social Conflicts Arising from the Transformation of Property Relations in Hungary," *Journal of Communist Studies*, vol. 10, no. 3: 56–77.

Szelenyi, Ivan and Eric Kostello, 1996, "The Market Transition Debate: Toward a Synthesis?" *American Journal of Sociology*, vol. 101, no. 4: 1082–1096.

Szelenyi, Ivan, 1995, "The Rise of Managerialism: The "New Class" after the Fall of Communism," Discussion Paper 16, Collegiums Budapest, Public Lecture Series.

Ta, Huu-Phuong, Hwee-Ling Choo, and Chee-Chuong Sun, 2000, "Transportation Concerns of Foreign Firms in China," *International Journal of Physical Distribution & Logistics Management*, vol. 30, no. 1: 35.

Tae, Hoon Oum, W.G. Waters II, and Chunyan Yu, 1999, "A Survey of Productivity and

Efficiency Measurement in Rail Transport," *Journal of Transport Economics and Policy*, vol. 33, no. 1: 9–42.

Tanzer, Andrew, 12 November 2001, "Chinese Walls," *Forbes Global*, www.forbes.com/ global/2001/1112/091.html.

"Technical Assistance: People's Republic of China—Railway Passenger and Freight Policy Reform Study," Technical Assistance Report, Asian Development Bank, Project Number 37628, November 2005, www.adb.org/Documents/TARs/PRC/37628-PRC-TAR.pdf.

"Telecommunication Reform: How to Succeed," *Public Policy Journal*, vol. 130, (1997), http://rru.worldbank.org/Documents/PublicPolicyJournal/130welle.pdf.

"The Brilliant 50 Years History of China's Railway Development," *China Railway Monthly*, vol. 2, no. 13 (1999): 3–14.

"The Core of the Reform Involves Property Rights and Property Rights Transaction Brings in a New Wave of Change," Sina.net, 11 August 2006, http://gov.finance.sina. com.cn/chanquan/2006-08-11/13769.html.

Thompson, Louis S., 2000, "Railway Restructuring in China: The Great Railway Challenge," Presentation to Railway Minister Fu Zhihuan Beijing, www.worldbank.org/ transport/rail/china/presentation.htm.

Thompson, Louis S. and Karim-Jacques Budin, 2001, "Directions of Railway Reform," Paper presented at the International Railway Congress Association meeting in Vienna, Austria, 25–28 September.

Thompson, Louis S. and Julie Fraser, 1993, "Notes on World Bank's Railway Database," Transport No.RW-6, www.worldbank.org/transport/publicat/td-rw6.htm.

"*Tiedao buzhang liu zhijun tan chexiao tielu fenju yuanyin,*" ("Railway Minister Liu Zhijun Discusses the Reasons of the Removal of Railway Sub-administration," *People Daily*, 19 March 2005.

"*Tielu duojing bahuayuan zhong de yiduo qiba*" ("One of the Many Railway Business Diversifications"), *Renmin tiedao bao*, 29 December 2002.

"*Tielu gaige xianru kunjing*" ("Railway Reform in Difficulties"), *China Economic Information Network*, 27 August 2002, Wisenews, http://libwisenews.wisers.net.

"*Tielu gaige zhou huitoulu*" ("The Railway Reform Turn Around"), *People's Daily*, 2 September 2002, www.people.com.cn/BIG5/jingji/1038/2066629.html.

"*Tielu gaige zhouchu chenmo jijiang chonglai*" ("Railway Reform Revives and Will be Back to the Stage Soon"), *Caijing*, 2 August 2004, http://finance.sina.com.cn/b/ 20040802/1101918481.shtml.

"*Tielu goujian duoyuan jingyin geju,*" ("The Railway Encourages Business Diversification") *Jingji Renbao*, 30 November 1999.

"*Tielu niannei quanmian shixian san fenkai*" ("The Policy of 'Three Separation' Rolls Out in the Railway Sector this Year"), *People's Daily*, 26 March 2001, www.people. com.cn/GB/jinji/32/180/20010326/425801.html.

"*Tielu xitong gaige saomiao*" ("Details of the Reform of the Railway System"), *People's Daily*, 17 January 2001, www.people.com.cn/BIG5/jinji/32/180/20010117/380412.html.

"*Tielu yunshu qiye jianyuan zhengxiao shishi yijian*" ("Opinion on Implementation of the Policy of Reducing the Establishment and Improving the Efficiency in the Transport Sub-sector of Ministry of Railways"), www.lawbook.com.cn/lawhtm/1997/64213.htm.

"*Tietong shiduo zhongguo dianxun ¼ guhua fen'e*" ("Railcom Swire to Take Away One-Fourth Market Share from China Telecom"), ChinaByte, 9 May 2001, http://news. chinabyte.com/124/1220124.shtml.

"*Tieyiyuan shili honghou gongji zuoyue*" ("The First Survey & Design Institute of the

Ministry of Railways is Well Established with Excellent Business Record"), *Lanzhou Morning Post*, 22 November 2005.

"*Tupoxing jingzhan: tielu sanda huoyun gongsi jiepa*" ("Breakthrough Development: The Opening of the Three Big Railway Freight Transport Companies"), *21st Century*, 11 January 2004, http://channel.eastday.com/epublish/gb/paper94/20040111/class009400 004/hwz1386376.htm.

Villalonga, Belen, 2000, "Privatization and Efficiency: Differentiating Ownership Effects from Political, Organizational, and Dynamic Effects," *Journal of Economic Behavior & Organization*, vol. 42: 43–47.

Voszka, Eva, 1995, "Centralization, Re-Nationalization, and Redistribution: Government's Role in Changing Hungary's Ownership Structure," in Jerzy Hausner, Bob Jessop, and Klaus Nielsen, ed., *Strategic Choice and Path-Dependency in Post-Socialism: Institutional Dynamics in the Transformation Process*, Aldershot: Edward Elgar.

Walder, Andrew, 1995, "Local Governments as Industrial Firms: An Organizational Analysis of China's Transitional Economy," *American Journal of Sociology*, vol. 101, no. 2: 263–301.

Walder, Andrew, 1997, *Zouping in Transition: The Process of Reform in Rural North China*, Cambridge, MA: Harvard University Press.

Walder, Andrew G., 2002, "Privatization and Elite Mobility: Rural China, 1979–1996," Asia/Pacific Research Center Working Paper, http://aparc.stanford.edu/publications/20205.

Walder, Andrew, 2003, "Politics and Property in Transitional Economies: A Theory of Elite Opportunity," Working Paper, Asia/Pacific Research Center.

Walder, Andrew and Jean Oi, 1999, "Property Rights in the Chinese Economy: Contours of the Process of Change," in Jean Oi and Andrew Walder, eds., *Property Rights and Economic Reform in China*, Stanford: Stanford University Press.

Wan, Zheng and Liu, Xiang, "Chinese Railway Transportation: Opportunity and Challenge," Transportation Research Board Annual Meeting 2009 Paper #09-2279, http://trid.trb.org/view.aspx?id=881652.

Wan, Xiaobing, 2001, "*Tielu xiang zhiji huiqi shoushudao*" ("Railway Undertook Operations Itself"), *Caijing Magazine*, vol. 4, www.chinanews.com.cn/zhonghuawenzhai/2001-06-01/txt/16.htm.

Wang, Chenbo and Lin Yingli, 2003, "*Tielu gaige huigui tubian*" ("The Railway Reform Back to Square One"), *China's News Week*, vol. 32, www.chinanewsweek.com.cn/2003-09-05/1/2160.html.

Wang, Lingfeng, 16 January 2003, "*Zhongguo tielu gaige de zongdian*" ("The Main Points of China's Railway Reform"), *21st Century Business Herald*, www.chinainfobank.com.

Wang, Shaoguang, 1995, "The Rise of the Regions: Fiscal Reform and the Decline of Central State Capacity in China," in Andrew Walder, ed., *The Waning of the Communist State*, Berkeley, CA: University of California Press, pp. 87–113.

Wang, Shengke and Mo Fei, 16 May 2005, "*Guozi 'guanwang' gushi gaige*" ("The SASAC 'Wait and See' on Equity Market Reforms"), *21 shiji jingji baodao*, http://finance.sina.com.cn/stock/y/20050514/10581587629.shtml.

Wang, Whing-Chun, 1910, "Why the Chinese Oppose Foreign Railway Loans?" *The American Political Science Review*, vol. 4, no. 3: 365–373.

Wang, Ying, 4 January 2005, "Shortfall in Coal Supply to Remain," *China Daily*, www.chinadaily.com.cn/english/doc/2005-01/04/content_405663.htm.

"*Wangyun fenli tielaoda zaici tixu*" ("Separating between Rail Road and Transport Services, the Ministry of Railways will Catch up on the Speed Again,") *China Enterprise News*, 16 April 2001, Wisesnews, http://libwisesearch.wisers.net.

Waverman, Leonard, Meloria Meschi, and Melvyn Fuss, 2005, "The Impact of Telecoms on Economic Growth in Developing Countries," The Vodafone Policy Paper Series, no. 2: 10–23.

Wei, Heping, 18 December 2002, "*Fu Zhihuan: tielu xitong de jianshe, tiaozheng yu fazhang*," China.com.cn, http://big5.china.com.cn/chinese/2002/Oct/219610.htm.

Wei, Yingtao, 1981, *Sichuan baolu yundong shi* (Railway Recovery Campaign in Sichuan), Chengdu: Sichuan People's Publisher.

Weimer, David L., 1997, "The Political Economy of Property Rights," in David L. Weimer, ed., *The Political Economy of Property Rights*, Cambridge: Cambridge University Press.

White, Tyrene, 1987 "Implementing the 'One-Child-per-Couple' Population Program in Rural China: National Goals and Local Politics," in D. Lampton, ed., *Policy Implementation in Post-Mao China*, Berkeley, CA: University of California Press.

Whiting, Susan H., 1999 "The Regional Evolution of Ownership Forms: Shareholding Cooperatives and Rural Industry in Shanghai and Wenzhou" in Jean C. Oi and Andrew G. Walder, eds., *Property Rights and Economic Reform in China*, Stanford, CA: Stanford University Press.

Wilbur Smith and Associates, 1973, *New Zealand Transport Policy Study*, New Zealand: Ministry of Transport, Government of New Zealand.

Williamson, Oliver E., 1971, "The Vertical Integration of Production: Market Failure Considerations," *American Economic Review*, vol. 61: 112–123.

Williamson, Oliver E., 1990, "A Comparison of Alternative Approaches to Economic Organization," *Journal of Institutional and Theoretical Economics*, vol. 146: 61–71.

Williamson, Oliver E., 1994, "Transaction Cost Economics and Organization Theory," in Neil J. Smelser and Richard Swedberg, eds., *The Handbook of Economic Sociology*, Princeton, NJ: Princeton University Press.

Wong, Christine, 1987, "Between Plan and Market: The Role of the Local Sector in Post-Mao China," *Journal of Comparative Economics*, vol. 11: 385–398.

Wong, Christine, 1997, "Overview of Issues in Local Public Finance in the PRC," in Christine Wong, ed., *Financing Local Government in the People's Republic of China*, Hong Kong: Oxford University Press.

Wong, Christine, 2000, "Central–Local Relations Revisited: The 1994 Tax-haring Reform and Public Expenditure Management in China," *China Perspectives*, vol. 31.

Woo, Wing Thye, 1999, "The Real Reasons for China's Growth," *The China Journal*, vol. 41: 115–137.

"WTO Entry Unleashes Greater Opportunity and Competition in Logistics Sector," *Hong Kong Trade Development Council*, vol. 8, 15 August 2002, www.tdctrade.com/alert/cba-e0208sp.htm.

Wu, Jian Hong and Chris Nash, 2000, "Railway Reform in China," *Transport Reviews*, vol. 20, no. 1: 25–48.

Wu, Jianzhong, 1988, *Tielu yunshu qiye shichanghua guanli* (The Market-oriented Management of Railway Transport Enterprises), Beijing: Zhongguo ttiedao chubanshe.

Wu, Jianzhong, 1998, *Tielu yunshu jiye shichanghua guanli* (Management of Railway Transport Enterprises during the Transition Towards Market Economy), Beijing: Zhongguo tiedao chubanshe.

"*Xiang dabo dianxun canye de longduan: tietong ping sheme jingzheng*" ("Want to Break the Telecommunications Monopoly—How Could Tietong Compete"), *Zhongguo jingying bao*, 16 Janaury 2001, http://big5.china.com.cn/chinese/EC-c/17010.htm.

Xiao, Yang, 10 August 2002, "Order Essential in Telecom Market," *China Daily* (North American edition).

Xiao, Yilin, 23 October 2002, "*Teilu gaige de miju: 'hengqie' yu 'shuqie' liunian zhizheng*" ("The Myth of the Railway Reform: The Six Year's Fight between "Horizontal Separation" and "Vertical Separation"), People.com.cn, www.people.com.cn/GB/jinji/222/9285/9287/20021023/849272.html.

"'*Xibei Ronglian' ronglian chule sheme*" ("What had the 'Northwest Furnace' Produced"), *Renmin tiedao bao*, 25 February 2003.

Xie, Ruhe, Haibo Chen, and Chris Nash, 2002, "Migration of Railway Freight Transport from Command Economy to Market Economy: The Case of China," *Transport Reviews*, vol. 22, no. 2: 159–177.

X. Xue, F. Schmid, and R. Smith, "An Introduction to China's Rail Transport Part 1: History, Present and Future of China's Railways," in *Proceedings of the Institution of Mechanical Engineers. Part F, Journal of Rail and Rapid Transit*, vol. 216, no. 1: 153–163.

"*Yangqi chongzu buru 'jiaoshaqi'*" ("The Restructuring of the Centralized Enterprises is Entering a Stage of 'Competition and Demolition'"), *Canquan shichang*, 29 November 2005, http://sme.sina.com.hk/cgi-bin/news/show_news.cgi?type=build&date=2005-11-29&id=223076.

Yang, Qin, 6 December 2002, "*Zhongguo tielu gaige dati queding: gaoceng qingxiang congqie luwang*" ("China's Railway Reform Largely Confirmed: Leadership Inclined to Vertically Separate the Network"), *Caijing shibao*, http://finance.sina.com.cn/b/20021206/1626287174.shtml.

Yu, Chuan, 1999, ed., *Zhongguo tielu caiwu kuaiji* (Finance and Account of China's Railways), Beijing: Zhongguo tielu chubanshe.

Yu, Jun, 2003, *Tielu chongzu de lilun yu shijian* (Theory and Implementation of Railway Restructuring), Beijing: Jingji kexue chubanshe.

Zen, E-Tu, Sun, 1955, "The Pattern of Railway Development in China," *The Far Eastern Quarterly*, vol. 14, no. 2: 179–199.

Zeng, Qingkai, 18 February 2003, "*Three Regional Firms to Deal with Railway Business*," *China Daily HK edition*, www.chinadaily.com.cn.

Zhao, Anying, 12 April 2004, "*Teilaoda kumi gaige luxiantu*" ("The Railway Big Brother is Endeavoring to Look for the Reform Strategy"), *China Economic Net*, www.ce.cn/ztpd/hqmt/gnmt/cjj/more/200504/12/t20050412_3585578.shtml.

Zhao, Yanling, 8 June 2001, "*Zhongguo tielu xitong dapo longduan kunnan chongchong*" ("Numerous Difficulties in Breaking the Monopoly of China's Railway System"), China Infobank.

Zhao, Yun, 30 September 2005, "*Zhongguo tielu gaige fang'an geqian*," ("The Termination of China's Railway Reform"), *The Economic Observer*, www.chinainfobank.com.

"*Zhonggongsi, zhonggongsi dangwei fachu tongzhi gongbu zhenghe zhongzu huazuan zhonggongsi guanli de yuantielu sigong sheji danwei*" ("The China Railway Construction Corporation and the Party Secretary of the China Railway Construction Corporation Announce the Restructuring of the Construction and Design Units under the Ministry of Railways"), *Zhongguo tiedao jianzhu bao*, 12 February 2004.

"*Zhongguo jianzuye de duiwai kaifang zhiyi*" ("Open up China's Construction Industry, Part I"), *Zhongguo jianshe bao*, 8 January 2007, China Infobank, http://210.177.11.50/

gate/big5/www.chinainfobank.com/ifbase643-L0lyaXNCaW4~/-VGV4dC5kbGw~?-
ZGI9Qkcmbm89MjI5Njc3JmNzPTI2MzQ0Njcmc3RyPc3i18q9qNb+#.

Zhongguo jianzu nianjian 1997 and 1998 (China Construction Annual Report 1997 and 1998), Beijing: China Construction Industry Publisher, Ministry of Construction.

"*Zhongguo shixian tielu kuayueshi fazhan shuoyao jiejue de zhuyao maodun shi yunli duanque wenti*" ("The Major Problem for China's Great Leap Approach in Railway Development is to Solve the Transport Incapacity"), *Wuliu shidai*, 3 September 2003.

Zhongguo tielu chubanshe, 1999, ed., *Xin zhongguo tielu wushinian* (Fifty-Year Review of the New China Railway), Beijing: Zhongguo tielu chubanshe.

"*Zhongguo teilu gaige congxing tisu*" ("Speeding Up China's Railway Reform Again"), *Caijing shibao*, 18 October 2002, http://finance.sina.com.cn/roll/20021018/1002268255.html.

"*Zhongguo tielu bumen nanxia kaizhan duoyuan jingying huatie nanfang jituan zhaishen choujian*" ("The Chinese Railway Units go South to Start the Diversified Business and Prepare the Establishment of Huatie Nanfang Corporation in Shenzhen"), *Shenzhen Special Zone Daily*, 7 August 1995, www.chinainfobank.com.

"*Zhongguo tielu duoyuan jinying shiwu nian chuangshou RMB 230 billion*" ("Chinese Railway's Business Diversification Gained RMB 230 Billion in 15 years"), *Jingji Rebao*, 22 November 1999.

"*Zhongguo tielu zongzu wangyun fengli taolun gao chulong*" ("The Announcement of the Discussion Paper of the Separation between Network and Transport in China's Railway Reform"), *Zhongguo dianli bao*, 1 April 2003, China Infobank, http://210.177.11.50/gate/big5/www.chinainfobank.com/ifbase643-L0lyaXNCaW4~/-VGV4dC5kbGw~?-ZGI9SEsmbm89MTk5NzI5MCZjcz0yMTg5NDEmc3RyPdbQufrM+sK3K9bY1+krzfj Uy7fWwOsrzNbC2w~~.

"*Zhongguo tietong: lizhu tielu zhuanwang, kaizhang teshe yewu*" ("China Railcom: Based on the Railway Network to Develop Businesses with Special Features"), *Tongxun shijie*, 30 November 2006, www.51telecom.com/Get/syyw/200611304922.htm.

"*Zhongjia qianyue chengli gangsusheng shoujia wuliu gongsi*" ("Chinese and Canadian Companies Sign Contract to Establish the First Logistics Company in Gangsu"), http://unn.people.com.cn/BIG5/channel22/37/183/200111/30/132513.html.

"'*Zhongtie hangmu' yao yuanhang: Zhongguo tiedao jianzhu zonggongsi zongjingli Wang Zhenhou tan rushi*" ("'Chinese Railway's Flagship' are Sailing: Wang Zhenghou, the General Manager of China Railway Construction Corporation Talks about the Entry into the WTO"), *Zhongguo jiaotong bao*, 22 January 2002.

"*Zhongtie jianshe jituan wuzi gongsi kaizhan duoyuan jingying jiesheguo*" ("Successful Results of the Development of Diversified Businesses of the China Railway Construction Material Supply Corporation"), *Zhongguo jianshe bao*, 7 February 2007, China Infobank, http://210.177.11.50/gate/big5/www.chinainfobank.com/ifbase643-L0lyaXN CaW4~/-VGV4dC5kbGw~?-ZGI9SEsmbm89MjY5MDQ1MCZjcz0zMjYzNzUx JnN0cj3W0Mz6vajJ6LyvzcXO79fKuavLvg~~.

Zhongnanhai Reform and Development Research Center, 22 November 2000, "*Weilai wu-shi nian zhongguo jingji gaige zhongdian*" ("China's Major Economic Reform in the Future 5–10 Years"), *Ta Kung Pao*.

"*Zhongyang qiye zhongzu tisu*" ("Speeding up the restructuring of Central Enterprises"), *Shanghai Securities News*, 17 December 2004.

Zhou, Qiren, 2002, "*Renli zhiben dechangquan*" ("Property Rights of Human Capital"), in Zhou Qiren, *Zhengshi shijie de jingjixue*, Beijing: Zhongguo fazhan chubanshe.

"*Zhufu fengli, tielu gaige de zhuyao moshi*" ("Separation between the Core and the Ancillary Businesses: The Major Model for the Railway Reform"), *Zhongguo jingyingbao*, 19 March 2004, http://news1.jrj.com.cn/news/2004-03-22/000000775268.html.

"*Zonggongsi chuangru xianggang ditie jianshe shichang*" ("China Railway Construction Corporation Enters into the Market of the Construction of the Mass Transit Railway in Hong Kong"), *Zhongguo tiedao jianzhu bao*, 16 September 2002, www.wisers.com. ezproxy.ust.hk.

Zweig, David, "Context and Content in Policy Implementation: Household Contracts and Decollectivizaton, 1977–1983," in D. Lampton, ed., *Policy Implementation in Post-Mao China*, Berkeley, CA: University of California Press.

Zweig, David and Jianhai Bi, 2005, "China's Global Hunt for Energy," *Foreign Affairs*, September–October.

Index

Page numbers in *italics* denote tables, those in **bold** denote figures.

archival documents 19
Asset Management System 42, 50

Barzel, Yorman 9
Beijing 21, 42, 61, 64, 70, 78, *90*, 92, 98,
    125, 128, 136, 150, *159*, 179, 196
big bang reform 12, 17, 208
Boykco, M. 6
business diversification 122–30, 186
business groups 155, 199, 208–9;
    construction business group 163–8

Campos, Javier 61
Cantos, Pedro 61
case studies 20
centralization 44–7, 89, 107–11, 142, 163,
    190–1, 197, 206
centralized enterprises 16, 118–20, 149,
    155–6, 160, 165, 168, 199, 210–11
Chandler, Alfred D. 44
China Civil Engineering Construction
    Corporation 131, 161
China Mobile Corporation 178, **186**
China Network Communications Group
    Corporation 178–9, **186**; *see also*
    China Netcom
China Netcom 181–2, **183**, **186**, 194–6
China Railcom 179–201, 210; *see also*
    China TieTong
China Railway Communication Company
    131, **132**, 149
China Railway Construction Corporation
    53–5, 148, *153*, 157, **162**
China Railway Container Transport
    Center 141–2
China Railway Corporation 21, 43, 61,
    111, 207

China Railway Engineering Corporation
    55, 53, 63, 157, 168; *see also* CREC
China Railway Express Ltd. 137
China Railway Foreign Services
    Company 141
China Railway Locomotive and Rolling
    Stock Industry Corporation 50, 63, 80,
    131
China Railway Material Corporation 64,
    161
China Railway Parcel Express Company
    Ltd. 141
China Railway Special Cargo Company
    Ltd. 141
China Railways Communications
    Corporation 179
China Satellite Communications
    Corporation 178, **188**; *see also* China
    Satcom
China Satcom 179
China Telecom 177–201, **182**, **183**, **188**
China TieTong 182–201, 210; *see also*
    China Railcom
China Unicom 177, 178, 179, 182, 187,
    192, 194, 201, 204, 210
China United Communications
    Corporation 177; *see also* China
    Unicom
coal transport 91
container transport 88, 104, 126, 128,
    141–2, *159*; container cars 104
convergence theory 1, 3, 4, 11, 12, 67, 201
CRCC 131, 134, 148–73; *see also* China
    Railway Construction Corporation; joint
    ventures *169*; organizational chart **166**
CREC 131, 148, 149; *see also* China
    Railway Engineering Corporation

Cultural Revolution 47, 73

dabaogan 75–80, 112; *see also* responsibility system
de-collectivization 6–7
de-politicization 5–7, 30, 42, 48, 65–7, 108, 148, 167
Demsetz, Harold 12
distribution system 92, 137–8; distribution network 35, 92
diversified businesses 119, 126, **127**, 128, **129**, 130, 131, 132, 135, 143, 151, 152, 161, 174, 208; *see also duojing* enterprises
duojing enterprises 132
dual-track system 51–2, 107, 118–25, 135, 142, 147–8, 151, 175, 186, 208

Eastern Europe 7, 12, 15, 17, 19, 25, 66, 82, 163, 217, 222, 225
economic integration 111, 154, 164, 209
enterprise groups 155, 175
extra-budgetary production resources 120–1
Eyal, Gil 15

Five-Year Plan 46, 87, 89–90, 108, 124, 126, 158–9, 163, 176
for-profit enterprises *65*
foreign investment 108, *180*
France *106*
freight transport 29–37, 64–9, 71, 78, 87, 92–5, 102–10, 122, 137–9, 149; freight cars *104*; market share **70**
Fu, Zhihuan 42, 60, 70, 129

Going out policy 163
gradualists 13
Great-Leap-Forward approach 21, 42, 121
Guang-shen Railway 10, 18, 50–5, 107, 122
Guangzhou Railway (Group) Corporation 50, 53–5, 80, 189

hidden assets 8, 120–1; extra-budgetary production resources 120–1; "floating" resources 9; intangible resources 8–9, 120
high-speed rail 42, 90, 111, 207
Hong Kong Stock Exchange 53
Hong Kong Trade Development Council 100, 159, 218
horizontal associations 155
Hu, Xiaobo 10
hypotheses 2–5, 28, 48–9, 56, 174

idle assets 2, 5, 9–11, 21, 49, 56, 81, 86, 119, 125–6, 129–30, 135, 143, 147, 160–3, 177, 182, 190, 208
institutional theory 14, 18

Kopicki, Ron 30
Kornai, Janos 6, 51, 59, 64, 220
Kostello, Eric 15

Li, Hongbin 11
Liu, Zhijun 42–3, 54, 61, 110–11
local cadres' survival strategies 2, 8, 19–20, 52, 56
logistics 69, 89–101, 107–8, 114–15, 129, 132, 137–43, 147, 161; cost *100*; handling time *104*; operating cost **123**

Ministry of Posts and Telecommunications 177
moral hazard 11

negative externalities 29
New Silk Road 111, 117
New York Stock Exchange 53

Oi, Jean 17, 223
Organization for Economic Co-operation and Development 30, 39, 42, 61, 175
ownership: communal ownership 6, 46; private ownership 5, 30, 31, 44, 110; state ownership 6–7, 10, 14, 38, 49, 55, 67, 130, 148, 164, 168, 170, 175, 177, 207–11
ownership changes 17; efficiency model 4, 9, 12–21, *18*, 28, 31, 41, 43, 61–7, 73, 85, 88, 163, 176, 207; ownership concentration 12; ownership conversion model *18*; ownership delineation 12; volutionary model 13–17, *18*

path dependency theory 13, 18, 25
"pick the right assets" 2, 49, 56, 112, 119, 132, 147
"pick the right owner" 2, 16, 112
political capitalism 14, 16, 18
Porta, Rafael La 11
principle-agent problems 10
private ownership 5, 30, 31, 44, 110
privatization 1–19, 24, 30, 38, 49, 52–6, 61–7, 85–7, 112, 121, 147, 154, 163–76, 198, 206–11; empty shares 167; insider privatization 11; real shares 168
profit sharing 1, 71, 74, 79, 80, 85, 107, 118, 122, 206–8

property rights 5–11, 174, 206; collective property rights 6; control and income rights 67, 71–9; economic theory 5, 30; income rights 5, 50, 74–9, 206; property relations 8, 16, 17; property rights hybrid 5, 15, 168–70, **190**; the trio of rights 5–10

railway: administrative integration 62, 64, 65; ancillary sectors 65, 130, 147–9, 154; arbitrary charges 125–6; bottleneck 88–107, 143; break-bulk 104–6; density 108; economic integration 111, 154, 164, 209; fixed asset investment 94, 158, 176; functional integration 62–3; handling volume **68**, 73, 78; heterogeneous services 29; Japanese railway 36; luggage cars 135, 136, 142; lumpy 29; market share **68, 69**; natural monopoly 30, 42, 65; New Zealand railway 37; railway administrations and sub-administrations *109*; sideline businesses 21, 51–6, 107, 119–52, 161, 201; sideline sector *65*; sidelines 122, 127, 130; social integration 62, **63**, 64; spinning off **55**, **123**, 130, **149**, 176, **187**; Swedish railway 35; troop 150, 151; US railways 35, 65; vertical integration 28; workforces **132**

railway reform: assets discovery 1–8, 15–20, 49, 52, 56, 118–19, 147, 158, 174–5, 208; assets recovery 1–5, 17, *18*, 49, 56, 147, 155, 158, 209–10; best reform model 1, 3, 30–1, 62, 67, 207; decentralization 1–2, 4, 15–17, **18**, 48–56, 61–2, 66–7, 71, 74, 79, 85–6, 108–21, 142–54, 170–8, 182, 190–201, 206–10; disintegration 30, 42; economic imperatives 2, 48–51, 56, 62, 66–8, 79, 88, 170, 207; economic model of railway reform 28; geographical separation 31; horizontal separation 31; monopolistic myth 29; passenger transport companies 32, 87; pre-centralization period 44; re-centralization 1, 18–21, 44–67, 85, 118–20, 130, 139, 147–9, 154, 174, 201, 207–8; spinning off **55**, **123**, 130, **149**, 176, **187**; structural separation 31, 34–7, *38*; telecommunications sub-sector 174–205; Three Separations 131; vertical separation 21, 31, 34, 35, 42, *43*, 54, 61, 86–7, 206; vertical and horizontal separation 88

Railway Troop 150, 151

reform of loan for funding 75

responsibility system 50, 71–81, 107, 122, **123**, 206; responsibility contract 13, 17, 49–50, 67, 71–80, 127, 151, 206–7; responsibility saystem of assets management 50

rural enterprises 3, 4, 11, 52

Roberts, John 11

Rozelle, Scott 11

SAMC 53, 148, 149; *see also* State Assets Management Commission

SASAC 119, 131, 148, 155–227; *see also* State-owned Assets Supervision and Administration Commission

Shanghai 21, 44, 80, *90*, 92, 93, 104, 125, 135

Sheng, Guangzhu 61

shock therapy 12

shortage economy 6, 51, 64, 73

Sinotrans 108, 115, 116, 139, 217

Smith, Adam 12

Staniszkis, Jadwiga 14

Stark, David 17

State Assets Management Commission 53

State Council 42, 48, 52, 61, 86–9, 121, 151–6, 170, 177–9, 189, 197–9, 209–12, 218

state ownership 6–7, 10, 14, 38, 49, 55, 67, 130, 148, 164, 168–70, 175–7, 207–11; dilution 168

State-owned Assets Supervision and Administration Commission 131, 148, 155, 174

Sun, Rongfu 104, 106, 139

Szalai, Erzsebet 15

Szelenyi, Ivan 15, 225

tax for profit 74

technocratic managerialism 15, 18

technology transfer 108

telecommunications reform 176, 204

telecommunication sector: personnel reshuffle 181, **183**

Thompson, Louis S. 30, 39, 42, 65

trio of rights, the 5–10

Walder, Andrew 15, 17, 173

Weimer, David L. 10

Wen, Jiabao 89, 108

Williamson, Oliver E. 7, 81

World Bank 30, 38–9, 42, 61, 65, 70, 78–81, 87, 175–6, 199, 202

World Trade Organization 41–2, 85, 98, *100*, 114, 138–40, 143, 145, 149, 154, 158–9, 164, 176, 179–80, 201–2
WTO *see* World Trade Organization
Wu, Jian Hong 70

Wu, Jichuan 179, 192

Xi, Jinping 111

Zhu, Rongji 53, 87, 113, 123, 130, 197